Spanish

Phrasebook & Dictionary

Acknowledgments
Product Editor Bruce Evans
Language Writers Marta López, Cristina Hernández Montero
Cover Image Researcher Naomi Parker

Thanks
James Hardy, Campbell McKenzie, Angela Tinson, Clifton Wilkinson, Juan Winata

Published by Lonely Planet Global Limited
CRN 554153

8th Edition – September 2018
ISBN 978 1 78701 465 7
Text © Lonely Planet 2018
Cover Image Marbella nightlife. Maurizio Rellini/4Corners©

Printed in China   10 9 8 7 6 5

Contact lonelyplanet.com/contact

Although the authors and Lonely Planet try to make the information as accurate as possible, we accept no responsibility for any loss, injury or inconvenience sustained by anyone using this book.

Paper in this book is certified against the Forest Stewardship Council™ standards. FSC™ promotes environmentally responsible, socially beneficial and economically viable management of the world's forests.

MIX
Paper from
responsible sources
FSC™ C021741

Look out for the following icons throughout the book:

 'Shortcut' Phrase
Easy-to-remember alternative to the full phrase

 Q&A Pair
Question-and-answer pair – we suggest a
response to the question asked

 Look For
Phrases you may see on signs, menus etc

 Listen For
Phrases you may hear from officials, locals etc

 Language Tip
An insight into the foreign language

Culture Tip
An insight into the local culture

How to read the phrases:
- Coloured words and phrases throughout the book are
  phonetic guides to help you pronounce the foreign language.
- Lists of phrases with tinted background are options you
  can choose to complete the phrase above them.

These abbreviations will help you choose the right words and phrases in this book:

a	adjective	m	masculine	sg	singular
f	feminine	n	noun	v	verb
inf	informal	pl	plural		
lit	literal	pol	polite		

Contents

PAGE 6

About Spanish

Learn about Spanish, build your own sentences and pronounce words correctly.

PAGE 31

Travel Phrases

Ready-made phrases for every situation – buy a ticket, book a hotel and much more.

Basics 31

Practical 41

PAGE 190

📖 Menu Decoder
Dishes and ingredients explained – order with confidence and try new foods.

PAGE 205

📖 Two-Way Dictionary
Quick reference vocabulary guide – 3500 words to help you communicate.

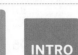

Spanish

español es·pa·*nyol*

Who Speaks Spanish?
Official Language

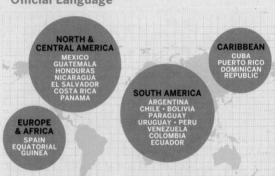

NORTH & CENTRAL AMERICA
MEXICO
GUATEMALA
HONDURAS
NICARAGUA
EL SALVADOR
COSTA RICA
PANAMA

CARIBBEAN
CUBA
PUERTO RICO
DOMINICAN REPUBLIC

SOUTH AMERICA
ARGENTINA
CHILE · BOLIVIA
PARAGUAY
URUGUAY · PERU
VENEZUELA
COLOMBIA
ECUADOR

EUROPE & AFRICA
SPAIN
EQUATORIAL GUINEA

Widely Understood USA

Why Bother

You'll be seduced by this melodic language and have fun trying to roll your *rr*'s like the locals – not to mention ordering scrumptious tapas or engaging in all the shouting at the *fútbol*.

Distinctive Sounds

The strong and rolled r, harsh and guttural kh and, in European Spanish, 'lisping' th.

Spanish in the World

Over the last 500 years, Spanish in Latin America has evolved differently to the

300 MILLION
speak Spanish as their
first language

100 MILLION
speak Spanish as their
second language

Spanish of Europe. Among other differences, you'll easily recognise Latin Americans by the lack of lisp in their speech – ie *cerveza* (beer) is ther·*ve*·tha in Europe but ser·*ve*·sa across the Atlantic.

Spanish in Spain

Spanish, or Castilian (*castellano* ka·ste·*lya*·no) is primarily the language of Castille (covering the largest territory in Spain). However, Catalan, Galician and Basque are also official languages, and locals in these regions are very proud of their own language.

False Friends

Warning: many Spanish words look like English words but have a different meaning altogether, eg *suburbio* soo·*boor*·byo is a slum district, not a suburb (which is *barrio* ba·ryo in Spanish).

Language Family

Romance (developed from Vulgar Latin spoken by Roman soldiers and merchants during the conquest from the 3rd to the 1st century BC). Close relatives include Portuguese, Italian, French and Romanian.

Must-Know Grammar

Spanish has a formal and informal word for 'you' (*Usted* oo·*ste* and *tú* too respectively). The verbs also have a different ending for each person, like the English 'I do' vs 'he/she do**es**'.

Donations to English

Thanks to Columbus' discovery of the New World in 1492, a large corpus of words from indigenous American languages has entered English via Spanish. You may recognise *canyon*, *guerrilla*, *ranch*, *tornado*...

5 Phrases to Learn Before You Go

1 **What time does it open/close?**
¿A qué hora abren/cierran? a ke o·ra ab·ren/thye·ran

The Spanish tend to observe the siesta (midday break), so opening times may surprise you.

2 **Are these complimentary?**
¿Son gratis? son gra·tees

Tapas (bar snacks) are available pretty much around the clock at Spanish bars. You'll find they're free in some places.

3 **When is admission free?**
¿Cuándo es la entrada gratuita?
kwan·do es la en·tra·da gra·twee·ta

Many museums and galleries in Spain have admission-free times, so check before buying tickets.

4 **Where can we go (salsa) dancing?**
¿Dónde podemos ir a bailar (salsa)?
don·de po·de·mos eer a bai·lar (sal·sa)

Flamenco may be the authentic viewing experience in Spain, but to actively enjoy the music you'll want to do some dancing.

5 **How do you say this in (Catalan/Galician/Basque)?**
¿Cómo se dice ésto en (catalán/gallego/euskera)?
ko·mo se dee·the es·to en (ka·ta·lan/ga·lye·go/e·oos·ke·ra)

Spain has four official languages, and people in these regions will appreciate it if you try to use their local language.

10 Phrases to Sound Like a Local

What's up?	¿Qué pasa?	ke *pa*·sa
Great!	¡Genial!	khe·*nyal*
How cool!	¡Qué guay!	ke gwai
That's fantastic!	¡Estupendo!	es·too·*pen*·do
Really?	¿En serio?	en *se*·ryo
You don't say!	¡No me digas!	no me *dee*·gas
Sure.	Seguro.	se·*goo*·ro
OK.	Vale.	*va*·le
Of course!	¡Por supuesto!	por soo·*pwes*·to
Whatever.	Lo que sea.	lo ke *se*·a

ABOUT Spanish

Pronunciation

Spanish pronunciation isn't difficult, as most sounds are similar to the sounds found in English. The relationship between Spanish sounds and their spelling is straightforward and consistent. There are some easy rules to follow and once you learn them you shouldn't have problems being understood. As in most languages, Spanish pronunciation can vary according to region – this book focuses on Castilian Spanish.

Vowel Sounds

SYMBOL	ENGLISH EQUIVALENT	SPANISH EXAMPLE	TRANSLITERATION
a	alms	agua	a·gwa
ai	aisle	bailar	bai·lar
e	red	número	noo·me·ro
ee	bee	día	dee·a
ey	hey	seis	seys
o	go	ojo	o·kho
oo	book	gusto	goo·sto
ow	cow	autobús	ow·to·boos
oy	boy	hoy	oy

Consonant Sounds

SYMBOL	ENGLISH EQUIVALENT	SPANISH EXAMPLE	TRANSLITERATION
b	big	barco	*bar*·ko
ch	chilli	chica	*chee*·ka
d	din	dinero	dee·*ne*·ro
f	fun	fiesta	*fye*·sta
g	go	gato	*ga*·to
k	kick	cabeza, queso	ka·*be*·tha, *ke*·so
kh	as in the Scottish *loch*	jardín, gente	khar·*deen*, *khen*·te
l	loud	lago	*la*·go
ly	million	llamada	lya·*ma*·da
m	man	mañana	ma·*nya*·na
n	no	nuevo	*nwe*·vo
ny	canyon	señora	se·*nyo*·ra
p	pig	padre	*pa*·dre
r	run (but stronger and rolled)	ritmo, burro, mariposa	*reet*·mo, *boo*·ro, ma·ree·*po*·sa
s	so	semana	se·*ma*·na
t	tin	tienda	*tyen*·da
th	thin	Barcelona, manzana	bar·the·*lo*·na, man·*tha*·na
v	soft 'b', between 'v' and 'b'	vaca	*va*·ka
w	win	guardia	*gwar*·dya
y	yes	viaje, ya	*vya*·khe, ya

Reading & Writing

There are some key things to remember about consonants in written Spanish:

» The letter *c* is pronounced with a lisp, eg *cerveza* ther·ve·tha, except when it comes before *a, o* and *u* or a consonant. Then, it's pronounced hard like the *k* in 'king'.

» When ending a word, the letter *d* is also pronounced soft, like a th, or is so slight that it hardly gets pronounced at all.

» The letter *j* stands for a harsh and guttural sound, and we use the kh symbol in our pronunciation guides.

» Try to roll your double *r*'s.

» The letter *q* is pronounced hard, like a k.

» The letter *v* sounds more like a b, said with the lips pressed together.

» There are a few letter combinations which you may find slightly unusual: *ch, ll* and *ñ*. The *ch* (che) and *ll* (e·lye) are no longer considered separate letters in the Spanish alphabet, so in dictionaries and the like, you'll find words starting with *ch* amongst the *c* listings, and those starting with *ll*, amongst the *l* listings. The letter *ñ* (e·nye) is considered a separate letter in the Spanish alphabet.

~ SPANISH ALPHABET ~

A	a	a	B	b	be	C	c	the
D	d	de	E	e	e	F	f	e·fe
G	g	khe	H	h	a·che	I	i	ee
J	j	*kho·ta*	K	k	ka	L	l	e·le
M	m	e·me	N	n	e·ne	Ñ	ñ	e·nye
O	o	o	P	p	pe	Q	q	koo
R	r	e·re	S	s	e·se	T	t	te
U	u	oo	V	v	oo·ve	W	w	oo·ve do·ble
X	x	e·kees	Y	y	ee·grye·ga	Z	z	*the·ta*

Word Stress

There is word stress in Spanish, which means you emphasise one syllable in a word over another. Rule of thumb: when a written word ends in *n*, *s* or a vowel, the stress falls on the second-last syllable, eg *lejos* le·khos (far), *casa* ka·sa (house). Otherwise, the final syllable is stressed, eg *hablar* a·*blar* (talk). If you see an accent mark over a syllable, it cancels out these rules and you just stress that syllable instead, eg *número* noo·me·ro (number).

LANGUAGE TIP · **False Friends**

Beware of false friends – those words that sound like familiar English, but could land you in a bit of trouble if you use them unwittingly in Spanish. Here are some mistakes that it's a little too easy to make:

el suburbio	el soo·*boor*·byo slum district, not 'suburb' which is *el barrio*, el ba·ryo
Estoy constipado/a. m/f	es·toy kons·tee·*pa*·do/a I have a cold, not 'I'm constipated', which is *estoy estreñido/a* m/f es·toy es·tre·*nyee*·do/a
Estoy embarazada.	es·toy em·ba·ra·*tha*·da I'm pregnant, not 'I'm embarassed', which is *estoy avergonzado/a* m/f es·toy a·ver·gon·*tha*·do/a
la injuria	la een·*khoo*·ree·a insult, not 'injury', which is *la herida*, la e·ree·da
los parientes	los pa·ree·*yen*·tes relatives, not 'parents', which is *los padres*, los pa·dres
sensible	sen·*see*·ble sensitive, not 'sensible', which is *prudente*, proo·den·te

ABOUT Spanish

Grammar

This chapter is designed to explain the main grammatical structures you need in order to make your own sentences. Look under each heading for information on functions which these grammatical categories express in a sentence. For example, demonstratives are used for giving instructions, so you'll need them to tell the taxi driver where your hotel is, etc. A glossary of grammatical terms is included at the end of this chapter to help you.

Adjectives & Adverbs

Describing People/Things • Doing Things

When using an adjective to describe a noun, you need to use a different ending depending on whether the noun is masculine or feminine, and singular or plural (see **gender** and **plurals**). Most adjectives use the following four endings:

~ ADJECTIVES ~

	singular		plural	
m	fantástico	fan·*tas*·tee·ko	fantásticos	fan·*tas*·tee·kos
f	fantástica	fan·*tas*·tee·ka	fantásticas	fan·*tas*·tee·kas

a fantastic hotel   un hotel fantástico (lit: a-**m-sg** hotel fantastic-**m-sg**)
oon o·*tel* fan·*tas*·tee·ko

a fantastic meal	una comida fantástica (lit: a-**f-sg** meal fantastic-**f-sg**) oo·na ko·mee·da fan·tas·tee·ka
some fantastic books	unos libros fantásticos (lit: some-**m-pl** books fantastic-**m-pl**) oo·nos lee·bros fan·tas·tee·kos
some fantastic tapas	unas tapas fantásticas (lit: some-**f-pl** tapas fantastic-**f-pl**) oo·nas ta·pas fan·tas·tee·kas

Adjectives generally come after the noun in Spanish. However, adjectives expressing quantity (such as 'much', 'a lot', 'little', 'few', 'many') always precede the noun. See also **demonstratives** and **possessives**.

a comfortable hotel	un hotel cómodo (lit: a-**m-sg** hotel comfortable-**m-sg**) oon o·tel ko·mo·do
many tourists	muchos turistas (lit: many-**m-pl** tourists) moo·chos too·rees·tas

Most adverbs in Spanish are derived from adjectives by adding the ending -*mente* ·*men*·te to the singular feminine form of the adjective (ie the form ending in -*a*), just like you add the ending '-ly' to the adjective in English. In Spanish, adverbs are generally placed after the verb they refer to.

a slow train	un tren lento (lit: a-**m-sg** train slow-**m-sg**) oon tren len·to
to speak slowly	hablar lentamente (lit: to-speak slowly) ab·lar len·ta·men·te

Articles

Naming People/Things

There are four words for the definite article (ie equivalents of 'the' in English) in Spanish, used depending on the gender and the number of the noun (see **gender** and **plurals**). The masculine singular form of the definite article is joined to some prepositions when it's placed after them, so *a el* (to the-m-sg) becomes *al* al and *de el* (of the-m-sg) becomes *del* del. See also **prepositions**.

~ DEFINITE ARTICLES ~

m sg	**the car**	el coche	el ko·che
m pl	**the cars**	los coches	los ko·ches
f sg	**the shop**	la tienda	la tyen·da
f pl	**the shops**	las tiendas	las tyen·das

Similarly, Spanish has four words for the indefinite article (ie 'a/an' in English), depending on the gender and number of the noun.

~ INDEFINITE ARTICLES ~

m sg	**an egg**	un huevo	oon we·vo
m pl	**some eggs**	unos huevos	oo·nos we·vos
f sg	**a house**	una casa	oo·na ka·sa
f pl	**some houses**	unas casas	oo·nas ka·sas

Be

Describing People/Things • Making Statements

Spanish has two words for the English verb 'be': *ser* ser and *estar* es·tar, which are used depending on the context.

~ USE OF *SER* (TO BE) ~

permanent characteristics of persons/things	Liz es muy guapa. leez es mooy *gwa*·pa	Liz is very pretty.
occupations or nationality	Ana es de España. *a*·na es de e·*spa*·nya	Ana is from Spain.
time or location of events	Son las tres. son las tres	It's 3 o'clock.
possession	¿De quién es este bolso? de kyen es *es*·te *bol*·so	Whose bag is this?

~ USE OF *ESTAR* (TO BE) ~

temporary characteristics of persons/things	La sopa está fría. la *so*·pa es·*ta free*·a	The soup is cold.
time or location of persons/things	Estamos en Madrid. es·*ta*·mos en ma·*dreeth*	We're in Madrid.
mood of a person	Estoy contento/a. m/f es·toy kon·*ten*·to/a	I'm happy.

~ SER (TO BE) – PRESENT TENSE ~

I	am	yo	soy	yo	soy
you sg inf	are	tú	eres	too	e·res
you sg pol	are	Usted	es	oo·*ste*	es
he	is	él	es	el	es
she	is	ella	es	e·lya	es
we	are	nosotros m nosotras f	somos	no·so·tros no·so·tras	*so*·mos
you pl inf	are	vosotros m vosotras f	sois	vo·so·tros vo·so·tras	soys
you pl pol	are	Ustedes	son	oo·*ste*·des	son
they	are	ellos m ellas f	son	e·lyos e·lyas	son

~ *ESTAR* (TO BE) – PRESENT TENSE ~				
I	**am**	yo	estoy	yo	es·*toy*
you sg inf	**are**	tú	estás	too	es·*tas*
you sg pol	**are**	Usted	está	oo·*ste*	es·*ta*
he	**is**	él	está	el	es·*ta*
she	**is**	ella	está	e·*lya*	es·*ta*
we	**are**	nosotros m nosotras f	estamos	no·so·tros no·so·tras	es·*ta*·mos
you pl inf	**are**	vosotros m vosotras f	estáis	vo·so·tros vo·so·tras	es·*tais*
you pl pol	**are**	Ustedes	están	oo·*ste*·des	es·*tan*
they	**are**	ellos m ellas f	están	e·*lyos* e·*lyas*	es·*tan*

Demonstratives

Giving Instructions • Indicating Location • Pointing
Things Out

To point something out, the easiest phrases to use are *es* es (it
is), *esto es* es·to es (this is) or *eso es* e·so es (that is).

It's a guide to Seville.   Es una guía de Sevilla.
                                       (lit: is a-f-sg guide of Seville)
                                       es oo·na gee·a de se·vee·lya

The Spanish words for 'this' and 'that' vary, depending on whether
something is close (ie 'this'), away from you (ie 'that'), or even
further away in time or space (ie 'that over there'). Each of these
words changes form depending on the gender and number of the
noun it refers to. See also **gender** and **plurals**.

~ DEMONSTRATIVES ~

	m sg		m pl	
this (close)	éste	e·ste	éstos	e·stos
that (away)	ése	e·se	ésos	e·sos
that (further away)	aquél	a·kel	aquéllos	a·ke·lyos

	f sg		f pl	
this (close)	ésta	e·sta	éstas	e·stas
that (away)	ésa	e·sa	ésas	e·sas
that (further away)	aquélla	a·ke·lya	aquéllas	a·ke·lyas

Gender

Naming People/Things

In Spanish, all nouns (words which denote a thing, person or idea) have either masculine or feminine gender. You can recognise the noun's gender by the article, demonstrative, possessive or any other adjective accompanying the noun, as they all change form to agree with the noun's gender (see **adjectives & adverbs**, **articles**, **demonstratives**, **possessives**). The gender of words is also indicated in the dictionary, but here are some general rules:

» a word is masculine/feminine if it refers to a man/woman
» words ending in -o or -or are generally masculine
» words ending in -a, -d, -z or -ión are usually feminine

The masculine and feminine forms of words are indicated with m and f throughout this book where relevant. See also p138.

Have

Possessing

Possession can be indicated in various ways in Spanish (see also **possessives**). One way is by using the verb *tener* te·*ner* (have). For negative forms with 'have', see **negatives**.

~ TENER (TO HAVE) ~

I	have	yo	tengo	yo	*ten*·go
you sg inf	have	tú	tienes	too	*tye*·nes
you sg pol	have	Usted	tiene	oo·*ste*	*tye*·ne
he	has	él	tiene	el	*tye*·ne
she	has	ella	tiene	e·*lya*	*tye*·ne
we	have	nosotros m nosotras f	ten·emos	no·*so*·tros no·*so*·tras	te·*ne*·mos
you pl inf	have	vosotros m vosotras f	tenéis	vo·*so*·tros vo·*so*·tras	te·*neys*
you pl pol	have	Ustedes	tienen	oo·*ste*·des	*tye*·nen
they	have	ellos m ellas f	tienen	e·*lyos* e·*lyas*	*tye*·nen

The word *hay* ai – which is the impersonal form of the verb *haber* ha·*ber* (have) – is used to mean 'there is/are' and in questions for 'is/are there ...?':

Is there hot water? ¿Hay agua caliente?
(lit: is-there water hot-**f-sg**)
ai *a*·gwa ka·*lyen*·te

Negatives

Negating

To make a negative statement in Spanish, just add the word *no* no (not) before the main verb of the sentence:

I'm not going to try that.	No voy a probarlo. (lit: not I-go to to-try-it) no voy a pro·*bar*·lo

Contrary to English, Spanish uses double negatives:

I have nothing to declare.	No tengo nada que declarar. (lit: not I-have nothing that to-declare) no *ten*·go *na*·da ke dek·la·*rar*

Personal Pronouns

Making Statements • Naming People/Things

Personal pronouns ('I', 'you' etc) change form in Spanish depending on whether they're the subject or the object of a sentence. It's the same in English, which has 'I' and 'me' as subject and object pronouns (eg 'I see her' and 'She sees me'). Note, however, that the subject pronoun is usually omitted in Spanish as the subject is understood from the corresponding verb form (see **verbs**).

I'm a student.	Soy estudiante. (lit: I-am student-**m&f-sg**) soy es·too·*dyan*·te

~ SUBJECT PRONOUNS ~

I	yo	yo	we	nosotros m nosotras f	no·so·tros no·so·tras
you sg inf	tú	too	**you** pl inf	vosotros m vosotras f	vo·so·tros vo·so·tras
you sg pol	Usted	oo·*ste*	**you** pl pol	Ustedes	oo·*ste*·des
he **she**	él ella	el e·lya	**they**	ellos m ellas f	e·lyos e·lyas

As the tables show, Spanish has two 'you' forms. With people familiar to you or younger than you, it's usual to use the informal form of 'you', *tú* too, rather than the polite form, *Usted* oo·*ste*. Phrases in this book use the form that is appropriate to the situation. Where both forms are used, they are indicated by pol and inf. See also the box **addressing people**, p95.

~ OBJECT PRONOUNS ~

me	me	me	**us**	nos	nos
you sg inf	te	te	**you** pl inf	vos	vos
you sg pol	lo/le m la/le f	lo/le la/le	**you** pl pol	los/les m las/les f	los/les las/les
him **it**	lo/le	lo/le	**them**	los/les m las/les f	los/les las/les
her **it**	la/le	la/le			

In this table, the forms separated by a slash are direct/indirect object pronouns.

The direct and indirect object pronouns differ only for the third person ('he', 'she', 'it', 'they') and the polite 'you' forms.

I don't know her.	No la conozco. (lit: not her I-know)
	no la ko·*noth*·ko
I'm talking to her.	Le hablo. (lit: to-her I-talk)
	le *a*·blo

The object pronouns generally come before the verb. The indirect object pronoun comes before the direct object pronoun.

I'll show it to you.	Te lo mostraré. (lit: to-you-sg-inf
	it-m-sg I-will-show)
	te lo mos·tra·*re*

Plurals

Naming People/Things

To form plurals in Spanish, add *-s* if the noun ends in a vowel and *-es* if it ends in a consonant. In this book singular and plural forms are shown with sg and pl respectively where needed.

~ SINGULAR ~			~ PLURAL ~		
bed	cama	*ka*·ma	**beds**	camas	*ka*·mas
woman	mujer	moo·*kher*	**women**	mujeres	moo·*khe*·res

Possessives

Possessing

A common way of indicating possession is by using possessive adjectives before the noun they refer to. Like other adjectives, they agree with the noun in number, and in case of 'our' and 'your' they also agree in gender (see also **gender** and **plurals**).

| **our daughter** | nuestra hija (lit: our-f-sg daughter) |
| | *nwes*·tra ee·kha |

~ POSSESSIVE ADJECTIVES ~

my	mi/mis	mee/ mees	**our**	nuestro/ nuestros m nuestra/ nuestras f	nwes·tro/ nwes·tros nwes·tra/ nwes·tras
your sg inf	tu/tus	too/ toos	**your** pl inf	vuestro/ vuestros m vuestra/ vuestras f	vwes·tro/ vwes·tros vwes·tra/ vwes·tras
your sg pol	su/sus	soo/ soos	**your** pl pol	su/sus	soo/soos
his **her** **its**	su/sus	soo/ soos	**their**	su/sus	soo/soos

Note that in the table above, the Spanish possessive adjective forms separated by a slash are used with a singular and plural noun respectively.

my child	mi hijo (lit: my-m-sg child) mee *ee*·kho
my children	mis hijos (lit: my-m-pl children) mees *ee*·khos

Another way to indicate possession is by using possessive pronouns (see the table opposite), which also agree in gender and number with the noun.

The book is mine.	El libro es mío. (lit: the-m-sg book is mine-m-sg) el *lee*·bro es *mee*·o

~ POSSESSIVE PRONOUNS ~

mine	mío/ míos m mía/ mías f	mee·o/ mee·os mee·a/ mee·as	**ours**	nuestro/ nuestros m nuestra/ nuestras f	nwes·tro/ nwes·tros nwes·tra/ nwes·tras
yours sg inf	tuyo/ tuyos m tuya/ tuyas f	too·yo/ too·yos too·ya/ too·yas	**yours** pl inf	vuestro/ vuestros m vuestra/ vuestras f	vwes·tro/ vwes·tros vwes·tra/ vwes·tras
yours sg pol	suyo/ suyos m suya/ suyas f	soo·yo/ soo·yos soo·ya/ soo·yas	**yours** pl pol	suyo/ suyos m suya/ suyas f	soo·yo/ soo·yos soo·ya/ soo·yas
his **hers** **its**			**theirs**		

The four alternatives in this table are used with m sg, m pl, f sg and f pl nouns.

Ownership can also be expressed in Spanish using the construction '*de* de (of) + noun', just like in English. See also **have**.

my friend's bag	el bolso de mi amigo (lit: the-m-sg bag of my friend-m-sg) el *bol*·so de mee a·*mee*·go

Prepositions

Giving Instructions • Indicating Location • Pointing Things Out

Like English, Spanish uses prepositions to explain where things are in time or space. Some common prepositions are listed in the table that follows. For more prepositions, see the **dictionary**.

When certain prepositions are followed by a definite article, they are contracted into a single word (see **articles**).

~ PREPOSITIONS ~					
after	después de	des·*pwes* de	**from**	de	de
at (time)	a	a	**in (place)**	en	en
before	antes de	*an*·tes de	**to**	a	a

Questions

Asking Questions • Negating

The easiest way of forming 'yes/no' questions in Spanish is to add the phrase *verdad* ver·*da* (literally 'truth') to the end of a statement, similar to 'isn't it?' in English. You can also turn a statement into a question by putting the verb before the subject of the sentence, just like in English.

This is the right stop, isn't it?	¿Ésta es la parada, verdad? (lit: this-f-sg is the-f-sg stop truth) *es*·ta es la pa·*ra*·da ver·*da*
Is this the right stop?	¿Es ésta la parada? (lit: is this-f-sg the-f-sg stop) es *es*·ta la pa·*ra*·da

As in English, there are also question words for more specific questions. These words go at the start of the sentence.

~ QUESTION WORDS ~					
how	cómo	*ko*·mo	**where**	dónde	*don*·de
what	qué	ke	**who**	quién sg	kyen
				quiénes pl	*kye*·nes
when	cuándo	*kwan*·do	**why**	por qué	por ke

Verbs

Doing Things

There are three verb categories in Spanish, depending on whether the infinitive ends in -*ar*, -*er* or -*ir*, eg *hablar* ab·*lar* (talk), *comer* ko·*mer* (eat), *vivir* vee·*veer* (live). Tenses are formed by adding various endings for each person to the verb stem (after removing -*ar*, -*er* or -*ir* from the infinitive) or to the infinitive, and for most verbs these endings follow regular patterns. The verb endings for the present, past and future tenses are presented in the tables on the following pages. For negative forms of verbs, see **negatives**.

~ PRESENT TENSE ~

		hablar	**comer**	**vivir**
I	yo	hablo	como	vivo
you sg inf	tú	hablas	comes	vives
you sg pol	Usted	habla	come	vive
he/she	él/ella	habla	come	vive
we	nosotros m nosotras f	hablamos	comemos	vivimos
you pl inf	vosotros m vosotras f	habláis	coméis	vivís
you pl pol	Ustedes	hablan	comen	viven
they	ellos m ellas f	hablan	comen	viven

See also **be** and **have**.

~ PAST TENSE ~

		hablar	comer	vivir
I	yo	hablé	comí	viví
you sg inf	tú	hablaste	comiste	viviste
you sg pol	Usted	habló	comió	vivió
he/she	él/ella	habló	comió	vivió
we	nosotros m nosotras f	hablamos	comimos	vivimos
you pl inf	vosotros m vosotras f	hablasteis	comisteis	vivisteis
you pl pol	Ustedes	hablaron	comieron	vivieron
they	ellos m ellas f	hablaron	comieron	vivieron

In case of the future tense, the endings follow the same pattern for all three verb categories, and they are simply added to the infinitive (dictionary form of the verb), not the verb stem:

~ FUTURE TENSE ~

		hablar	comer	vivir
I	yo	hablaré	comeré	viviré
you sg inf	tú	hablarás	comerás	vivirás
you sg pol	Usted	hablará	comerá	vivirá
he/she	él/ella	hablará	comerá	vivirá
we	nosotros m nosotras f	hablaremos	comeremos	viviremos
you pl inf	vosotros m vosotras f	hablaréis	comeréis	viviréis
you pl pol	Ustedes	hablarán	comerán	vivirán
they	ellos m ellas f	hablarán	comerán	vivirán

Word Order

Making Statements

Spanish has a basic word order of subject–verb–object, just like English. However, the subject pronoun is usually omitted in Spanish because the subject is understood from the corresponding verb form (see **verbs**). Both of the following examples are correct, but the second one is more common:

I study business.　Yo estudio comercio.
(lit: I I-study business)
yo es·*too*·dyo ko·*mer*·thyo

Estudio comercio. (lit: I-study business)
es·*too*·dyo ko·*mer*·thyo

See also **negatives** and **questions**.

Proverbs in Spain

Proverbs are big in Spain. The Marqués de Santillana compiled a national collection in the second half of the 15th century, and one of the characters in *Don Quixote*, Sancho Panza, speaks almost entirely in proverbs. The novel's author, Cervantes, described these popular sayings as 'short sentences based on long experience'.

Ser como el perro del hortelano, que ni las come las berzas, ni las deja comer al amo.

ser *ko*·mo el *pe*·ro del or·te·*la*·no ke nee *ko*·me las *ber*·thas nee las *de*·kha ko·*mer* al *a*·mo
(lit: to be like the market gardener's dog, who doesn't eat the cabbages and won't let his master eat them either)

~ GRAMMAR GLOSSARY ~

adjective	a word that describes something – 'he was the **greatest** toreador of his time'
adverb	a word that explains how an action is done – 'he turned around **quickly**'
article	the words 'a', 'an' and 'the'
demonstrative	a word that means 'this' or 'that'
direct object	the thing or person in the sentence that has the action directed to it – 'and the bull missed **him**'
gender	classification of *nouns* into classes (like masculine and feminine), requiring other words (eg *adjectives*) to belong to the same class
indirect object	the person or thing in the sentence that is the recipient of the action – 'the public yelled to **him**'
infinitive	dictionary form of a verb – 'to **be** careful'
noun	a thing, person or idea – 'the **fight** was exciting'
number	whether a word is singular or plural – 'and they sent in new **toreadors**'
personal pronoun	a word that means 'I', 'you' etc
possessive adjective	a word that means 'my', 'your' etc
possessive pronoun	a word that means 'mine', 'yours' etc
preposition	a word like 'for' or 'before' in English
subject	the thing or person in the sentence that does the action – '**his cape** fell on the ground'
tense	form of a *verb* that tells you whether the action is in the present, past or future – eg 'run' (present), 'ran' (past), 'will run' (future)
verb	a word that tells you what action happened – 'when the bull **charged** again'
verb stem	part of a *verb* that doesn't change – eg '**move**' in '**mov**ing' and '**mov**ed'

Basics

Understanding

KEY PHRASES

Do you speak English?	¿Habla inglés? pol	ab·la een·gles
I (don't) understand.	(No) Entiendo.	(no) en·tyen·do
What does ... mean?	¿Qué significa ...?	ke seeg·nee·fee·ka ...

There are two words for 'Spanish': *español* es·pa·nyol and *castellano* kas·te·lya·no. *Español* is used in Spain, whereas *castellano* is more likely to be used by Latin Americans.

Q Do you speak (English)?	¿Habla (inglés)? ab·la (een·gles)
Q Does anyone speak (English)?	¿Hay alguien que hable (inglés)? ai al·gyen ke ab·le een·gles
A I (don't) speak Spanish.	(No) Hablo español. (no) ab·lo es·pa·nyol
A I speak a little (Spanish).	Hablo un poco de (español). ab·lo oon po·ko de (es·pa·nyol)
I'd like to practise Spanish.	Me gustaría practicar español. me goos·ta·ree·a prak·tee·kar es·pa·nyol
I need an interpreter who speaks (English).	Necesito un intérprete que hable (inglés). ne·the·see·to oon in·ter·pre·te ke ab·le (een·gles)

BASICS · UNDERSTANDING

🔊 LISTEN FOR

¿Cómo?	ko·mo	Pardon?
No.	no	No.
Sí.	see	Yes.

Would you like me to teach you some English?
¿Quieres que te enseñe algo de inglés? inf
kye·res ke te en·se·nye al·go de een·gles

Q Do you understand?
¿Me entiende/entiendes? pol/inf
me en·tyen·de/en·tyen·des

A I (don't) understand.
(No) Entiendo.
(no) en·tyen·do

How do you pronounce this word?
¿Cómo se pronuncia esta palabra?
ko·mo se pro·noon·thya es·ta pa·lab·ra

How do you write 'ciudad'?
¿Cómo se escribe 'ciudad'?
ko·mo se es·kree·be thyu·da

What does ... mean?
¿Qué significa ...?
ke seeg·nee·fee·ka ...

Could you repeat that?
¿Puede repetirlo?
pwe·de re·pe·teer·lo

Could you please write it down?
¿Puede escribirlo, por favor?
pwe·de es·kree·beer·lo por fa·vor

Could you please speak more slowly?
¿Puede hablar más despacio, por favor?
pwe·de ab·lar mas des·pa·thyo por fa·vor

Slowly, please!	Más despacio, por favor.	mas des·pa·thyo por fa·vor

Numbers & Amounts

KEY PHRASES

How much?	¿Cuánto?	kwan·to
a little	un poquito	oon po·kee·to
some	algunos/as m/f	al·goo·nos/as

Cardinal Numbers

0	cero	the·ro
1	uno	oo·no
2	dos	dos
3	tres	tres
4	cuatro	kwa·tro
5	cinco	theen·ko
6	seis	seys
7	siete	sye·te
8	ocho	o·cho
9	nueve	nwe·ve
10	diez	dyeth
11	once	on·the
12	doce	do·the
13	trece	tre·the
14	catorce	ka·tor·the
15	quince	keen·the
16	dieciséis	dye·thee·seys
17	diecisiete	dye·thee·sye·te
20	veinte	veyn·te

21	veintiuno	veyn·tee·*oo*·no
22	veintidós	veyn·tee·*dos*
30	treinta	*treyn*·ta
40	cuarenta	kwa·*ren*·ta
50	cincuenta	theen·*kwen*·ta
60	sesenta	se·*sen*·ta
70	setenta	se·*ten*·ta
80	ochenta	o·*chen*·ta
90	noventa	no·*ven*·ta
100	cien	thyen
101	ciento uno	*thyen*·to oo·no
500	quinientos	kee·*nyen*·tos
1000	mil	mil
1,000,000	un millón	oon mee·*lyon*

Ordinal Numbers

1st	primero/a m/f	pree·*me*·ro/a
2nd	segundo/a m/f	se·*goon*·do/a
3rd	tercero/a m/f	ter·*the*·ro/a

Amounts

How much?	¿Cuánto?	*kwan*·to
a little	un poquito	oon po·*kee*·to
many	muchos/as m/f	*moo*·chos/as
some	algunos/as m/f	al·*goo*·nos/as
more/less	más/menos	mas/*me*·nos
a quarter/half	un cuarto/medio	oon *kwar*·to/*me*·dyo
a third	un tercio	oon *ter*·thyo
all/none	todo/nada	*to*·do/*na*·da

For other amounts, see **self-catering** (p184).

Times & Dates

BASICS TIMES & DATES

What time is it?	¿Qué hora es?	ke o·ra es
At what time ...?	¿A qué hora ...?	a ke o·ra ...
What date?	¿Qué día?	ke dee·a

Telling the Time

Q **What time is it?**	¿Qué hora es? ke o·ra es
A **It's one o'clock.**	Es la una. es la oo·na
A **It's (10) o'clock.**	Son las (diez). son las (dyeth)
Quarter past one.	Es la una y cuarto. es la oo·na ee kwar·to
Twenty past one.	Es la una y veinte. es la oo·na ee veyn·te
Half past one.	Es la una y media. es la oo·na ee me·dya
Twenty to one.	Es la una menos veinte. es la oo·na me·nos veyn·te
Quarter to one.	Es la una menos cuarto. es la oo·na me·nos kwar·to
It's early.	Es temprano. es tem·pra·no
It's late.	Es tarde. es tar·de

Q At what time?	¿A qué hora? a ke o·ra
A At ...	A las ... a las ...
am	de la mañana de la ma·nya·na
pm	de la tarde de la tar·de

The Calendar

Monday	lunes m	loo·nes
Tuesday	martes m	mar·tes
Wednesday	miércoles m	myer·ko·les
Thursday	jueves m	khwe·ves
Friday	viernes m	vyer·nes
Saturday	sábado m	sa·ba·do
Sunday	domingo m	do·meen·go
January	enero m	e·ne·ro
February	febrero m	fe·bre·ro
March	marzo m	mar·tho
April	abril m	a·breel
May	mayo m	ma·yo
June	junio m	khoo·nyo
July	julio m	khoo·lyo
August	agosto m	a·gos·to
September	septiembre m	sep·tyem·bre
October	octubre m	ok·too·bre
November	noviembre m	no·vyem·bre
December	diciembre m	dee·thyem·bre

BASICS TIMES & DATES

summer	verano m	ve·ra·no
autumn	otoño m	o·to·nyo
winter	invierno m	een·vyer·no
spring	primavera f	pree·ma·ve·ra

What date?	¿Qué día? ke dee·a
🇶 **What date is it today?**	¿Qué día es hoy? ke dee·a es oy
🇦 **It's (18 October).**	Es (el dieciocho de octubre). es (el dye·thee·o·cho de ok·too·bre)

Present

now	ahora	a·o·ra
right now	ahora mismo	a·o·ra mees·mo
this afternoon	esta tarde	es·ta tar·de
this month	este mes	es·te mes
this morning	esta mañana	es·ta ma·nya·na
this week	esta semana	es·ta se·ma·na
this year	este año	es·te a·nyo
today	hoy	oy
tonight	esta noche	es·ta no·che

Past

(three) days ago	hace (tres) días	a·the (tres) dee·as
half an hour ago	hace media hora	a·the me·dya o·ra
a while ago	hace un rato	a·the un ra·to
(five) years ago	hace (cinco) años	a·the (theen·ko) a·nyos

day before yesterday	anteayer	an·te·a·*yer*
last month	el mes pasado	el mes pa·*sa*·do
last night	anoche	a·*no*·che
last week	la semana pasada	la se·*ma*·na pa·*sa*·da
last year	el año pasado	el *a*·nyo pa·*sa*·do
since (May)	desde (mayo)	*des*·de (*ma*·yo)
yesterday	ayer	a·*yer*
yesterday afternoon	ayer por la tarde	a·*yer* por la *tar*·de
yesterday evening	ayer por la noche	a·*yer* por la *no*·che
yesterday morning	ayer por la mañana	a·*yer* por la ma·*nya*·na

Future

in (six) days	dentro de (seis) días	*den*·tro de (seys) *dee*·as
in an hour	dentro de una hora	*den*·tro de *oo*·na *o*·ra
in (five) minutes	dentro de (cinco) minutos	*den*·tro de (*theen*·ko) mee·*noo*·tos
in a month	dentro de un mes	*den*·tro de oon mes
next month	el mes que viene	el mes ke *vye*·ne
next week	la semana que viene	la se·*ma*·na ke *vye*·ne
next year	el año que viene	el *a*·nyo ke *vye*·ne
tomorrow	manana	ma·*nya*·na
tomorrow morning	mañana por la mañana	ma·*nya*·na por la ma·*nya*·na

tomorrow afternoon	mañana por la tarde	ma·*nya*·na por la *tar*·de
tomorrow evening	mañana por la noche	ma·*nya*·na por la *no*·che
day after tomorrow	pasado manana	pa·*sa*·do ma·*nya*·na
until (June)	hasta (junio)	*as*·ta (*khoo*·nyo)

During the Day

afternoon	tarde f	*tar*·de
day	día m	*dee*·a
evening	noche f	*no*·che
midday	mediodía m	me·dyo·*dee*·a
midnight	medianoche f	me·dya·*no*·che
early morning (midnight to 5am)	madrugada f	ma·droo·*ga*·da
morning	mañana f	ma·*nya*·na
night	noche f	*no*·che
sunrise	amanecer m	a·ma·ne·*ther*
sunset	puesta f del sol	*pwes*·ta del sol

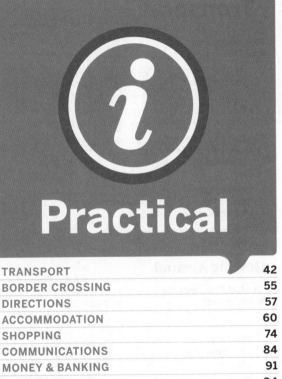

Practical

Transport

KEY PHRASES

At what time's the next bus?	¿A qué hora es el próximo autobús?	a ke o·ra es el *prok*·see·mo ow·to·*boos*
One ... ticket, please.	Un ... billete, por favor.	oon ... bee·*lye*·te, por fa·*vor*
Can you tell me when we get to (Valladolid)?	¿Puede avisar-me cuando lleguemos a (Valladolid)?	*pwe*·de a·vee·*sar*·me *kwan*·do lye·*ge*·mos a (va·lya·do·*leeth*)
Please take me to this address.	Por favor, lléveme a esta dirección.	por fa·*vor*, *lye*·ve·me a es·ta dee·rek·*thyon*
I'd like to hire a car.	Quisiera alquilar un coche.	kee·*sye*·ra al·kee·*lar* oon *ko*·che

Getting Around

At what time does the ... leave/arrive?
¿A qué hora sale/llega el ...?
a ke o·ra *sa*·le/*lye*·ga el ...

boat	barco	*bar*·ko
bus (city)	autobús	ow·to·*boos*
bus (intercity)	autocar	ow·to·*kar*
plane	avión	a·*vyon*
train	tren	tren
tram	tranvía	tran·*vee*·a

At what time's the first (bus)?	¿A qué hora es el primer (autobús)? a ke o·ra es el pree·*mer* (ow·to·*boos*)
At what time's the last (train)?	¿A qué hora es el último (tren)? a ke o·ra es el *ool*·tee·mo (tren)
At what time's the next (boat)?	¿A qué hora es el próximo (barco)? a ke o·ra es el *prok*·see·mo (*bar*·ko)
How long will it be delayed?	¿Cuánto tiempo se retrasará? *kwan*·to *tyem*·po se re·tra·sa·ra
Is this seat free?	¿Está libre este asiento? es·*ta lee*·bre es·te a·*syen*·to
✂ **Is it free?**	¿Está libre? es·*ta lee*·bre
That's my seat.	Ése es mi asiento. *e*·se es mee a·*syen*·to
I'd like to get off at (Aranjuez).	Me gustaría bajarme en (Aranjuez). me goos·ta·*ree*·a ba·*khar*·me en (a·ran·*khweth*)
I want to get off here!	¡Quiero bajarme aquí! *kye*·ro ba·*khar*·me a·*kee*
I'd prefer to walk there.	Prefiero ir a pie. pre·*fye*·ro eer a pye
Can we get there by public transport?	¿Se puede ir en transporte público? se *pwe*·de eer en trans·*por*·te *poo*·blee·ko

Buying Tickets

Do I need to book?	¿Tengo que reservar? *ten*·go ke re·ser·*var*
How much is it?	¿Cuánto cuesta? *kwan*·to *kwes*·ta
Where can I buy a ticket?	¿Dónde puedo comprar un billete? *don*·de *pwe*·do kom·*prar* oon bee·*lye*·te
Is it a direct route?	¿Es un viaje directo? es oon *vya*·khe dee·*rek*·to
Is there a toilet?	¿Hay servicios? ai ser·*vee*·thyos
How long does the trip take?	¿Cuánto se tarda? *kwan*·to se *tar*·da
Can I get a stand-by ticket?	¿Puede ponerme en la lista de espera? *pwe*·de po·*ner*·me en la *lees*·ta de es·*pe*·ra
I'd like an aisle seat.	Quisiera un asiento de pasillo. kee·*sye*·ra oon a·*syen*·to de pa·*see*·lyo
I'd like a window seat.	Quisiera un asiento junto a la ventana. kee·*sye*·ra oon a·*syen*·to *khoon*·to a la ven·*ta*·na
I'd like a (non)smoking seat.	Quisiera un asiento de (no) fumadores. kee·*sye*·ra oon a·*syen*·to de (no) foo·ma·*do*·res

Buying a Ticket

What time is the next ...?

¿A qué hora sale el próximo ...?
a ke *o·ra sa·*le el *prok·*see·mo ...

boat
barco
*bar·*ko

bus
autobús
ow·to·*boos*

train
tren
tren

One ... ticket, please.

Un billete ..., por favor.
oon bee·*lye·*te ... por fa·*vor*

one-way
sencillo
sen·*thee·*lyo

return
de ida y vuelta
de ee·da ee *vwel·*ta

I'd like a/an ... seat.

Quisiera un asiento ...
kee·*sye·*ra oon a·*syen·*to ...

aisle
de pasillo
de pa·*see·*lyo

window
junto a la
ventana
*khoon·*to a la
ven·*ta·*na

Which platform does it depart from?

¿De cuál andén sale?
de kwal an·*den sa·*le

I'd like to ... my ticket.

Me gustaría ... mi billete.
me goos·ta·*ree*·a ... mee bee·*lye*·te

cancel	cancelar	kan·the·*lar*
change	cambiar	kam·*byar*
collect	recoger	re·ko·*kher*
confirm	confirmer	kon·feer·*mar*

(Two) ... tickets, please.

(Dos) billetes ..., por favor.
(dos) bee·*lye*·tes ... por fa·*vor*

1st-class	de primera clase	de pree·*me*·ra *kla*·se
2nd-class	de segunda clase	de se·*goon*·da *kla*·se
child's	infantil	een·fan·*teel*
return	de ida y vuelta	de ee·da ee *vwel*·ta
student's	de estudiante	de es·too·*dyan*·te

A one-way ticket to (Barcelona).

Un billete sencillo a (Barcelona).
oon bee·*lye*·te sen·*thee*·lyo a (bar·the·*lo*·na)

Luggage

My luggage has been damaged/lost.

Mis maletas han sido dañadas/perdidas.
mees ma·*le*·tas an *see*·do da·*nya*·das/per·*dee*·das

🔊 LISTEN FOR

Esta parada es ...	es·ta pa·*ra*·da es ... This stop is ...
La próxima parada es ...	la *prok*·see·ma pa·*ra*·da es ... The next stop is ...
Está completo.	es·ta kom·*ple*·to It's full.
El ... está retrasado/ cancelado.	el ... es·ta re·tra·*sa*·do/ kan·the·*la*·do The ... is delayed/ cancelled.

My luggage has been stolen.	Mis maletas han sido robadas. mees ma·*le*·tas an *see*·do ro·*ba*·das
I'd like a luggage locker.	Quisiera un casillero de consigna. kee·*sye*·ra oon ka·see·*lye*·ro de kon·*seeg*·na

Bus

Which bus goes to (Madrid)?	¿Qué autobús va a (Madrid)? ke ow·to·*boos* va a (ma·*dreeth*)
Where's the bus stop?	¿Dónde está la parada del autobús? *don*·de es·ta la pa·*ra*·da del ow·to·*boos*
What's the next stop?	¿Cuál es la próxima parada? kwal es la *prok*·see·ma pa·*ra*·da

Please tell me when we get to (Valladolid).	¿Puede avisarme cuando lleguemos a (Valladolid)? *pwe·*de a·vee·*sar·*me *kwan·*do lye·*ge·*mos a (va·lya·do·*leeth*)
Bus number ...	El autobús número ... el ow·to·*boos* noo·me·ro ...

For bus numbers, see **numbers & amounts**, p34.

Train

What station is this?	¿Cuál es esta estación? kwal es *es·*ta es·ta·*thyon*
What's the next station?	¿Cuál es la próxima estación? kwal es la *prok·*see·ma es·ta·*thyon*
Does this train stop at (Valencia)?	¿Para el tren en (Valencia)? *pa·*ra el tren en (va·*len·*thya)
Do I need to change trains?	¿Tengo que cambiar de tren? *ten·*go ke kam·*byar* de tren
Which carriage is for (Bilbao)?	¿Cuál es el coche para (Bilbao)? kwal es el *ko·*che *pa·*ra (beel·*bow*)

Boat

Are there life jackets?	¿Hay chalecos salvavidas? ai cha·*le·*kos sal·va·*vee·*das
What's the sea like today?	¿Cómo está el mar hoy? *ko·*mo es·*ta* el mar oy
I feel seasick.	Estoy mareado/a. **m/f** es·*toy* ma·re·a·do/a

Taxi

I'd like a taxi at (9am).	Quisiera un taxi a (las nueve de la mañana).
	kee·*sye*·ra oon *tak*·see a (las *nwe*·ve de la ma·*nya*·na)
I'd like a taxi tomorrow.	Quisiera un taxi manana.
	kee·*sye*·ra oon *tak*·see ma·*nya*·na
Where's the taxi stand?	¿Dónde está la parada de taxis?
	don·de es·*ta* la pa·*ra*·da de *tak*·sees
Is this taxi free?	¿Está libre este taxi?
	es·*ta lee*·bre es·te *tak*·see
✂ **Is it free?**	¿Está libre? es·*ta lee*·bre

Where's the bus stop?
don·de es·*ta* la pa·*ra*·da del ow·to·*boos*
¿Dónde está la parada del autobús?

How much is the flag fall/ hiring charge?	¿Cuánto es la tasa de alquiler? *kwan·*to es la *ta·*sa de al·kee·*ler*
Please put the meter on.	Por favor, ponga el taxímetro. por fa·*vor* pon·ga el tak·see·me·tro
How much is it to (the Prado)?	¿Cuánto cuesta ir (al Prado)? *kwan·*to *kwes·*ta eer (al *pra·*do)
Please take me to (this address).	Por favor, lléveme a (esta dirección). por fa·*vor lye·*ve·me a (es·ta dee·rek·*thyon*)
✂ **To ...**	A ... · · · a ...
How much is the final fare?	¿Cuánto es en total? *kwan·*to es en to·*tal*
Please slow down.	Por favor vaya más despacio. por fa·*vor va·*ya mas des·*pa·*thyo
Please wait here.	Por favor espere aquí. por fa·*vor* es·*pe·*re a·*kee*
Stop here!	¡Pare aquí! *pa·*re a·*kee*

For other useful phrases, see **directions**, p57.

Car & Motorbike

Where can I hire a ...?	¿Dónde se puede alquilar ...?	*don*·de se *pwe*·de al·*kee*·lar ...
Does that include insurance/mileage?	¿Incluye el seguro/ kilometraje?	een·*kloo*·ye el se·*goo*·ro/ kee·lo·me·*tra*·khe
I'd like to hire a/an ...	Quisiera alquilar ...	kee·*sye*·ra al·*kee*·lar ...

4WD	un todoterreno	oon to·do·te·*re*·no
automatic car	un coche automático	oon *ko*·che ow·to·*ma*·tee·ko
manual car	un coche manual	oon *ko*·che man·*wal*
motorbike	una moto	*oo*·na *mo*·to

How much for hourly/ daily hire?	¿Cuánto cuesta el alquiler por hora/día?	*kwan*·to *kwes*·ta el al·*kee*·ler por o·ra/*dee*·a
How much for weekly hire?	¿Cuánto cuesta el alquiler por semana?	*kwan*·to *kwes*·ta el al·*kee*·ler por se·*ma*·na
Is this the road to (Seville)?	¿Se va a (Sevilla) por esta carretera?	se va a (se·*vee*·lya) por *es*·ta ka·re·*te*·ra
Where's a petrol station?	¿Dónde hay una gasolinera?	*don*·de ai *oo*·na ga·so·lee·*ne*·ra

🔍 LOOK FOR

Acceso	ak·*the*·so	Entrance
Aparcamiento	a·par·ka·*myen*·to	Parking
Ceda el Paso	*the*·da el *pa*·so	Give Way
Desvío	des·*vee*·o	Detour
Dirección Única	dee·rek·*thyon* oo·nee·ka	One Way
Frene	*fre*·ne	Slow Down
Peaje	pe·*a*·khe	Toll
Peligro	pe·*lee*·gro	Danger
Prohibido Aparcar	pro·ee·*bee*·do a·par·*kar*	No Parking
Prohibido el Paso	pro·ee·*bee*·do el *pa*·so	No Entry
Stop	es·*top*	Stop
Vía de Acceso	*vee*·a de ak·*the*·so	Exit Freeway

What's the (city) speed limit?	¿Cuál es el límite de velocidad (en la ciudad)? kwal es el *lee*·mee·te de ve·lo·thee·*da* (en la thyu·*da*)
Please fill it up.	Por favor, lléneme el depósito. por fa·*vor* *lye*·ne·me el de·*po*·see·to
I'd like (20) litres of ...	Quiero (veinte) litros de ... *kye*·ro (*veyn*·te) *lee*·tros de ...
Please check the oil/water.	Por favor, revise el nivel del aceite/agua. por fa·*vor* re·*vee*·se el nee·*vel* del a·*they*·te/*a*·gwa

windscreen
parabrisas m
pa·ra·*bree*·sas

petrol
gasolina f
ga·so·*lee*·na

battery
batería f
ba·ta·*ree*·a

engine
motor m
mo·*tor*

headlight
faro m
fa·ro

tyre
rueda f
rwe·da

Please check the tyre pressure.	Por favor, revise la presión de los neumáticos. por fa·*vor* re·*vee*·se la pre·*syon* de los ne·oo·*ma*·tee·kos
(How long) Can I park here?	¿(Por cuánto tiempo) Puedo aparcar aquí? (por *kwan*·to *tyem*·po) *pwe*·do a·par·*kar* a·*kee*
I need a mechanic.	Necesito un/una mecánico/a. **m/f** ne·the·*see*·to oon/*oo*·na me·ka·*nee*·ko/a
The car has broken down (at Salamanca).	El coche se ha averiado (en Salamanca). el *ko*·che se a a·ve·*rya*·do (en sa·la·*man*·ka)
I had an accident.	He tenido un accidente. e te·*nee*·do oon ak·thee·*den*·te

Bicycle

Can we get there by bike?	¿Se puede ir en bici? se *pwe*·de eer en *bee*·thee
Where can I hire a bicycle?	¿Dónde se puede alquilar una bicicleta? *don*·de se *pwe*·de al·kee·*lar* oo·na bee·thee·*kle*·ta
Where can I buy a (secondhand) bike?	¿Dónde se puede comprar una bicicleta (de segunda mano)? *don*·de se *pwe*·de kom·*prar* oo·na bee·thee·*kle*·ta (de se·*goon*·da *ma*·no)
How much is it per day?	¿Cuánto cuesta por un día? *kwan*·to *kwes*·ta por oon *dee*·a
How much is it per hour?	¿Cuánto cuesta por una hora? *kwan*·to *kwes*·ta por oo·na *o*·ra
I have a puncture.	Se me ha pinchado una rueda. se me a peen·*cha*·do oo·na *rwe*·da
I'd like to have my bicycle repaired.	Me gustaría arreglar mi bicicleta. me goo·sta·*ree*·a a·reg·*lar* mee bee·thee·*kle*·ta
Are there cycling paths?	¿Hay carril bicicleta? ai ka·*reel* bee·thee·*kle*·ta
Is there bicycle parking?	¿Hay aparcamiento de bicicletas? ai a·par·ka·*myen*·to de bee·thee·*kle*·tas
Can I take my bike on the train?	¿Puedo llevar mi bicicleta en el tren? *pwe*·do lye·*var* mee bee·thee·*kle*·ta en el tren

Border Crossing

KEY PHRASES

I'm here for ... days.	Estoy aquí por ... días.	es·*toy* a·*kee* por ... *dee*·as
I'm staying at ...	Me estoy alojando en ...	me es·*toy* a·lo·*khan*·do en ...
I have nothing to declare.	No tengo nada que declarar.	no *ten*·go *na*·da ke de·kla·*rar*

Passport Control

I'm here on business.	Estoy aquí de negocios. es·*toy* a·*kee* de ne·*go*·thyos
I'm here on holiday.	Estoy aquí de vacaciones. es·*toy* a·*kee* de va·ka·*thyo*·nes
I'm here in transit.	Estoy aquí en tránsito. es·*toy* a·*kee* en *tran*·see·to
I'm here for ... days.	Estoy aquí por ... días. es·*toy* a·*kee* por ... *dee*·as
I'm here for ... weeks.	Estoy aquí por ... semanas. es·*toy* a·*kee* por ... se·*ma*·nas
I'm here for ... months.	Estoy aquí por ... meses. es·*toy* a·*kee* por ... *me*·ses
I'm going to (Salamanca).	Voy a (Salamanca). voy a (sa·la·*man*·ka)
I'm staying at ...	Me estoy alojando en ... me es·*toy* a·lo·*khan*·do en ...

🔊 LISTEN FOR

Su pasaporte, por favor.	soo pa·sa·*por*·te por fa·*vor* Your passport, please.
Su visado, por favor.	soo vee·*sa*·do por fa·*vor* Your visa, please.
¿Está viajando en un grupo?	es·*ta* vya·*khan*·do en oon *groo*·po Are you travelling in a group?
¿Está viajando con familia?	es·*ta* vya·*khan*·do kon fa·*mee*·lya Are you travelling with family?
¿Está viajando solo/a? m/f	es·*ta* vya·*khan*·do *so*·lo/a Are you travelling on your own?

Customs

I have nothing to declare.	No tengo nada que declarar. no *ten*·go *na*·da ke de·kla·*rar*
I have something to declare.	Quisiera declarar algo. kee·*sye*·ra de·kla·*rar al*·go
That's (not) mine.	Eso (no) es mío. e·so (no) es *mee*·o
I didn't know I had to declare it.	No sabía que tenía que declararlo. no sa·*bee*·a ke te·*nee*·a ke de·kla·*rar*·lo

For phrases on payments and receipts, see **money & banking**, p91.

Directions

KEY PHRASES

Where's ...?	¿Dónde está ...?	*don*·de es·*ta* ...
What's the address?	¿Cuál es la direc-ción?	kwal es la dee·rek·*thyon*
How far is it?	¿A cuánta distancia está?	a *kwan*·ta dees·*tan*·thya es·*ta*

Excuse me.	Perdón. per·*don*
Could you help me, please?	¿Perdón, puede ayudarme, por favor? per·*don* pwe·de a·yoo·*dar*·me por fa·*vor*
Where's ...?	¿Dónde está ...? *don*·de es·*ta* ...
I'm looking for ...	Busco ... *boos*·ko ...
Which way is ...?	¿Por dónde se va a ...? por *don*·de se va a ...
How can I get there?	¿Cómo se puede ir? *ko*·mo se *pwe*·de eer
How far is it?	¿A cuánta distancia está? a *kwan*·ta dees·*tan*·thya es·*ta*
What's the address?	¿Cuál es la dirección? kwal es la dee·rek·*thyon*

| **Can you show me (on the map)?** | ¿Me lo puede indicar (en el mapa)?
me lo *pwe*·de een·dee·*kar* (en el *ma*·pa) |
| **It's ...** | Está ...
es·*ta* ... |

behind ...	detrás de ...	de·*tras* de ...
far away	lejos	*le*·khos
here	aquí	a·*kee*
in front of ...	enfrente de ...	en·*fren*·te de ...
left	por la izquierda	por la eeth·*kyer*·da
near	cerca	*ther*·ka
next to ...	al lado de ...	al *la*·do de ...
opposite ...	frente a ...	*fren*·te a ...
right	por la derecha	por la de·*re*·cha
straight ahead	todo recto	*to*·do *rek*·to
there	ahí	a·*ee*

Turn at the corner.	Doble en la esquina. *do*·ble en la es·*kee*·na
Turn at the traffic lights.	Doble en el semáforo. *do*·ble en el se·*ma*·fo·ro
Turn left/right.	Doble a la izquierda/derecha. *do*·ble a la eeth·*kyer*·da/ de·*re*·cha
(two) kilometres	(dos) kilómetros (dos) kee·*lo*·me·tros
(three) metres	(tres) metros (tres) *me*·tros
(six) minutes	(seis) minutos (seys) mee·*noo*·tos

PRACTICAL DIRECTIONS

traffic lights
semáforo m
se·ma·fo·ro

shop
tienda f
tyen·da

pedestrian crossing
paso de cebra m
pa·so de the·bra

bus
autobús m
ow·to·boos

intersection
cruce m
kroo·the

corner
esquina f
es·kee·na

taxi
taxi m
tak·see

by bus	por autobús por ow·to·boos
by taxi	por taxi por tak·see
by train	por tren por tren
on foot	a pie a pye
avenue	avenida f a·ve·nee·da
lane	callejón m ka·lye·khon
street	calle f ka·lye

For locations and compass directions, see the **dictionary**.

Accommodation

KEY PHRASES

Where's a hotel?	¿Dónde hay un hotel?	*don*·de ai on o·*tel*
Do you have a double room?	¿Tiene una habitación doble?	*tye*·ne *oo*·na a·bee·ta·*thyon* *do*·ble
How much is it per night?	¿Cuánto cuesta por noche?	*kwan*·to *kwes*·ta por *no*·che
Is breakfast included?	¿El desayuno está incluído?	el de·sa·*yoo*·no es·*ta* een·kloo·ee·do
What time is checkout?	¿A qué hora hay que dejar libre la habitación?	a ke o·ra ai ke de·*khar lee*·bre la a·bee·ta·*thyon*

Finding Accommodation

Where's a ...?		¿Dónde hay ...? *don*·de ai ...
bed & breakfast	una pensión con desayuno	*oo*·na pen·*syon* kon de·sa·*yoo*·no
camping ground	terreno de cámping	te·*re*·no de *kam*·peeng
guesthouse	una pensión	*oo*·na pen·*syon*
hotel	un hotel	oon o·*tel*
youth hostel	un albergue juvenil	oon al·*ber*·ge khoo·ve·*neel*

Can you recommend somewhere (cheap)?	¿Puede recomendar algún sitio (barato)? *pwe·de re·ko·men·dar al·goon see·tyo (ba·ra·to)*
Can you recommend somewhere (nearby)?	¿Puede recomendar algún sitio (cercano)? *pwe·de re·ko·men·dar al·goon see·tyo (ther·ka·no)*
Can you recommend somewhere (luxurious)?	¿Puede recomendar algún sitio (de lujo)? *pwe·de re·ko·men·dar al·goon see·tyo (de loo·kho)*
What's the address?	¿Cuál es la dirección? *kwal es la dee·rek·thyon*

For more on how to get there, see **directions** (p57).

Booking Ahead & Checking In

I'd like to book a room, please.	Quisiera reservar una habitación. *kee·sye·ra re·ser·var oo·na a·bee·ta·thyon*

✂	**Are there rooms?**	¿Hay habitaciones?	ai a·bee·ta·thyo·nes

I have a reservation.	He hecho una reserva. *e e·cho oo·na re·ser·va*
My name's ...	Me llamo ... *me lya·mo ...*
For (three) nights/weeks.	Por (tres) noches/semanas. *por (tres) no·ches/se·ma·nas*
From (July 2) to (July 6).	Desde (el dos de julio) hasta (el seis de julio). *des·de (el dos de khoo·lyo) as·ta (el seys de khoo·lyo)*

PRACTICAL ACCOMMODATION

🔊 LISTEN FOR

Lo siento, está completo.	lo *syen*·to es·*ta* kom·*ple*·to I'm sorry, we're full.
¿Por cuántas noches?	por *kwan*·tas *no*·ches For how many nights?
Su pasaporte, por favor.	soo pa·sa·*por*·te por fa·*vor* Your passport, please.

Do I need to pay upfront?	¿Necesito pagar por adelantado? ne·the·*see*·to pa·*gar* por a·de·lan·*ta*·do
Do you offer (long-stay) discounts?	¿Ofrecen descuentos (por larga estancia)? of·*re*·then des·*kwen*·tos (por *lar*·ga es·*tan*·thya)
Is breakfast included?	¿El desayuno está incluído? el de·sa·*yoo*·no es·*ta* een·kloo·*ee*·do
Is there parking?	¿Hay aparcamiento? ai a·par·ka·*myen*·to
Is there wireless internet access here?	¿Hay acceso inalámbrico a internet aquí? ai ak·*the*·so een·a·*lam*·bree·ko a *een*·ter·net a·*kee*
How much is it per person?	¿Cuánto cuesta por persona? *kwan*·to *kwes*·ta por per·*so*·na
How much is it per night/ week?	¿Cuánto cuesta por noche/semana? *kwan*·to *kwes*·ta por *no*·che/se·*ma*·na

Finding a Room

Do you have a ... room?
¿Tiene una habitación ...?
tye·ne oo·na a·bee·ta·thyon ...

 double
doble
do·ble

 single
individual
een·dee·vee·dwal

How much is it per ...?
¿Cuánto cuesta por ...?
kwan·to kwes·ta por ...

 night
noche
no·che

 person
persona
per·so·na

Is breakfast included?
 ¿El desyauno está incluído?
el de·sa·yoo·no es·ta een·kloo·ee·do

Can I see the room?
 ¿Puedo verla?
pwe·do ver·la

I'll take it.
 La alquilo.
la al·kee·lo

I won't take it.
No la alquilo.
no la al·kee·lo

Can I pay by credit card?	¿Puedo pagar con tarjeta de crédito? *pwe·do pa·gar con tar·khe·ta de kre·dee·to*

For other methods of payment, see **money & banking**, p91.

Do you have a double room?	¿Tiene una habitación doble? *tye·ne oo·na a·bee·ta·thyon do·ble*
Do you have a single room?	¿Tiene una habitación individual? *tye·ne oo·na a·bee·ta·thyon een·dee·vee·dwal*
Do you have a twin room?	¿Tiene una habitación con dos camas? *tye·ne oo·na a·bee·ta·thyon con dos ka·mas*
Do you have a room with/ without (a) ...?	¿Tiene una habitación con/sin ...? *tye·ne oo·na a·bee·ta·thyon kon/seen ...*
Can I see it?	¿Puedo verla? *pwe·do ver·la*
It's fine, I'll take it.	Vale, la alquilo. *va·le la al·kee·lo*

Requests & Queries

When/Where's breakfast served?	¿Cuándo/Dónde se sirve el desayuno? *kwan·do/don·de se seer·ve el de·sa·yoo·no*
Please wake me at (seven).	Por favor, despiérteme a (las siete). *por fa·vor des·pyer·te·me a (las sye·te)*

Can I get another ...?	¿Puede darme otro/a ...? m/f
	pwe·de dar·me o·tro/a ...

Can I use the ...?	¿Puedo usar ...?
	pwe·do oo·sar ...

internet	el internet	el een·ter·net
kitchen	la cocina	la ko·thee·na
laundry	el lavadero	el la·va·de·ro
telephone	el teléfono	el te·le·fo·no

Is there a/an ...?	¿Hay ...?
	ai ...

lift (elevator)	ascensor	as·then·sor
message board	tablón de anuncios	ta·blon de a·noon·thyos
safe	una caja fuerte	oo·na ka·kha fwer·te
swimming pool	piscina	pees·thee·na

Do you arrange tours here?	¿Aquí organizan recorridos?
	a·kee or·ga·nee·than re·ko·ree·dos

Do you change money here?	¿Aquí cambian dinero?
	a·kee kam·byan dee·ne·ro

Is there a message for me?	¿Tiene un mensaje para mí?
	tye·ne oon men·sa·khe pa·ra mee

I'm locked out of my room.	Cerré la puerta y se me olvidaron las llaves dentro.
	the·re la pwer·ta y se me ol·vee·da·ron las lya·ves den·tro

The (bathroom) door is locked.	La puerta (del baño) está cerrada.
	la *pwer*·ta (del *ba*·nyo) es·*ta* the·*ra*·da
There's no need to change my sheets.	No hace falta cambiar las sábanas.
	no *a*·the *fal*·ta kam·*byar* las *sa*·ba·nas

Complaints

It's too ... Es demasiado ...
es de·ma·*sya*·do ...

cold	fría f	*free*·a
dark	oscura f	os·*koo*·ra
light/bright	clara f	*kla*·ra
noisy	ruidosa f	rwee·*do*·sa
small	pequeña f	pe·*ke*·nya

The ... doesn't work. No funciona ...
no foon·*thyo*·na ...

air-conditioning	el aire acondicionado	el *ai*·re a·kon·dee·thyo·*na*·do
fan	el ventilador	el ven·tee·la·*dor*
heater	la estufa	la es·*too*·fa
toilet	el retrete	el re·*tre*·te
window	la ventana	la ven·*ta*·na

This ... isn't clean.	Éste/Ésta ... no está limpio/a. m/f
	es·te/es·ta ... no es·*ta* *leem*·pyo/a
There's no hot water.	No hay agua caliente.
	no ai *a*·gwa ka·*lyen*·te

TV
televisión f
te·le·vee·*syon*

fan
ventilador m
ven·tee·la·*dor*

air-conditioning
aire acondicionado m
ai·re a·kon·dee·thyo·*na*·do

bed
cama f
ka·ma

key
llave f
lya·ve

toilet
retrete m
re·*tre*·te

bathroom
baño m
ba·nyo

Answering the Door

Who is it?	¿Quién es? kyen es
Just a moment.	Un momento. oon mo·*men*·to
Come in.	Adelante. a·de·*lan*·te
Can you come back later, please?	¿Puede volver más tarde, por favor? *pwe*·de vol·*ver* mas *tar*·de por fa·*vor*

Checking Out

What time is check out?	¿A qué hora hay que dejar libre la habitación? *a ke o·ra ai ke de·khar lee·bre la a·bee·ta·thyon*
How much extra to stay until (6 o'clock)?	¿Cuánto más cuesta quedarse hasta (las seis)? *kwan·to mas kwes·ta ke·dar·se as·ta (las seys)*
Can I have a late check out?	¿Puedo dejar la habitación más tarde? *pwe·do de·khar la a·bee·ta·thyon mas tar·de*
Can I leave my bags here?	¿Puedo dejar las maletas aquí? *pwe·do de·khar las ma·le·tas a·kee*
There's a mistake in the bill.	Hay un error en la cuenta. *ai oon e·ror en la kwen·ta*
I'm leaving now.	Me voy ahora. *me voy a·o·ra*
Can you call a taxi for me (for 11 o'clock)?	¿Me puede pedir un taxi (para las once)? *me pwe·de pe·deer oon tak·see (pa·ra las on·the)*
Could I have my deposit, please?	¿Me puede dar mi depósito, por favor? *me pwe·de dar mee de·po·see·to por fa·vor*

Could I have my passport, please?	¿Me puede dar mi pasaporte, por favor? me *pwe*·de dar mee pa·sa·*por*·te por fa·*vor*
Could I have my valuables, please?	¿Me puede dar mis objetos de valor, por favor? me *pwe*·de dar mees ob·*khe*·tos de va·*lor* por fa·*vor*
I'll be back on (Tuesday).	Volveré el (martes). vol·ve·*re* el (*mar*·tes)
I'll be back in (three) days.	Volveré en (tres) días. vol·ve·*re* en (tres) *dee*·as

Where's a hotel?
don·de ai oon o·*tel*

¿Dónde hay un hotel?

I had a great stay, thank you.	He tenido una estancia muy agradable, gracias. *e te·nee·do oo·na es·tan·thya mooy a·gra·da·ble gra·thyas*
You've been terrific.	Han sido estupendos. *an see·do es·too·pen·dos*
I'll recommend it to my friends.	Se lo recomendaré a mis amigos. *se lo re·ko·men·da·re a mees a·mee·gos*

Camping

Where's the nearest camp site?	¿Dónde está el terreno de cámping más cercano? *don·de es·ta el te·re·no de kam·peeng mas ther·ka·no*
Can I camp here?	¿Se puede acampar aquí? *se pwe·de a·kam·par a·kee*
Can I park next to my tent?	¿Se puede aparcar al lado de la tienda? *se pwe·de a·par·kar al la·do de la tyen·da*
Do you have ...?	¿Tiene ...? *tye·ne ...*

electricity	electricidad	e·lek·tree·thee·da
shower facilities	duchas	doo·chas
a site	un sitio	oon see·tyo
tents for hire	tiendas de campaña para alquilar	tyen·das de kam·pa·nya pa·ra al·kee·lar

How much is it per ...?	¿Cuánto vale por ...?	
	kwan·to va·le por ...	

caravan	caravana	ka·ra·va·na
person	persona	per·so·na
tent	tienda	tyen·da
vehicle	vehículo	ve·ee·koo·lo

Is the water drinkable?	¿Se puede beber el agua?
	se *pwe*·de *be*·ber el *a*·gwa

I'm looking for the nearest showers.	Estoy buscando las duchas más cercanas.
	es·*toy* boos·*kan*·do las *doo*·chas mas ther·*ka*·nas

I'm looking for the nearest toilet block.	Estoy buscando los servicios más cercanos.
	es·*toy* boos·*kan*·do los ser·*vee*·thyos mas ther·*ka*·nos

Could I borrow ...?	¿Me puede prestar ...?
	me *pwe*·de pres·*tar* ...

For cooking utensils, see **self-catering** (p186) and the **dictionary**.

🔍 **LOOK FOR**

Caballeros	ka·ba·*lye*·ros	Men
Caliente	ka·*lyen*·te	Hot
Dirección Prohibida	dee·rek·*thyon* pro·hee·*bee*·da	No Entry
Frío	*free*·o	Cold
Señoras	se·*nyo*·ras	Women

Sidebar: PRACTICAL ACCOMMODATION

Renting

Do you have a/an ... for rent?	¿Tiene ... para alquilar? tye·ne ... pa·ra al·kee·lar

apartment	un piso	oon pee·so
cabin	una cabaña	oo·na ka·ba·nya
house	una casa	oo·na ka·sa
room	una habitación	oo·na a·bee·ta·thyon
villa	un chalet	oon cha·le

furnished	amueblado/a m/f a·mwe·bla·do/a
partly furnished	semi amueblado/a m/f se·mee a·mwe·bla·do/a
unfurnished	sin amueblar seen a·mwe·blar

Staying with Locals

Can I stay at your place?	¿Me puedo quedar en su/tu casa? pol/inf me pwe·do ke·dar en soo/too ka·sa
Thanks for your hospitality.	Gracias por su/tu hospitalidad. pol/inf gra·thyas por soo/too os·pee·ta·lee·da
I have my own mattress.	Tengo mi propio colchón. ten·go mee pro·pyo kol·chon
I have my own sleeping bag.	Tengo mi propio saco de dormir. ten·go mee pro·pyo sa·ko de dor·meer

Can I bring anything for the meal?	¿Puedo traer algo para la comida? *pwe·*do tra·*er al·*go pa·ra la ko·*mee·*da
Can I use your telephone?	¿Puedo usar su/tu teléfono? pol/inf *pwe·*do oo·*sar* soo/too te·*le·*fo·no
Can I help?	¿Puedo ayudar? *pwe·*do a·yoo·*dar*
Can I set/clear the table?	¿Puedo poner/quitar la mesa? *pwe·*do po·*ner*/kee·*tar* la *me·*sa
Can I do the dishes?	¿Puedo lavar los platos? *pwe·*do la·*var* los *pla·*tos
Can I take out the rubbish?	¿Puedo sacar la basura? *pwe·*do sa·*kar* la ba·*soo·*ra

For compliments to the chef, see **eating out** (p174).

Shopping

KEY PHRASES

I'd like to buy ...	Quisiera comprar ...	kee·sye·ra kom·prar ...
Can I look at it?	¿Puedo verlo?	pwe·do ver·lo
Can I try it on?	¿Me lo puedo probar?	me lo pwe·do pro·bar
How much?	¿Cuánto cuesta?	kwan·to kwes·ta
That's too expensive.	Es muy caro.	es mooy ka·ro

Looking For ...

Where's a (super)market?	¿Dónde está un (super)mercado? don·de es·ta oon (soo·per·)mer·ka·do
Where's a camping store?	¿Dónde está una tienda de camping? don·de es·ta oo·na tyen·da de kam·peeng
Where can I buy locally produced goods/souvenirs?	¿Dónde puedo comprar recuerdos de la zona? don·de pwe·do kom·prar re·kwer·dos de la tho·na
Where can I buy ...?	¿Dónde puedo comprar ...? don·de pwe·do kom·prar ...

For more on shops and how to get there, see **directions** (p57) and the **dictionary**.

Making a Purchase

How much is this?	¿Cuánto cuesta esto? *kwan·to kwes·ta es·to*
✂ **How much?** ¿Cuánto cuesta? *kwan·to kwes·ta*	
I'd like to buy ...	Quisiera comprar ... *kee·sye·ra kom·prar ...*
I'm just looking.	Sólo estoy mirando. *so·lo es·toy mee·ran·do*
Can I look at it?	¿Puedo verlo? *pwe·do ver·lo*
Do you have any others?	¿Tiene otros? *tye·ne o·tros*
What is this made from?	¿De qué está hecho? *de ke es·ta e·cho*
Do you accept credit/debit cards?	¿Aceptan tarjetas de crédito/débito? *a·thep·tan tar·khe·tas de kre·dee·to/de·bee·to*
Could I have a bag, please?	¿Podría darme una bolsa, por favor? *po·dree·a dar·me oo·na bol·sa por fa·vor*
Could I have a receipt, please?	¿Podría darme un recibo, por favor? *po·dree·a dar·me oon re·thee·bo por fa·vor*
✂ **Receipt, please.**	El recibo, por favor. *el re·thee·bo por fa·vor*

🔊 LISTEN FOR

¿En qué le puedo servir?	en ke le *pwe*·do ser·*veer* Can I help you?
No tengo.	no *ten*·go I don't have any.
¿Algo más?	*al*·go mas Anything else?

I don't need a bag, thanks.	No necesito bolsa, gracias. no ne·the·*see*·to *bol*·sa *gra*·thyas
Can you write down the price?	¿Puede escribir el precio? *pwe*·de es·kree·*beer* el *pre*·thyo
Could I have it wrapped?	¿Me lo podría envolver? me lo po·*dree*·a en·vol·*ver*
Does it have a guarantee?	¿Tiene garantía? *tye*·ne ga·ran·*tee*·a
Can I pick it up later?	¿Puedo recogerlo más tarde? *pwe*·do re·ko·*kher*·lo mas *tar*·de
Can I have it sent overseas?	¿Pueden enviarlo por correo a otro país? *pwe*·den en·vee·*ar*·lo por ko·*re*·o a *o*·tro pa·*ees*
It's faulty.	Es defectuoso. es de·fek·*two*·so
I'd like my change, please.	Quisiera mi cambio, por favor. kee·*sye*·ra mee *kam*·byo por fa·*vor*

Making a Purchase

I'd like to buy ...
Quisiera comprar ...
kee·*sye*·ra kom·*prar* ...

How much is it?
¿Cuánto cuesta esto?
kwan·to *kwes*·ta es·to

········· **OR** ·········

Can you write down the price?
¿Puede escribir el precio?
pwe·de es·kree·*beer* el *pre*·thyo

Do you accept credit cards?
¿Aceptan tarjetas de crédito?
a·*thep*·tan tar·*khe*·tas de *kre*·dee·to

Could I have a ..., please?
¿Podría darme ..., por favor?
po·*dree*·a *dar*·me ... por fa·*vor*

 receipt
un recibo
oon re·*thee*·bo

 bag
una bolsa
oo·na *bol*·sa

🔊 LISTEN FOR

cazador m **de ofertas**	ka·tha·*dor* de o·*fer*·tas	bargain hunter
estafa f	es·*ta*·fa	rip-off
ganga f	*gan*·ga	bargain
rebajas f pl	re·*ba*·khas	specials
ventas f pl	*ven*·tas	sale

I'd like my money back, please.	Quisiera que me devuelva el dinero, por favor. kee·*sye*·ra ke me de·*vwel*·va el dee·*ne*·ro por fa·*vor*
I'd like to return this, please.	Quisiera devolver esto, por favor. kee·*sye*·ra de·vol·*ver es*·to por fa·*vor*

Bargaining

That's too expensive.	Es muy caro. es mooy *ka*·ro
Do you have something cheaper?	¿Tiene algo más barato? *tye*·ne *al*·go mas ba·*ra*·to
Can you lower the price?	¿Podría bajar un poco el precio? po·*dree*·a ba·*khar* oon *po*·ko el *pre*·thyo
I'll give you ...	Le/Te daré ... **pol/inf** le/te da·*re* ...

Clothes

Can I try it on?	¿Me lo puedo probar? me lo *pwe*·do *pro*·bar
My size is ...	Uso la talla ... *oo*·so la *ta*·lya ...
It doesn't fit.	No me queda bien. no me *ke*·da byen
small	pequeño/a m/f pe·*ke*·nyo/a
medium	mediano/a m/f me·*dya*·no/a
large	grande m&f *gran*·de

For clothing items, see the **dictionary**. For sizes, see **numbers & amounts** (p34).

> *I'm just looking.*
> *so*·lo es·*toy* mee·*ran*·do
> *Sólo estoy mirando.*

Repairs

Can I have my (camera) repaired here?	¿Puede reparar mi (cámara) aquí? *pwe·*de re·pa·*rar* mee (*ka·*ma·ra) a·*kee*
When will my (sun)glasses be ready?	¿Cuándo estarán listas mis gafas (de sol)? *kwan·*do es·ta·*ran lees·*tas mees *ga·*fas (de sol)
When will my shoes be ready?	¿Cuándo estarán listos mis zapatos? *kwan·*do es·ta·*ran lees·*tos mees tha·*pa·*tos

Books & Reading

Is there a/an (English-language) bookshop?	¿Hay una librería (en inglés)? ai *oo·*na lee·bre·*ree·*a (en een·*gles*)
Is there a/an (English-language) section?	¿Hay una sección (en inglés)? ai *oo·*na sek·*thyon* (en een·*gles*)
I (don't) like ...	(No) Me gusta/gustan ... sg/pl (no) me *goos·*ta/*goos·*tan ...
I'm looking for something by (Javier Marías).	Estoy buscando algo de (Javier Marías). es·*toy* boos·*kan·*do *al·*go de (kha·*vyer* ma·*ree·*as)

For more on books and reading, see **interests** (p124).

CULTURE TIP

Hispanic Literature
Spanish-language literature has a long history, dating from the 12th century and written across the Spanish-speaking world. Today's thriving industry includes such authors as Ana María Matute, Isabel Allende, Jorge Luis Borges, Miguel de Unamuno, Carmen Martín Gaite, Juan Goytisolo, Miguel Delibes, 1982 Nobel Prize winner Gabriel García Márquez and the 1989 Nobel Prize winner, Camilo José Cela.

Music & DVD

I heard a band called ...	Escuché a un grupo que se llama ... es·koo·*che* a oon *groo*·po ke se *lya*·ma ...
What's their best recording?	¿Cuál es su mejor disco? kwal es soo me·*khor dees*·ko
Can I listen to this?	¿Puedo escuchar esto? *pwe*·do es·koo·*char es*·to
What region is this DVD for?	¿Para qué región es este DVD? *pa*·ra ke re·*khyon* es *es*·te de·oo·ve·de
I'd like a CD/DVD.	Quisiera un compact/DVD. kee·*sye*·ra oon *kom*·pak/de·oo·ve·de
Is this a pirated copy?	¿Es copia pirata? es *ko*·pya pee·*ra*·ta
I'd like some headphones.	Quisiera unos auriculares. kee·*sye*·ra oo·nos ow·ree·koo·*la*·res

Video & Photography

Can you print digital photos?	¿Podría imprimir fotos digitales? po·*dree*·a eem·pree·*meer* fo·tos dee·khee·*ta*·les
Can you transfer my photos from camera to CD?	¿Podría pasar las fotos de mi cámara a un compact? po·*dree*·a pa·*sar* las fo·tos de mee *ka*·ma·ra a oon kom·pak
How much is it to develop this film?	¿Cuánto cuesta revelar este carrete? *kwan*·to *kwes*·ta re·ve·*lar* es·te ka·re·te
Do you have slide film?	¿Tiene diapositivas? *tye*·ne dee·a·po·see·*tee*·vas
I need a cable to connect my camera to a computer.	Necesito un cable para conectar mi cámara al ordenador. ne·the·*see*·to oon *ka*·ble pa·ra ko·nek·*tar* mee *ka*·ma·ra al or·de·na·dor
I need a cable to recharge this battery.	Necesito un cable para recargar esta batería. ne·the·*see*·to oon *ka*·ble pa·ra re·kar·*gar* es·ta ba·te·*ree*·a
Do you have batteries for this camera?	¿Tiene pilas para esta cámara? *tye*·ne *pee*·las pa·ra es·ta *ka*·ma·ra
Do you have memory cards for this camera?	¿Tiene tarjetas de memoria para esta cámara? *tye*·ne tar·*khe*·tas de me·*mo*·rya pa·ra es·ta *ka*·ma·ra

CULTURE TIP

The Spanish Lisp

According to a popular legend, one Spanish king – some say Felipe IV, others Ferdinand I – was unable to pronounce the s sound properly and his court, and eventually all of Spain, mimicked his lisp. Of course, the tale is a myth. Indeed, only the letters *c* and *z* are pronounced th (when they precede an *i* or an *e*), while the letter *s* remains the same as in English – a selectiveness due to the way Spanish evolved from Latin. So when you hear someone say *gracias gra·*thyas, they are no more lisping than when you say 'thank you' in English.

Do you have (a) ... for this camera?	¿Tiene ... para esta cámara? *tye·*ne ... *pa·*ra es·ta *ka·*ma·ra
I need a B&W film for this camera.	Necesito película en blanco y negro para esta cámara. ne·the·*see·*to pe·*lee·*koo·la en *blan·*ko y *ne·*gro *pa·*ra es·ta *ka·*ma·ra
I need a colour film for this camera.	Necesito película en color para esta cámara. ne·the·*see·*to pe·*lee·*koo·la en ko·*lor pa·*ra es·ta *ka·*ma·ra
I need a (400) speed film for this camera.	Necesito película de sensibilidad (cuatrocientos) para esta cámara. ne·the·*see·*to pe·*lee·*koo·la de sen·see·bee·lee·*da* (*kwa·*tro·*thyen·*tos) *pa·*ra es·ta *ka·*ma·ra
I need a passport photo taken.	Necesito fotos de pasaporte. ne·the·*see·*to *fo·*tos de pa·sa·*por·*te

Communications

KEY PHRASES

Where's the local internet cafe?	¿Dónde hay un cibercafé cercano?	*don*·de ai oon thee·ber·ka·*fe* ther·*ka*·no
I'd like to check my email.	Quisiera revisar mi correo electrónico.	kee·*sye*·ra re·vee·*sar* mee ko·*re*·o e·lek·*tro*·nee·ko
I want to send a parcel.	Quisiera enviar un paquete.	kee·*sye*·ra en·vee·*ar* oon pa·*ke*·te
I'd like a SIM card.	Quisiera una tarjeta SIM.	kee·*sye*·ra oo·na tar·*khe*·ta seem

Post Office

I want to send a parcel.	Quisiera enviar un paquete. kee·*sye*·ra en·vee·*ar* oon pa·*ke*·te
I want to send a postcard.	Quisiera enviar una postal. kee·*sye*·ra en·vee·*ar* oo·na pos·*tal*
I want to buy an envelope.	Quisiera comprar un sobre. kee·*sye*·ra kom·*prar* oon *so*·bre
I want to buy stamps.	Quisiera comprar sellos. kee·*sye*·ra kom·*prar* se·lyos
Please send it by air/ surface mail to ...	Por favor, mándelo por vía aérea/terrestre a ... por fa·*vor* man·de·lo por *vee*·a a·*e*·re·a/te·*res*·tre a ...

🔊 LISTEN FOR

buzón m	boo·*thon*	mail box
código m **postal**	*ko*·dee·go pos·*tal*	postcode
correo m **certificado**	ko·*re*·o ther·tee·fee·*ka*·do	registered mail
por vía aérea	por *vee*·a a·*e*·re·a	airmail
correo m **urgente**	ko·*re*·o oor·*khen*·te	express mail
declaración f **de aduana**	de·kla·ra·*thyon* de a·*dwa*·na	customs declaration
frágil	*fra*·kheel	fragile
internacional	een·ter·na·thyo·*nal*	international
nacional	na·thyo·*nal*	domestic

It contains ...	Contiene ...
	kon·*tye*·ne ...
Where's the poste restante section?	¿Dónde está la lista de correos?
	don·de es·*ta* la *lees*·ta de ko·*re*·os
Is there any mail for me?	¿Hay alguna carta para mí?
	ai al·*goo*·na *kar*·ta *pa*·ra mee

Phone

Q What's your phone number?	¿Cuál es su/tu número de teléfono? pol/inf
	kwal es soo/too *noo*·me·ro de te·*le*·fo·no
A The number is ...	El número es ...
	el *noo*·me·ro es ...

Where's the nearest public phone?	¿Dónde hay una cabina telefónica? *don·de ai oo·na ka·bee·na te·le·fo·nee·ka*
Can I look at a phone book?	¿Puedo mirar la guía de teléfonos? *pwe·do mee·rar la gee·a de te·le·fo·nos*
What's the area code for ...?	¿Cuál es el prefijo de la zona de ...? *kwal es el pre·fee·kho de la tho·na de ...*
What's the country code for ...?	¿Cuál es el prefijo del país de ...? *kwal es el pre·fee·kho del pa·ees de ...*

For telephone numbers, see **numbers & amounts**, page 34.

I want to...	Quiero ... *kye·ro ...*

make a call to (Singapore)	hacer una llamada a (Singapur)	*a·ther oo·na lya·ma·da a (seen·ga·poor)*
make a local call	hacer una llamada local	*a·ther oo·na lya·ma·da lo·kal*
a reverse-charge/ collect call	una llamada a cobro revertido	*oo·na lya·ma·da a ko·bro re·ver·tee·do*
buy a phone card	comprar una tarjeta telefónica	*kom·prar oo·na tar·khe·ta te·le·fo·nee·ka*

It's engaged.	Está comunicando. *es·ta ko·moo·nee·kan·do*

🔊 LISTEN FOR

¿De parte de quién?	de *par*·te de kyen	Who's calling?
¿Con quién quiere hablar?	kon kyen *kye*·re a·*blar*	Who do you want to speak to?
Lo siento, pero ahora no está.	lo *syen*·to *pe*·ro a·*o*·ra no es·*ta*	I'm sorry, he/she is not here.
Lo siento, tiene el numero equivocado.	lo *syen*·to *tye*·ne el *noo*·me·ro e·kee·vo·*ka*·do	Sorry, you have got the wrong number.

The connection's bad.	Es mala conexión. es *ma*·la ko·nek·*syon*
Hello. (calling)	Hola. o·la
Hello? (answering)	¿Diga? *dee*·ga
Can I speak to ...?	¿Está ...? es·*ta* ...
It's (Julio) ...	Soy (Julio) ... soy (*Julio*) ...
I've been cut off.	Me han cortado. me an kor·*ta*·do
Can I leave a message?	¿Puedo dejar un mensaje? *pwe*·do de·*khar* oon men·*sa*·khe
Please tell him/her I called.	Sí, por favor, dile que he llamado. see por fa·*vor dee*·le ke e lya·*ma*·do
I'll call back later.	Ya llamaré más tarde. ya lya·ma·*re* mas *tar*·de

Mobile/Cell Phone

| I'd like a/an ... | Quisiera ...
kee·*sye*·ra ... |

charger for my phone	un cargador para mi teléfono	oon kar·ga·*dor* *pa*·ra mee te·*le*·fo·no
mobile/cell phone for hire	un móvil para alquilar	oon *mo*·veel *pa*·ra al·kee·*lar*
prepaid phone	una tarjeta prepagada	*oo*·na tar·*khe*·ta pre·pa·*ga*·da
SIM card (for your network)	una tarjeta SIM (para su red)	*oo*·na tar·*khe*·ta seem (*pa*·ra soo red)

| **What are the rates?** | ¿Cuál es la tarifa?
kwal es la ta·*ree*·fa |

The Internet

Where's the local internet cafe?	¿Dónde hay un cibercafé cercano? *don*·de ai oon thee·ber·ka·*fe* ther·*ka*·no
Do you have public internet access here?	¿Tiene acceso público a internet? *tye*·ne ak·*the*·so *poo*·blee·ko a *een*·ter·net
Is there wireless internet access here?	¿Hay acceso inalámbrico a internet aquí? ai ak·*the*·so een·a·*lam*·bree·ko a *een*·ter·net a·*kee*

Can I connect my laptop here?	¿Puedo conectar mi ordenador portátil aquí? *pwe·do ko·nek·tar mee or·de·na·dor por·ta·teel a·kee*
Do you have headphones (with a microphone)?	¿Tiene auriculares (con micrófono)? *tye·ne ow·ree·koo·la·res (kon mee·kro·fo·no)*
I'd like to buy a card/ USB for prepaid mobile internet.	Quisiera comprar una tarjeta/USB para internet móvil de prepago. *kee·sye·ra kom·prar oo·na tar·khe·ta/oo·e·se·be pa·ra een·ter·net mo·veel de pre·pa·go*

🔍 LOOK FOR

Here are some Spanish substitutes for common internet-related terms.

charlar	*char·lar*	chat
ciberespacio m	*thee·ber·e·spa·thyo*	cyberspace
correr tabla por la red	*ko·rer ta·bla por la re*	surf
descargar	*des·kar·gar*	download
en línea	*en lee·ne·a*	online
nombre m **de usuario**	*nom·bre de oo·swa·ryo*	username
página f **Web inicial**	*pa·khee·na web ee·nee·thyal*	homepage
sistema f **de búsqueda**	*sees·te·ma de boos·ke·da*	search engine
sitio m **Web**	*see·tyo web*	website

I'd like to …	Quisiera … kee·sye·ra …	
burn a CD	copiar un disco	ko·pyar oon dees·ko
check my email	revisar mi correo electrónico	re·vee·sar mee ko·re·o e·lek·tro·nee·ko
download my photos	descargar mis fotos	des·kar·gar mees fo·tos
use a printer	usar una impresora	oo·sar oo·na eem·pre·so·ra
use a scanner	usar un escáner	oo·sar oon es·ka·ner
use Skype	usar Skype	oo·sar es·kaip

How much per hour/page?	¿Cuánto cuesta por hora/página? kwan·to kwes·ta por o·ra/pa·khee·na
How do I log on?	¿Cómo entro al sistema? ko·mo en·tro al sees·te·ma
It's crashed.	Se ha quedado colgado. se a ke·da·do kol·ga·do
I've finished.	He terminado. e ter·mee·na·do
media player (MP3)	equipo m MP3 e·kee·po e·me·pe·tres
portable hard drive	disco duro m portátil dees·ko doo·ro por·ta·teel
PSP	PSP m pe·e·se·pe
USB flash drive (memory stick)	memoria f USB me·mo·rya oo·e·se·be

Money & Banking

KEY PHRASES

How much is it?	¿Cuánto cuesta esto?	*kwan*·to *kwes*·ta *es*·to
What's the exchange rate?	¿Cuál es el tipo de cambio?	kwal es el *tee*·po de *kam*·byo
Where's the nearest ATM?	¿Dónde está el cajero automático más cercano?	*don*·de es·*ta* el ka·*khe*·ro ow·to·*ma*·tee·ko mas ther·*ka*·no

Paying the Bill

Q How much is it?	¿Cuánto cuesta esto? *kwan*·to *kwes*·ta *es*·to
A It's (12) euros.	Son (doce) euros. son (*do*·the) e·oo·ros
A It's free.	Es gratis. es *gra*·tees
There's a mistake in the bill.	Hay un error en la cuenta. ai oon e·*ror* en la *kwen*·ta
Do you accept credit/ debit cards?	¿Aceptan tarjetas de crédito/débito? a·*thep*·tan tar·*khe*·tas de *kre*·dee·to/*de*·bee·to
Do you accept travellers cheques?	¿Aceptan cheques de viajero? a·*thep*·tan *che*·kes de vya·*khe*·ro

| I'd like my change, please. | Quisiera mi cambio, por favor.
kee·*sye*·ra mee *kam*·byo por fa·*vor* |
| Could I have a receipt, please? | ¿Podría darme un recibo, por favor?
po·*dree*·a *dar*·me oon re·*thee*·bo por fa·*vor* |

See also **bargaining** (p78).

Banking

| Where can I ...? | ¿Dónde puedo ...?
don·de *pwe*·do ... |
| I'd like to ... | Me gustaría ...
me goos·ta·*ree*·a ... |

arrange a transfer	hacer una transferencia	ha·*ther* oo·na trans·fe·*ren*·thee·ya
get a cash advance	obtener un adelanto	ob·te·*ner* on a·de·*lan*·to
change money	cambiar dinero	kam·*byar* dee·*ne*·ro
change a travellers cheque	cambiar un cheque de viajero	kam·*byar* oon *che*·ke de vya·*khe*·ro
get change for this note	conseguir cambio para este billete	kon·se·*geer* *kam*·byo *pa*·ra es·te bee·*lye*·te
withdraw money	sacar dinero	sa·*kar* dee·*ne*·ro

| Where's the nearest ATM? | ¿Dónde está el cajero automático más cercano?
don·de es·*ta* el ka·*khe*·ro ow·to·*ma*·tee·ko mas *ther*·ka·no |

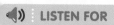

LISTEN FOR

No le quedan fondos.	no le *ke*·dan *fon*·dos You have no money left.
Hay un problema con su cuenta.	ai oon pro·*ble*·ma kon soo *kwen*·ta There's a problem with your account.
¿Puedo ver su identificación, por favor?	*pwe*·do ver soo ee·den·tee·fee·ka·*thyon* por fa·*vor* Can I see your ID, please?
Por favor firme aquí.	por fa·*vor feer*·me a·*kee* Please sign here.

Where's the nearest foreign exchange office?	¿Dónde está la oficina de cambio más cercano? *don*·de es·*ta* la o·fee·*thee*·na de *kam*·byo mas ther·*ka*·no
What's the exchange rate?	¿Cuál es el tipo de cambio? kwal es el *tee*·po de *kam*·byo
What's the charge for that?	¿Cuánto hay que pagar por eso? *kwan*·to ai ke pa·*gar* por *e*·so
The ATM took my card.	El cajero automático se ha tragado mi tarjeta. el ka·*khe*·ro ow·to·*ma*·tee·ko se a tra·*ga*·do mee tar·*khe*·ta
I've forgotten my PIN.	Me he olvidado del NPI. me e ol·vee·*da*·do del *e*·ne·pe·ee
Has my money arrived yet?	¿Ya ha llegado mi dinero? ya a lye·*ga*·do mee dee·*ne*·ro
How long will it take to arrive?	¿Cuánto tiempo tardará en llegar? *kwan*·to *tyem*·po tar·da·*ra* en lye·*gar*

Business

KEY PHRASES

I'm attending a conference.	Asisto a un congreso.	a·*sees*·to a oon kon·*gre*·so
I have an appointment with ...	Tengo una cita con ...	*ten*·go *oo*·na *thee*·ta kon ...
Can I have your business card?	¿Puede darme su tarjeta de visita?	*pwe*·de *dar*·me soo tar·*khe*·ta de vee·*see*·ta

People usually chit-chat for a while before they get down to business. For titles and greetings, see **meeting people** (p106).

| I'm attending a ... | Asisto a ... a·*sees*·to a ... |

conference	un congreso	oon kon·*gre*·so
course	un curso	oon *koor*·so
meeting	una reunión	*oo*·na re·oo·*nyon*
trade fair	una feria de muestras	*oo*·na *fe*·rya de *mwes*·tras

I'm with my colleagues.	Estoy con mis colegas. m&f es·*toy* kon mees ko·*le*·gas
I'm alone.	Estoy solo/a. m/f es·*toy* *so*·lo/a
Where's the business district?	¿Dónde está el centro financiero? *don*·de es·*ta* el *then*·tro fee·nan·*thye*·ro

LANGUAGE TIP

Addressing People

To show formality or respect, you should use the polite form of address *Usted* sg pol oo·*ste* or *Ustedes* pl pol oo·*ste*·des in business and with any service providers (be they kiosk attendants or doctors). It's best to take the lead from how people address you, and respond in the same way. For more on polite forms, see **personal pronouns** in the **grammar** chapter, p21.

Where's the conference?	¿Dónde está el congreso? *don*·de es·*ta* el kon·*gre*·so
Where's the meeting?	¿Dónde es la reunión? *don*·de es la re·oo·*nyon*
I have an appointment with ...	Tengo una cita con ... *ten*·go oo·na *thee*·ta kon ...
🔲 Can I have your business card?	¿Puede darme su tarjeta de visita? *pwe*·de *dar*·me soo tar·*khe*·ta de vee·*see*·ta
🔲 Here's my business card.	Aquí tiene mi tarjeta de visita. a·*kee tye*·ne mee tar·*khe*·ta de vee·*see*·ta
That went very well.	Eso fue muy bien. *e*·so fwe mooy byen
Thank you for your interest/time.	Gracias por su interés/tiempo. *gra*·thyas por soo een·te·*res*/ *tyem*·po
Shall we go for a drink/meal?	¿Vamos a tomar/comer algo? *va*·mos a to·*mar*/ko·*mer al*·go
It's on me.	Invito yo. een·*vee*·to yo

Sightseeing

KEY PHRASES

Can we hire a guide?	¿Podemos alquilar un guía?	po·*de*·mos al·kee·*lar* oon *gee*·a
Can I take photographs?	¿Puedo tomar fotos?	*pwe*·do to·*mar fo*·tos
When's the museum open?	¿A qué hora abren el museo?	a ke *o*·ra *ab*·ren el moo·*se*·o

Requests & Queries

I'd like a/an ... Quisiera ...
kee·*sye*·ra ...

audio set	un equipo audio	oon e·*kee*·po *ow*·dyo
catalogue	un catálogo	oon ka·*ta*·lo·go
guidebook in English	una guía turística en inglés	*oo*·na *gee*·a too·*rees*·tee·ka en een·*gles*
(local) map	un mapa (de la zona)	oon *ma*·pa (de la *tho*·na)

I'd like to see ... Me gustaría ver ...
me goos·ta·*ree*·a ver ...

Do you have information on local sights?	¿Tiene información sobre los lugares de interés local? *tye·ne een·for·ma·thyon so·bre los loo·ga·res de een·te·res lo·kal*
Do you have information on historical sights?	¿Tiene información sobre los lugares de interés histórico? *tye·ne een·for·ma·thyon so·bre los loo·ga·res de een·te·res ees·to·ree·ko*
Do you have information on religious sights?	¿Tiene información sobre los lugares de interés religioso? *tye·ne een·for·ma·thyon so·bre los loo·ga·res de een·te·res re·lee·khyo·so*
Can we hire a guide?	¿Podemos alquilar un guía? *po·de·mos al·kee·lar oon gee·a*
Can I take photographs (of you)?	¿(Le/Te) Puedo tomar fotos? pol/inf *(le/te) pwe·do to·mar fo·tos*
I'll send you the photograph.	Le/Te mandaré la foto. pol/inf *le/te man·da·re la fo·to*
Could you take a photograph of me?	¿Me puede hacer una foto? *me pwe·de a·ther oo·na fo·to*
What's that?	¿Qué es eso? *ke es e·so*
How old is it?	¿De qué época es? *de ke e·po·ka es*

Getting In

What time does it open/ close?	¿A qué hora abren/cierran? *a ke o·ra ab·ren/thye·ran*
What's the admission charge?	¿Cuánto cuesta la entrada? *kwan·to kwes·ta la en·tra·da*

Is there a discount for ...?	¿Hay descuentos para ...? ai des·*kwen*·tos *pa*·ra ...

children	niños	*nee*·nyos
families	familias	fa·*mee*·lyas
groups	grupos	*groo*·pos
older people	gente mayor	*khen*·te ma·*yor*
students	estudiantes	es·too·*dyan*·tes

Galleries & Museums

When's the gallery open?	¿A qué hora abren la galería? a ke o·ra a·bren la ga·le·*ree*·a
When's the museum open?	¿A qué hora abren el museo? a ke o·ra ab·ren el moo·*se*·o
Q What's in the collection?	¿Qué hay en la colección? ke ai en la ko·lek·*thyon*
A It's a/an ... exhibition.	Es una exposición de ... es oo·na eks·po·see·*thyon* de ...
I like the works of ...	Me gustan las obras de ... me *goos*·tan las o·bras de ...
It reminds me of ...	Me recuerda a ... me re·*kwer*·da a ...
... art	arte м ... *ar*·te ...

graphic	gráfico	*gra*·fee·ko
impressionist	impresionista	eem·pre·syo·*nees*·ta
modernist	modernista	mo·der·*nees*·ta
Renaissance	renacentista	re·na·then·*tees*·ta

🔑 LOOK FOR

Abierto	a·*byer*·to	Open
Cerrado	the·*ra*·do	Closed
Prohibido	pro·ee·*bee*·do	Prohibited

Tours

Are there organised walking tours?	¿Organizan recorridos a pie? or·ga·*nee*·than re·ko·*ree*·dos a pye
I'd like to take cooking/ language classes.	Me gustaría ir a clases de cocina/idiomas. me goos·ta·*ree*·a eer a *kla*·ses de ko·*thee*·na/ee·*dyo*·mas
Can you recommend a ...?	¿Puede recomendar algún/alguna ...? m/f *pwe*·de re·ko·men·*dar* al·*goon*/al·*goo*·na ...

Can I take photographs?
pwe·do to·*mar* fo·tos
¿Puedo tomar fotos?

When's the next ...?	¿Cuándo es el/la próximo/a ...? m/f *kwan*·do es el/la *prok*·see·mo/a ...

boat trip	paseo m en barca	pa·*se*·o en *bar*·ka
day trip	excursión f de un día	eks·koor·*syon* de oon *dee*·a
excursion	excursión f	eks·koor·*syon*
tour	recorrido m	re·ko·*ree*·do

Do I need to take (food) with me?	¿Necesito llevar (comida)? ne·the·*see*·to lye·*var* (ko·*mee*·da)
Is (equipment/transport) included?	¿Incluye (equipo/transporte)? een·*kloo*·ye (e·*kee*·po/trans·*por*·te)
How long is the tour?	¿Cuánto dura el recorrido? *kwan*·to *doo*·ra el re·ko·*ree*·do
What time should I be back?	¿A qué hora tengo que volver? a ke *o*·ra *ten*·go ke vol·*ver*
Be back here at ...	Vuelva ... *vwel*·va ...
I've lost my group.	He perdido a mi grupo. e per·*dee*·do a mee *groo*·po

Senior & Disabled Travellers

KEY PHRASES

I need assistance.	Necesito asistencia.	ne·the·*see*·to a·sees·*ten*·thya
Is there wheelchair access?	¿Hay acceso para la silla de ruedas?	ai ak·*the*·so pa·ra la *see*·lya de *rwe*·das
Are there toilets for people with a disablity?	¿Hay aseos para minusválidos?	ai a·*se*·os pa·ra mee·noos·*va*·lee·dos

I have a disability.	Soy minusválido/a. **m/f** soy mee·noos·*va*·lee·do/a
I need assistance.	Necesito asistencia. ne·the·*see*·to a·sees·*ten*·thya
Are guide dogs permitted?	¿Se permite la entrada a los perros lazarillos? se per·*mee*·te la en·*tra*·da a los pe·ros la·tha·*ree*·lyos
Is there wheelchair access?	¿Hay acceso para la silla de ruedas? ai ak·*the*·so pa·ra la *see*·lya de *rwe*·das
Are there parking spaces for people with a disability?	¿Tiene aparcamiento para minusválidos? *tye*·ne a·par·ka·*myen*·to pa·ra mee·noos·*va*·lee·dos
Are there rails in the bathroom?	¿Hay pasamanos en el baño? ai pa·sa·*ma*·nos en el *ba*·nyo

PRACTICAL SENIOR & DISABLED TRAVELLERS

 LOOK FOR

Acceso para Sillas de Ruedas	ak·*the*·so pa·ra *see*·lyas de *rwe*·das	Wheelchair Entrance
Ascensor	a·then·*sor*	Elevator/Lift

Are there toilets for people with a disability?	¿Hay aseos para minusválidos? ai a·*se*·os pa·ra mee·noos·*va*·lee·dos
Is there somewhere I can sit down?	¿Hay algun sitio dónde me pueda sentar? ai al·*goon* see·tyo *don*·de me *pwe*·da sen·*tar*
Could you help me cross this street?	¿Me puede ayudar a cruzar la calle? me *pwe*·de a·yoo·*dar* a kroo·*thar* la *ka*·lye
Could you call me a taxi for the disabled?	¿Podría llamar a un taxi para minusválidos? po·*dree*·a lya·*mar* a oon *tak*·see pa·ra mee·noos·*va*·lee·dos
crutches	muletas f pl moo·*le*·tas
guide dog	perro m lazarillo *pe*·ro la·tha·*ree*·lyo
ramp	rampa f *ram*·pa
walking frame	andador m an·da·*dor*
walking stick	bastón m bas·*ton*
wheelchair	silla f de ruedas *see*·lya de *rwe*·das

Travel with Children

KEY PHRASES

Are children allowed?	¿Se admiten niños?	se ad·mee·ten nee·nyos
Is there a child discount?	¿Hay descuento para niños?	ai des·kwen·to pa·ra nee·nyos
Is there a baby change room?	¿Hay una sala en la que cambiar el pañal al bebé?	ai oo·na sa·la en la ke kam·byar·le el pa·nyal al be·be

I need a ...

Necesito ...
ne·the·see·to ...

baby/child seat	un asiento de seguridad para bebés/niños	oon a·syen·to de se·goo·ree·da pa·ra be·bes/ nee·nyos
cot	una cuna	oo·na koo·na
potty	un orinal de niños	oon o·ree·nal de nee·nyos
stroller	un cochecito	oon ko·che·thee·to

Do you sell baby wipes?	¿Vende toallitas para bebés? ven·de to·a·lyee·tas pa·ra be·bes
Do you sell disposable nappies/diapers?	¿Vende pañales de usar y tirar? ven·de pa·nya·les de oo·sar ee tee·rar

| **Do you sell milk formula?** | ¿Vende leche de fórmula? *ven·*de *le·*che de for·moo·la |
| **Is there a/an ...?** | ¿Hay ...? ai ... |

baby change room	una sala en la que cambiarle el pañal al bebé	oo·na sa·la en la ke kam·byar·le el pa·nyal al be·be
child discount	descuento para niños	des·kwen·to pa·ra nee·nyos
child-minding service	servicio de cuidado de niños	ser·vee·thyo de kwee·da·do de nee·nyos
children's menu	menú infantil	me·noo een·fan·teel
family discount	descuento familiar	des·kwen·to fa·mee·lyar
highchair	trona	tro·na

Do you mind if I breastfeed here?	¿Le molesta que dé de pecho aquí? le mo·les·ta ke de de pe·cho a·kee
Are children allowed?	¿Se admiten niños? se ad·mee·ten nee·nyos
Is this suitable for (three)-year-old children?	¿Es apto para niños de (tres) años? es ap·to pa·ra nee·nyos de (tres) a·nyos

If your child is sick, see **health** (p158).

Social

SOCIAL MEETING PEOPLE

Meeting People

KEY PHRASES

My name is ...	Me llamo ...	me *lya*·mo ...
I'm from ...	Soy de ...	soy de ...
I work in (education).	Trabajo en (enseñanza).	tra·*ba*·kho en (en·se·*nyan*·tha)
I'm ... years old.	Tengo ... años.	*ten*·go ... *a*·nyos
And you?	¿Y Usted/tú? pol/inf	ee oos·*te*/too

Basics

Yes.	Sí. see
No.	No. no
Please.	Por favor. por fa·*vor*
Thank you (very much).	(Muchas) Gracias. (*moo*·chas) *gra*·thyas
You're welcome.	De nada. de *na*·da
Excuse me.	Perdón/Discúlpeme. per·*don*/dees·*kool*·pe·me
Sorry.	Lo siento. lo *syen*·to

Greetings

In Spain people are often quite casual in their social interactions.
It's fine to use the following expressions in both formal and informal
situations.

Hello/Hi.	Hola. *o·la*
Good morning.	Buenos días. *bwe·nos dee·as*
Good afternoon. **(until 8pm)**	Buenas tardes. *bwe·nas tar·des*
Good evening/night.	Buenas noches. *bwe·nas no·ches*
See you later.	Hasta luego. *as·ta lwe·go*
Goodbye./Bye.	Adiós. *a·dyos*
How are you?	¿Qué tal? *ke tal*
Fine, thanks. **And you?**	Bien, gracias. ¿Y Usted/tú? **pol/inf** *byen gra·thyas* *ee oos·te/too*
What's your name?	¿Cómo se llama Usted? **pol** *ko·mo se lya·ma oos·te* ¿Cómo te llamas? **inf** *ko·mo te lya·mas*
My name is ...	Me llamo ... *me lya·mo ...*
I'm pleased to meet you.	Mucho gusto. *moo·cho goos·to*

I'd like to introduce you to ...	Quisiera presentarle a ... **pol**
	kee·*sye*·ra pre·sen·*tar*·le a ...
	Quisiera presentarte a ... **inf**
	kee·*sye*·ra pre·sen·*tar*·te a ...

✂ **This is ...**   Ésto es...   *es*·to es ...

This is my friend.	Éste/a es mi amigo/a. **m/f**
	es·te/a es mee a·*mee*·go/a

Titles & Addressing People

Señor and *Señora* tend to be used in everyday speech. *Doña*, although rare, is used as a mark of respect towards older women, while *Don* is sometimes used to address men. An elderly neighbour, for example, might be called *Doña Lola*. For more on polite forms, see **addressing people** (p95), and **personal pronouns** (p21).

Mr	Señor
	se·*nyor*
Sir	Don
	don
Miss	Señorita
	se·nyo·*ree*·ta
Ms/Mrs	Señora
	se·*nyo*·ra
Madam	Doña
	do·nya

Making Conversation

Spain is known for its distinct regional personalities. A great conversation starter in Spain is to ask someone where they come from. Other good topics are sport, politics, history and travel.

Do you live here?	¿Vives aquí?
	vee·ves a·*kee*

LANGUAGE TIP — **Addressing Friends**

You may hear friends calling each other *tío* m *tee*·o, or *tía* f *tee*·a, but these words are usually used when talking about others. They're a bit crass (a little like using 'sheila' to describe a girl in Australia). Guys use *colega* ko·*le*·ga, and *hombre* *om*·bre, to address their workmates or male friends. In the south, people call their friends *pixas* *pee*·chas or *xoxos* *cho*·chos.

Where are you going?	¿Adónde vas? a·*don*·de vas
What are you doing?	¿Qué haces? ke *a*·thes
Q Are you here on holidays?	¿Estás aquí de vacaciones? es·*tas* a·*kee* de va·ka·*thyo*·nes
A I'm here for a holiday.	Estoy aquí de vacaciones. es·*toy* a·*kee* de va·ka·*thyo*·nes
A I'm here on business.	Estoy aquí en viaje de negocios. es·*toy* a·*kee* en *vya*·khe de ne·*go*·thyos
A I'm here to study.	Estoy aquí estudiando. es·*toy* a·*kee* es·too·*dyan*·do
That's (beautiful), isn't it?	¿Es (precioso), no? es (pre·*thyo*·so) no
Q How long are you here for?	¿Cuánto tiempo te vas a quedar? *kwan*·to *tyem*·po te vas a ke·*dar*
A I'm here for ... weeks/days.	Estoy aquí por ... semanas/días. es·*toy* a·*kee* por ... se·*ma*·nas/*dee*·as

Nationalities

You'll find that many country names are similar to English, so even if you don't know the Spanish name, it's more than likely you'll be understood. For more countries, see the **dictionary**.

Q **Where are you from?**	¿De dónde es Usted? pol de *don*·de es oos·*te* ¿De dónde eres? inf de *don*·de e·res
A **I'm from (Australia).**	Soy de (Australia). soy de (ow·*stra*·lya)
A **I'm from (Canada).**	Soy de (Canadá). soy de (ka·na·*da*)

Age

Q **How old are you?**	¿Cuántos años tienes? *kwan*·tos a·nyos *tye*·nes
A **I'm ... years old.**	Tengo ... años. *ten*·go ... a·nyos
Q **How old is your son/ daughter?**	¿Cuántos años tiene tu hijo/hija? *kwan*·tos a·nyos *tye*·ne too ee·*kho*/ee·*kha*
A **He's/She's ... years old.**	Tiene ... años. *tye*·ne ... a·nyos
I'm younger than I look.	Soy más joven de lo que parezco. soy mas *kho*·ven de lo ke pa·*reth*·ko
Too old!	¡Demasiado viejo! de·ma·*sya*·do *vye*·kho

For your age, see **numbers & amounts** (p34).

🔊 LISTEN FOR

¡Cojonudo!	ko·kho·*noo*·do	Great!
¿De veras?	de *ve*·ras	Really?
¡Enhorabuena!	e·no·ra·*bwe*·na	Congratulations!
¡Estupendo!	es·too·*pen*·do	That's fantastic!
¡No me digas!	no me *dee*·gas	You don't say!
¡Qué guay!	ke gwai	How cool!
¿Qué hay?	ke ai	What's up?
¡Qué interesante!	ke een·te·re·*san*·te	How interesting!

SOCIAL   MEETING PEOPLE

Occupations & Study

Q What do you do?

¿A qué te dedicas?
a ke te de·*dee*·kas

A I work in (education/ hospitality).

Trabajo en (enseñanza/ hostelería).
tra·*ba*·kho en (en·se·*nyan*·tha/ os·te·le·*ree*·a)

A I'm a/an ...

Soy ...
soy ...

architect	arquitecto/a m/f	ar·kee·*tek*·to/a
mechanic	mecánico/a m/f	me·*ka*·nee·ko/a
student	estudiante m&f	es·too·*dyan*·te
teacher	profesor/ profesora m/f	pro·fe·*sor*/ pro·fe·*so*·ra

A I'm self-employed.

Soy trabajador/ trabajadora autónomo/a. m/f
soy tra·ba·kha·*dor*/ tra·ba·kha·*do*·ra ow·*to*·no·mo/a

A	I'm retired.	Estoy jubilado/a. m/f
		es·*toy* khoo·bee·*la*·do/a

A	I'm unemployed.	Estoy en el paro.
		es·*toy* en el *pa*·ro

Q	What are you studying?	¿Qué estudias?
		ke es·*too*·dyas

A	I'm studying (languages).	Estudio (idiomas).
		es·*too*·dyo (ee·*dyo*·mas)

	I'm studying at ...	Estudio en ...
		es·*too*·dyo en ...

For more occupations and studies, see the **dictionary**.

Family

Q	Do you have (a) ...?	¿Tiene ...? pol
		tye·ne ...
		¿Tienes ...? inf
		tye·nes ...

A	I (don't) have (a) ...	(No) Tengo ...
		(no) *ten*·go ...

brother	un hermano	oon er·*ma*·no
children	hijos	*ee*·khos
family	una familia	*oo*·na fa·*mee*·lya
partner	una pareja m&f	*oo*·na pa·*re*·kha
sister	una hermana	*oo*·na er·*ma*·na

Q	Are you married?	¿Estás casado/a? m/f
		es·*tas* ka·*sa*·do/a

A	I'm married.	Estoy casado/a. m/f
		es·*toy* ka·*sa*·do/a

A	I'm single.	Soy soltero/a. m/f
		soy sol·*te*·ro/a

A I live with someone.

Vivo con alguien.
vee·vo kon al·gyen

A I'm separated.

Estoy separado/a. **m/f**
es·*toy* se·pa·*ra*·do/a

Talking with Children

Do you go to school or kindergarten?	¿Vas al colegio o a la guardería? vas al ko·*le*·khyo o a la gwar·de·*ree*·a
What grade are you in?	¿En qué curso estás? en ke *koor*·so es·*tas*
Do you like school?	¿Te gusta el colegio? te *goos*·ta el ko·*le*·khyo
Do you like sport?	¿Te gusta el deporte? te *goos*·ta el de·*por*·te
Do you learn (English)?	¿Aprendes (inglés)? a·*pren*·des (een·*gles*)
I come from very far away.	Vengo de muy lejos. *ven*·go de mooy *le*·khos

Farewells

It's been great meeting you.	Me ha encantado conocerte. me a en·kan·*ta*·do ko·no·*ther*·te
Keep in touch!	¡Nos mantendremos en contacto! nos man·ten·*dre*·mos en kon·*tak*·to
Are you on Facebook?	¿Estás en Facebook? es·*tas* en *feys*·book

> **LANGUAGE TIP**
>
> **Spanish Idioms**
> Even idioms translate across languages. Here are a few golden oldies:
>
> | | |
> |---|---|
> | **It's like casting pearls before swine.** | Es como echar margaritas a los cerdos. (lit: it's like feeding daisies to the pigs) *es ko·mo e·char mar·ga·ree·tas a los ther·dos* |
> | **When it rains, it pours.** | Éramos pocos y parió la abuela. (lit: there were a few of us then granny gave birth) *e·ra·mos po·kos y pa·ree·o la a·bwe·la* |
> | **This is like watching grass grow.** | Es más largo que un día sin pan. (lit: it's longer than a day without bread) *es mas lar·go ke oon dee·a seen pan* |

If you ever visit (South Africa), you can stay with me.	Si algún día visitas (Sudáfrica), te puedes quedar conmigo. *see al·goon dee·a vee·see·tas (soo·da·free·ka) te pwe·des ke·dar kon·mee·go*
Q **What's your (address)?**	¿Cuál es tu (dirección)? *kwal es too (dee·rek·thyon)*
A **Here's my ...**	Ésta es mi ... **m/f** *es·te/es·ta es mee ...*
A **Here's my address.**	Ésta es mi dirección. *es·ta es mee dee·rek·thyon*
A **Here's my email address.**	Ésta es mi dirección de email. *es·ta es mee dee·rek·thyon de ee·mayl*

For more on addresses, see **directions** (p57).

Basque

Basque (*euskara*, in Basque), is spoken at the western end of the Pyrenees and along the Bay of Biscay – from Bayonne in France to Bilbao in Spain, and inland, almost to Pamplona. Dialects are also spoken, including Bizkaian, Gipuzkoan, High Navarrese, Aezkoan, Salazarese, Lapurdian, Low Navarrese and Suberoan. No one quite knows its origin, but the most likely theory is that Basque is the lone survivor of a language family that once extended across Europe, and was wiped out by the languages of the Celts, Germanic tribes and Romans.

Speaking Spanish in the Basque-speaking towns might be expected from a foreigner, but is not as warmly received as an attempt at one of the most ancient languages of Europe.

Hi!	Kaixo! *kai*·sho
Good morning.	Egun on. e·goon *on*
Good afternoon/evening.	Arratsalde on. a·ra·chyal·de *on*
Goodbye.	Agur. a·*goor*
Take care.	Ondo ibili. on·do ee·*beel*·ee
How are you?	Zer moduz? ser mo·*doos*
Fine, thank you.	Ongi, eskerrik asko. on·gee e·*ske*·reek *as*·ko

🔊 **LISTEN FOR**

Euskal Herrian beti jai!	e·oos·*kal* e·*ree*·an *be*·tee yai The Basque Country's always partying!
Gora gu 'ta gutarrak!	*go*·ra goo ta *goo*·ta·rak Hurray for us!

SOCIAL

MEETING PEOPLE

Excuse me.	Barkatu. bar·*ka*·too
Please.	Mesedez. me·*se*·des
Thank you.	Eskerrik asko. es·*ke*·reek *as*·ko
You're welcome.	Ez horregatik. es o·*re*·ga·teek
Do you speak English?	Ingelesez ba al dakizu? een·*ge*·le·ses ba al da·kee·soo
I know a little Basque.	Euskara apur bat badakit. e·*oos*·ka·ra a·*poor* bat ba·da·*keet*
I don't understand.	Ez dut ulertzen. es toot oo·*ler*·tzen
Could you speak in Castillian, please?	Erdaraz egingo al didazu, mesedez? er·da·ras e·*geen*·go al dee·*da*·soo me·*se*·des
How do you say that in Basque?	Nola esaten da hori euskara? *no*·la e·*sa*·ten da o·ree e·oo·ska·ra

CULTURE TIP

Spanish in America

Columbus' arrival in the New World in 1492 launched the era of Spanish expansion in America, one which is also reflected in the language. *Patata*, *tomate*, *cacao* and *chocolate* are just a few examples of words that entered Spanish (and consequently English) from the indigenous American languages. Bear in mind that Spanish has evolved differently in the Americas, and it's a good idea to take Lonely Planet's *Latin American Spanish* phrasebook if that's your destination.

Catalan

Catalan (*català*, in Catalan) is spoken by up to 10 million people in the northeast of Spain, a territory that comprises Catalonia, coastal Valencia and the Balearic Islands (Majorca, Minorca and Ibiza).

Outside Spain, Catalan is also spoken in Andorra, the south of France and the town of Alguer in Sardinia. Many famous creatives have been Catalan speakers: painters like Dalí, Miró and Picasso, architects like Gaudí, and writers like Mercé Rodoreda.

Despite the fact that almost all Catalan speakers from Spain are bilingual, they appreciate it when visitors attempt to communicate, if even in the simplest way, in Catalan.

Hello!	Hola! o·la
Good morning.	Bon dia. bon *dee*·a
Good afternoon.	Bona tarda. bo·na *tar*·da
Good evening.	Bon vespre. bon *bes*·pra
Goodbye.	Adéu. a·*the*·oo
How are you?	Com estàs? kom as·*tas*
(Very) Well.	(Molt) Bé. (mol) be
Excuse me.	Perdoni. par·*tho*·nee
Sorry.	Ho sento. oo *sen*·to
Please.	Sisplau. sees·*pla*·oo
Thank you.	Gràcies. *gra*·see·as

🔊 LISTEN FOR

Això rai!	a·*sho* ra·ee	No problem!
Quin tip de riure!	kin tip da ri·a·oo·ra	What a laugh!

Yes./No.	Sí./No.
	see/no
Do you speak English?	Parla anglès?
	par·la an·*gles*
Could you speak in Castilian, please?	Pot parlar castellà sisplau?
	pot par·*la* kas·ta·*lya* sees·*pla*·oo
I (don't) understand.	(No) Ho entenc.
	(no) oo an·*teng*
How do you say ...?	Com es diu ...?
	kom az *dee*·oo ...

Galician

Galician (*galego,* in Galician), is an official language of the Autonomous Community of Galicias and is also widely understood in the neighbouring regions of Asturias and Castilla-Léon. It's very similar to Portuguese, as the two languages have roots in Vulgar Latin.

Galicians are likely to revert to Spanish when addressing a stranger, especially a foreigner, but making a small effort to communicate in Galician will always be welcomed.

Hello!	Ola!
	o·la
Good day.	Bon dia.
	bon *dee*·a
Good afternoon/evening.	Boa tarde.
	bo·a *tar*·de

Goodbye.	Adeus. *a·de·oos* Até logo. *a·te lo·go*
Excuse me.	Perdón. *per·don*
Please.	Por favor. *por fa·vor*
Thank you.	Grácias. *gra·see·as*
Many thanks.	Moitas grácias. *moy·tas gra·see·as*
That's fine.	De nada. *de na·da*
Yes./No.	Si./Non. *see/non*
Do you speak English?	Fala inglés? *fa·la een·gles*
Could you speak in Castilian, please?	Pode falar en español, por favor? *po·de fa·la en e·spa·nyol por fa·bor*
I (don't) understand.	(Non) Entendo. *(non) en·ten·do*
What's this called in Galician?	Como se chama iso en galego? *ko·mo se cha·ma ee·so en ga·le·go*

SOCIAL MEETING PEOPLE

Interests

KEY PHRASES

What do you do in your spare time?	¿Qué te gusta hacer en tu tiempo libre?	ke te *goos*·ta a·*ther* en too *tyem*·po *lee*·bre
Do you like (travelling)?	¿Te gusta (viajar)?	te *goos*·ta (vya·*khar*)
I (don't) like ...	(No) Me gusta ...	(no) me *goos*·ta ...

Common Interests

What do you do in your spare time?	¿Qué te gusta hacer en tu tiempo libre? ke te *goos*·ta a·*ther* en too *tyem*·po *lee*·bre
Q Do you like (travelling)?	¿Te gusta (viajar)? te *goos*·ta (vya·*khar*)
A I like (cooking).	Me gusta (cocinar). me *goos*·ta (ko·thee·*nar*)
A I don't like (hiking).	No me gusta (el excursionismo). no me *goos*·ta (el eks·koor·syo·*nees*·mo)
I (don't) like photography.	(No) Me gusta la fotografía. (no) me *goos*·ta la fo·to·gra·*fee*·a
I (don't) like shopping.	(No) Me gusta ir de compras. (no) me *goos*·ta eer de *kom*·pras

For more activities, see **sports** (p142) and the **dictionary**.

Music

Do you like to ...? ¿Te gusta ...?
te *goos*·ta ...

dance	ir a bailar	eer a bai·*lar*
go to concerts	ir a conciertos	eer a kon·*thyer*·tos
listen to music	escuchar música	es·koo·*char* moo·see·ka
play an instrument	tocar algún instrumento	*to*·kar al·*goon* eens·troo·*men*·to
sing	cantar	*kan*·tar

What music do you like?
ke *moo*·see·ka te *goos*·ta
¿Qué música te gusta?

Which bands do you like?	¿Qué grupos te gustan? ke *groo*·pos te *goos*·tan
Which singers do you like?	¿Qué cantantes te gustan? ke kan·*tan*·tes te *goos*·tan
What music do you like?	¿Qué música te gusta? ke *moo*·see·ka te *goos*·ta
classical music	música f clásica *moo*·see·ka *kla*·see·ka
jazz	jazz m khath
pop	música f pop *moo*·see·ka pop
rock	música f rock *moo*·see·ka rok
world music	música f étnica *moo*·see·ka *et*·nee·ka

Cinema & Theatre

I feel like going to (a comedy).	Tengo ganas de ir a (una comedia). *ten*·go *ga*·nas de eer a (*oo*·na ko·*me*·dya)
What's showing at the cinema (tonight)?	¿Qué película dan en el cine (esta noche)? ke pe·*lee*·koo·la dan en el *thee*·ne (*es*·ta *no*·che)
Is it in (English)?	¿Es en (inglés)? es en (een·*gles*)
Is it dubbed?	¿Está doblada? es·*ta* dob·*la*·da
Does it have (English) subtitles?	¿Tiene subtítulos (en inglés)? *tye*·ne soob·*tee*·too·los (en een·*gles*)

Have you seen ...?	¿Has visto ...? as *vees*·to ...
Q Who's in it?	¿Quién actúa? kyen ak·*too*·a
A It stars ...	Actúa ... ak·*too*·a ...
Are those seats taken?	¿Están ocupados estos asientos? es·*tan* o·koo·*pa*·dos *es*·tos a·*syen*·tos
Q Did you like the film/play?	¿Te gustó el cine/teatro? te goos·*to* el *thee*·ne/te·a·tro
A I thought it was excellent/OK.	Pienso que fue excelente/regular. *pyen*·so ke fwe eks·the·*len*·te/re·goo·*lar*
A I thought it was long.	Pienso que fue largo. *pyen*·so ke fwe *lar*·go
I (don't) like ...	(No) Me gusta/gustan ... sg/pl (no) me *goos*·ta/*goos*·tan ...

animated films	películas f pl de dibujos animados	pe·*lee*·koo·las de dee·*boo*·khos a·nee·*ma*·dos
comedy	comedia f	ko·*me*·dya
documentary	documentales m pl	do·koo·men·*ta*·les
drama	drama m	*dra*·ma
(Spanish) cinema	cine m (español)	*thee*·ne (es·pa·*nyol*)
horror movies	cine m de terror	*thee*·ne de te·*ror*
sci-fi	cine m de ciencia ficción	*thee*·ne de *thyen*·thya feek·*thyon*

)ff to a show? See **buying tickets** (p44) and **going out** (p130).

SOCIAL INTERESTS

Books & Reading

What kind of books do you read?	¿Qué tipo de libros lees? ke *tee*·po de *lee*·bros *le*·es
On this trip I'm reading ...	En este viaje estoy leyendo ... en es·te *vya*·khe es·*toy* le·*yen*·do ...
Have you read ...?	¿Has leído ...? as le·*ee*·do ...
Q Which (Spanish) author do you recommend?	¿Qué autor (español) recomiendas? ke ow·*tor* (es·pa·*nyol*) re·ko·*myen*·das
A I'd recommend ...	Recomiendo a ... re·ko·*myen*·do a ...
Where can I exchange books?	¿Dónde puedo cambiar libros? *don*·de *pwe*·do kam·*byar* *lee*·bros

For more on books and reading, see **shopping** (p80).

Volunteering

I'd like to volunteer my skills.	Me gustaría ofrecer mis conocimientos. me goos·ta·*ree*·a o·fre·*ther* mees ko·no·thee·*myen*·tos
Are there any volunteer programs available in the area?	¿Hay programas de voluntariado en la zona? ai pro·*gra*·mas de vo·loon·ta·*rya*·do en la *tho*·na

Feelings & Opinions

KEY PHRASES

Are you ...?	¿Tienes/Estás ...?	tye·nes/es·tas ...
I'm (not) ...	(No) Tengo/ Estoy ...	(no) ten·go/ es·toy ...
What did you think of it?	¿Qué pensaste de eso?	ke pen·sas·te de e·so?
I thought it was ...	Pienso que fue ...	pyen·so ke fwe ...
Did you hear about ...?	¿Has oído que ...?	as o·ee·do ke ...

SOCIAL

FEELINGS & OPINIONS

Feelings

Feelings are described with either nouns or adjectives: the nouns use 'have' in Spanish (eg, 'I have hunger') and the adjectives use 'be' (like in English).

Are you ...?		¿Tienes ...? tye·nes ...
I'm (not) ...		(No) Tengo ... (no) ten·go ...

cold	frío	free·o
hot	calor	ka·lor
hungry	hambre	am·bre
in a hurry	prisa	pree·sa
thirsty	sed	se

Q Are you ...?	¿Estás ...? es·*tas* ...
A I'm (not) ...	(No) Estoy ... (no) es·*toy* ...

annoyed	fastidiado/a m/f	fas·tee·*dya*·do/a
embarrassed	avergonzado/a m/f	a·ver·gon·*tha*·do/a
happy	feliz m&f	fe·*leeth*
sad	triste m&f	*trees*·te
tired	cansado/a m/f	kan·*sa*·do/a
well	bien m&f	byen

I'm a little (sad).	Estoy un poco (triste). m&f es·*toy* oon *po*·ko (*trees*·te)
I'm quite (disappointed).	Estoy bastante (decepcionado/a). m/f es·*toy* bas·*tan*·te (de·thep·thyo *na*·do/a)
I feel very (lucky).	Me siento muy (afortunado/a). m/f me *syen*·to mooy (a·for·too·*na*·do/a)

If you're not feeling well, see **health** (p158).

Opinions

Q Did you like it?	¿Te gustó? te goos·*to*
Q What did you think of it?	¿Qué pensaste de eso? ke pen·*sas*·te de e·so

| A I thought it was ... | Pienso que fue ...
pyen·so ke fwe ... |
| A It's ... | Es ...
es ... |

beautiful	bonito/a m/f	bo·*nee*·to/a
bizarre	raro/a m/f	*ra*·ro/a
entertaining	entretenido/a m/f	en·tre·te·*nee*·do/a
excellent	fantástico/a m/f	fan·*tas*·tee·ko/a
horrible	horrible m&f	o·*ree*·ble

I thought it was OK.	Pienso que estaba bien. *pyen*·so ke es·*ta*·ba byen
He's/She's the best.	Es un trozo de pan. (lit: he's/she's a piece of bread) es oon *tro*·tho de pan
I disagree!	No estoy de acuerdo! no es·*toy* de a·*kwer*·do
Yes, but ...	Sí, pero ... see *pe*·ro ...
Whatever.	Lo que sea. lo ke *se*·a

Politics & Social Issues

Q Who do you vote for?	¿A quién votas? a kyen *vo*·tas
A I support the ... party.	Apoyo al partido ... a·*po*·yo al par·*tee*·do ...
Did you hear about ...?	¿Has oído que ...? as o·*ee*·do ke ...
Are you in favour of ...?	¿Estás a favor de ...? es·*tas* a fa·*vor* de ...

🔊 LISTEN FOR

Claro.	*kla*·ro	Sure.
¡Claro que sí!	*kla*·ro ke see	Of course!
¡De ningún modo!	de neen·*goon mo*·do	No way!
Era broma.	*e*·ra *bro*·ma	Just joking.
Está bien.	es·*ta* byen	It's OK.
Estoy bien.	es·*toy* byen	I'm OK.
Quizás.	kee·*thas*	Maybe.
Sin problema.	seen pro·*ble*·ma	No problem.
Un momento.	oon mo·*men*·to	Just a minute.
Vale.	*va*·le	OK.
¡Ya lo creo!	ya lo *kre*·o	You bet!

How do people feel about ...?	¿Cómo se siente la gente de ...? *ko*·mo se *syen*·te la *khen*·te de ...
the economy	economía f e·ko·no·*mee*·a
health care	seguro m médico se·*goo*·ro *me*·dee·ko
immigration	inmigración f een·mee·gra·*thyon*
war in ...	guerra f en ... *ge*·ra en ...

The Environment

Is there an environmental problem here?	¿Aquí hay un problema con el medio ambiente? a·*kee* ai oon pro·*ble*·ma kon el *me*·dyo am·*byen*·te

Is this (forest) protected?	¿Está este (bosque) protegido? es·*ta* es·te (*bos*·ke) pro·te·*khee*·do
Where can I recycle this?	¿Dónde se puede reciclar esto? *don*·de se *pwe*·de re·thee·*klar* es·to
climate change	cambio m climático *kam*·byo klee·*ma*·tee·ko
pollution	contaminación f kon·ta·mee·na·*thyon*
recycling	reciclaje m re·thee·*kla*·khe

> **I'm happy.**
> es·*toy* fe·*leeth*
> **Estoy feliz.**

Going Out

KEY PHRASES

What's on tonight?	¿Qué hay esta noche?	ke ai es·ta no·che
Where are the clubs?	¿Dónde están las discotecas?	don·de es·tan las dees·ko·te·kas
Would you like to go for a coffee?	¿Quieres que vayamos a tomar un café?	kye·res ke va·ya·mos a to·mar oon ka·fe
What time shall we meet?	¿A qué hora quedamos?	a ke o·ra ke·da·mos
Where will we meet?	¿Dónde quedamos?	don·de ke·da·mos

Where to Go

What's there to do in the evenings?	¿Qué se puede hacer por las noches? ke se pwe·de a·ther por las no·ches
What's on ...?	¿Qué hay ...? ke ai ...

locally	en la zona	en la tho·na
this weekend	este fin de semana	es·te feen de se·ma·na
today	hoy	oy
tonight	esta noche	es·ta no·che

Where are there gay venues?	¿Dónde hay lugares gay? don·de ai loo·ga·res gai

Where are there places to eat?	¿Dónde hay lugares para comer? *don·de ai* loo·*ga·*res *pa·*ra ko·*mer*
Where are the clubs?	¿Dónde están las discotecas? *don·*de es·*tan* las dees·ko·*te·*kas
Where are there pubs?	¿Dónde hay pubs? *don·*de ai poobs
Is there a local ... guide?	¿Hay una guía ... de la zona? ai oo·na *gee·*a ... de la *tho·*na

entertainment	del ocio	del o·thyo
film	de cine	de *thee·*ne
gay	de lugares gay	de loo·*ga·*res gai
music	de música	de *moo·*see·ka

I feel like going to a/the ...   Tengo ganas de ir ...
*ten·*go *ga·*nas de eer ...

ballet	al ballet	al ba·*le*
bar	a un bar	a oon bar
cafe	a un café	a oon ka·*fe*
concert	a un concierto	a oon kon·*thyer·*to
karaoke bar	a un bar de karaoke	a oon bar de ka·ra·o·ke
movies	al cine	al *thee·*ne
nightclub	a una discoteca	a oo·na dees·ko·*te·*ka
party	a una fiesta	a oo·na *fyes·*ta
restaurant	a un restaurante	a oon res·tow·*ran·*te
theatre	al teatro	al te·*a·*tro

Invitations

What are you doing this evening?	¿Qué haces esta noche? ke *a*·thes es·ta *no*·che
What are you up to (right now)?	¿Qué haces (ahora)? ke *a*·thes (a·o·ra)
Would you like to go for a ...?	¿Quieres que vayamos a ...? *kye*·res ke va·*ya*·mos a ...

coffee	tomar un café	to·*mar* oon ka·*fe*
drink	tomar algo	to·*mar* al·go
meal	comer	ko·*mer*
walk	pasear	pa·se·*ar*

I feel like going dancing.	Me apetece ir a bailar. me a·pe·*te*·the eer a bai·*lar*
I feel like going out somewhere.	Me apetece salir. me a·pe·*te*·the sa·*leer*
My round.	Invito yo. een·*vee*·to yo
Do you know a good restaurant?	¿Conoces algún buen restaurante? ko·*no*·thes al·*goon* bwen res·tow·*ran*·te
Do you want to come to the (...) concert with me?	¿Quieres venir conmigo al concierto (de ...)? *kye*·res ve·*neer* kon·*mee*·go al kon·*thyer*·to (de ...)
We're having a party.	Vamos a dar una fiesta. *va*·mos a dar *oo*·na *fyes*·ta
Do you want to come?	¿Por qué no vienes? por ke no *vye*·nes
Are you ready?	¿Estás listo/a? **m/f** es·*tas lees*·to/a

CULTURE TIP

Movie Subtitles

Foreign movies are usually dubbed into Spanish, but in bigger cities you'll find that some films have Spanish subtitles. Look out for *v.o.* (*version original* ver·*syon* o·ree·khee·*nal*, 'original version') or *v.o.s.* (*version original subtitulada* ver·*syon* o·ree·khee·*nal* soob·tee·too·*la*·da, 'original version with subtitles') in listings.

Responding to Invitations

Sure!	¡Por supuesto! por soo·*pwes*·to
Yes, I'd love to.	Me encantaría. me en·kan·ta·*ree*·a
Where will we go?	¿A dónde vamos? a *don*·de va·*mos*
That's very kind of you.	Es muy amable por tu parte. es mooy a·*ma*·ble por too *par*·te
No, I'm afraid I can't.	Lo siento pero no puedo. lo *syen*·to *pe*·ro no *pwe*·do
Sorry, I can't sing/dance.	Lo siento, no sé cantar/bailar. lo *syen*·to no se kan·*tar*/bai·*lar*
What about tomorrow?	¿Qué tal mañana? ke tal ma·*nya*·na

🔊 LISTEN FOR

¡Eh, tú!	e too	Hey!
¡Escucha (esto)!	es·koo·cha (es·to)	Listen (to this)!
¡Mira!	mee·ra	Look!

Arranging to Meet

Q What time shall we meet?	¿A qué hora quedamos? a ke o·ra ke·da·mos
A Let's meet at (eight) o'clock.	Quedamos a las (ocho). ke·da·mos a las (o·cho)
Q Where will we meet?	¿Dónde quedamos? don·de ke·da·mos
A Let's meet at the (entrance).	Quedamos en (la entrada). ke·da·mos en (la en·tra·da)
I'll pick you up.	Paso a recogerte. pa·so a re·ko·kher·te
I'll be coming later.	Iré más tarde. ee·re mas tar·de
Where will you be?	¿Dónde estarás? don·de es·ta·ras
OK!	¡Hecho! e·cho
I'll see you then.	Nos vemos. nos ve·mos
See you later/tomorrow.	Hasta luego/mañana. as·ta lwe·go/ma·nya·na
I'm looking forward to it.	Tengo muchas ganas de ir. ten·go moo·chas ga·nas de eer

Sorry I'm late.	Siento llegar tarde. *syen*·to lye·*gar* tar·de
Never mind.	No pasa nada. no *pa*·sa *na*·da

Nightclubs & Bars

Where can we go (salsa) dancing?	¿Dónde podemos ir a bailar (la salsa)? *don*·de po·*de*·mos eer a bai·*lar* (la *sal*·sa)
Q What type of music do you like?	¿Qué tipo de música prefieres? ke *tee*·po de *moo*·see·ka pre·*fye*·res
A I really like (reggae).	Me encanta (el reggae). me en·*kan*·ta (el *re*·gai)
Come on!	¡Vamos! *va*·mos
This place is great!	¡Este lugar me encanta! *es*·te loo·*gar* me en·*kan*·ta

For more on bars and drinks, see **eating out** (p177).

Drugs

I don't take drugs.	No consumo ningún tipo de drogas. no kon·*soo*·mo neen·*goon* *tee*·po de *dro*·gas
I take ... occasionally.	Tomo ... de vez en cuando. *to*·mo ... de veth en *kwan*·do
Do you want to have a smoke?	¿Nos fumamos un porro? nos foo·*ma*·mos oon *po*·ro
Do you have a light?	¿Tienes fuego? *tye*·nes *fwe*·go

See also **police** (p156).

SOCIAL · GOING OUT

Romance

KEY PHRASES

Would you like to do something?	¿Quieres hacer algo?	kye·res a·ther al·go
I love you.	Te quiero.	te kye·ro
Leave me alone, please	Déjame en paz, por favor.	de·kha·me en path por fa·vor

Asking Someone Out

Don't be surprised if invitations come late in the day. Social life in Spain continues well into the night: sometimes people begin to eat dinner at 10pm and many clubs open at midnight.

Q	**Would you like to do something (tonight)?**	¿Quieres hacer algo (esta noche)? kye·res a·ther al·go (es·ta no·che)
A	**Yes, I'd love to.**	Me encantaría. me en·kan·ta·ree·a
A	**I'm busy.**	Estoy ocupado/a. m/f es·toy o·koo·pa·do/a

Pick-up Lines

Would you like a drink?	¿Te apetece una copa? te a·pe·te·the oo·na ko·pa
Do you have a light?	¿Tienes fuego? tye·nes fwe·go

You're great.	Eres estupendo/a. m/f e·res es·too·pen·do/a
You mustn't come here much, because I would have noticed you sooner.	No debes venir mucho por aquí porque me habría fijado en ti antes. no de·bes ve·neer moo·cho por a·kee por·ke me a·bree·a fee·kha·do en tee an·tes

Rejections

I'm here with my boyfriend/girlfriend.	Estoy aquí con mi novio/a. m/f es·toy a·kee kon mee no·vyo/a
Excuse me, I have to go now.	Lo siento, pero me tengo que ir. lo syen·to pe·ro me ten·go ke eer
Leave me alone, please.	Déjame en paz, por favor. de·kha·me en path por fa·vor
Go away!	¡Vete! ve·te
Hey, I'm not interested in talking to you.	Mira tío/a, es que no me interesa hablar contigo. m/f mee·ra tee·o/a es ke no me een·te·re·sa ab·lar kon·tee·go

Getting Closer

Can I kiss you?	¿Te puedo besar? te pwe·do be·sar
Do you want to come inside for a drink?	¿Quieres entrar a tomar algo? kye·res en·trar a to·mar al·go

LANGUAGE TIP

Masculine & Feminine

In this book, masculine forms appear before the feminine forms. If you see a word ending in *-o/a*, it means the masculine form ends in *-o* and the feminine form ends in *-a* (ie you replace the *-o* ending with the *-a* ending to make it feminine), eg hijo/a *ee*·kho/a m/f (son/daughter). The same goes for the plural endings *-os/as*, eg *hijos/as* *ee*·khos/as m/f (sons/daughters). If you see an *(a)* between brackets at the end of a word, it means you have to add it in order to make that word feminine, eg *español(a)* es·pa·*nyol*/es·pa·*nyo*·la m/f (Spanish). In other cases we spell out the whole word, eg *actor/actriz* ak·*tor*/ak·*treeth* m/f (actor/actress). See also **gender** (p19).

Do you want a massage?	¿Quieres un masaje? *kye*·res oon ma·*sa*·khe
Let's go to bed!	¡Vámonos a la cama! *va*·mo·nos a la *ka*·ma

Sex

Kiss me!	¡Dame un beso! *da*·me oon *be*·so
I want you.	Te deseo. te de·*se*·o
I want to make love to you.	Quiero hacerte el amor. *kye*·ro a·*ther*·te el a·*mor*
Do you have a condom?	¿Tienes un condón? *tye*·nes oon kon·*don*
Q **Do you like this?**	¿Esto te gusta? *es*·to te *goos*·ta
A **I (don't) like that.**	Eso (no) me gusta. *e*·so (no) me *goos*·ta

I think we should stop now.	Pienso que deberíamos parar. *pyen*·so ke de·be·*ree*·a·mos pa·*rar*
Oh yeah!	¡Así! a·*see*
That was amazing.	Eso fue increíble. e·so fwe een·kre·*ee*·ble
Can I stay over?	¿Puedo quedarme? *pwe*·do ke·*dar*·me

Love

Q Do you love me?	¿Me quieres? me *kye*·res
A I love you.	Te quiero. te *kye*·ro
I think we're good together.	Creo que estamos muy bien juntos. *kre*·o ke es·*ta*·mos mooy byen *khoon*·tos

LANGUAGE TIP

Endearments

Here are a few terms of endearment you might use with the one you love.

heart	corazón m&f	ko·ra·*thon*
heaven	cielo m&f	*thye*·lo
little love	amorcito/a m/f	a·mor·*thee*·to/a
my life	mi vida m&f	mee *vee*·da
my love	mi amor m&f	mee a·*mor*
treasure	tesoro m&f	te·*so*·ro

Beliefs & Culture

KEY PHRASES

What's your religion?	¿Cuál es su/tu religión? pol/inf	kwal es soo/too re·lee·*khyon*
I'm ...	Soy ...	soy ...
I'm sorry, it's against my beliefs.	Lo siento, eso va en contra de mis creencias.	lo *syen*·to e·so va en *kon*·tra de mees kre·*en*·thyas

Religion

Q What's your religion?   ¿Cuál es su/tu religión? pol/inf
kwal es soo/too re·lee·*khyon*

A I'm (not) ...   (No) Soy ...
(no) soy ...

agnostic	agnóstico/a m/f	ag·*nos*·tee·ko/a
Buddhist	budista m&f	boo·*dees*·ta
Catholic	católico/a m/f	ka·to·lee·ko/a
Christian	cristiano/a m/f	krees·*tya*·no/a
Hindu	hindú m&f	een·*doo*
Jewish	judío/a m/f	khoo·*dee*·o/a
Muslim	musulmán m	moo·sool·*man*
	musulmana f	moo·sool·*ma*·na

I'm (not) religious.   (No) Soy religioso/a. m/f
(no) soy re·lee·*khyo*·so/a

I (don't) believe in God.	(No) Creo en Dios. *(no) kre·o en dyos*
I (don't) believe in destiny/fate.	(No) Creo en el destino. *(no) kre·o en el des·tee·no*
Can I pray here?	¿Puedo rezar aquí? *pwe·do re·thar a·kee*

Cultural Differences

Is this a local custom?	¿Esto es una costumbre local? *es·to es oo·na kos·toom·bre lo·kal*
This is fun.	Esto es divertido. *es·to es dee·ver·tee·do*
This is (very) interesting.	Esto es (muy) interesante. *es·to es (mooy) een·te·re·san·te*
This is (very) different.	Esto es (muy) diferente. *es·to es (mooy) dee·fe·ren·te*
I'm not used to this.	No estoy acostumbrado/a a esto. m/f *no es·toy a·kos·toom·bra·do/a a es·to*
I'm sorry, it's against my beliefs.	Lo siento, eso va en contra de mis creencias. *lo syen·to e·so va en kon·tra de mees kre·en·thyas*
I'll try it.	Lo probaré. *lo pro·ba·re*
Sorry, I didn't mean to do/ say anything wrong.	Lo siento, lo hice/dije sin querer. *lo syen·to lo ee·the/dee·khe seen ke·rer*

Sports

KEY PHRASES

What sport do you play?	¿Qué deporte practicas?	ke de·*por*·te prak·*tee*·kas
What's your favourite team?	¿Cuál es tu equipo favorito?	kwal es too e·*kee*·po fa·vo·*ree*·to
What's the score?	¿Cómo van?	*ko*·mo van

Sporting Interests

Q **What sport do you play?**	¿Qué deporte practicas? ke de·*por*·te prak·*tee*·kas
Q **What sport do you follow?**	¿A qué deporte eres aficionado/a? **m/f** a ke de·*por*·te e·res a·fee·thyo·*na*·do/a
A **I play/do ...**	Practico ... prak·*tee*·ko ...
A **I follow ...**	Soy aficionado/a al ... **m/f** soy a·fee·thyo·*na*·do/a al ...

basketball	baloncesto m	ba·lon·*thes*·to
cycling	ciclismo m	thee·*klees*·mo
football (soccer)	fútbol m	*foot*·bol
tennis	tenis m	*te*·nis
volleyball	voleibol m	*vo*·ley·bol

For more sports, see the **dictionary**.

Do you like sport?	¿Te gustan los deportes? te *goos*·tan los de·*por*·tes
I like watching it.	Me gusta mirar. me *goos*·ta mee·*rar*
Who's your favourite sportsperson?	¿Quién es tu deportista favorito/a? **m/f** kyen es too de·por·*tees*·ta fa·vo·*ree*·to/a
What's your favourite team?	¿Cuál es tu equipo favorito? kwal es too e·*kee*·po fa·vo·*ree*·to

Going to a Game

Would you like to go to a (basketball) game?	¿Te gustaría ir a un partido de (baloncesto)? te goos·ta·*ree*·a eer a oon par·*tee*·do de (ba·lon·*thes*·to)
Who are you supporting?	¿Con qué equipo vas? kon ke e·*kee*·po vas
Who's playing?	¿Quién juega? kyen *khwe*·ga
Who's winning?	¿Quién gana? kyen *ga*·na
That was a (boring) game.	Ese partido fue (aburrido). *e*·se par·*tee*·do fwe (a·boo·*ree*·do)
That was a (great) game!	¡Ese partido fue (cojonudo)! *e*·se par·*tee*·do fwe (ko·kho·*noo*·do)
What's the score?	¿Cómo van? *ko*·mo van

SOCIAL SPORTS

Local Sports
If you hear the sounds of bat, ball and exertion, it may be *pelotari* (pelota players) enjoying the traditional game of *pelota vasca*, Basque handball. It's also known as *jai-alai* in Basque.

ball	pelota f	pe·*lo*·ta
striker	delantero/a m/f	de·lan·*te*·ro/a
wall	frontón m	fron·*ton*

Playing Sport

Q Do you want to play?	¿Quieres jugar?	kye·res khoo·*gar*
A Yeah, that'd be great.	Sí, me encantaría.	see me en·kan·ta·*ree*·a
A Not at the moment, thanks.	Ahora mismo no, gracias.	a·o·ra *mees*·mo no *gra*·thyas
A I have an injury.	Tengo una lesión.	*ten*·go oo·na le·*syon*
Can I join in?	¿Puedo jugar?	*pwe*·do khoo·*gar*
Where's the best place to run around here?	¿Cuál es el mejor sitio para hacer footing por aquí cerca?	kwal es el me·*khor see*·tyo *pa*·ra a·*ther foo*·teen por a·*kee ther*·ka
Where's the nearest gym?	¿Dónde está el gimnasio más cercano?	*don*·de es·*ta* el kheem·*na*·syo mas ther·*ka*·no
Do I have to be a member to attend?	¿Hay que ser socio/a para entrar? m/f	ai ke ser *so*·thyo/a *pa*·ra en·*trar*

Where's the nearest swimming pool?	¿Dónde está la piscina más cercana?	
	don·de es·*ta* la pees·*thee*·na mas ther·*ka*·na	
Where's the nearest tennis court?	¿Dónde está la pista de tenis más cercana?	
	don·de es·*ta* la pees·ta de *te*·nees mas ther·*ka*·na	
Where are the change rooms?	¿Dónde están los vestuarios?	
	don·de es·*tan* los ves·*twa*·ryos	
What's the charge per ...?	¿Cúanto cobran por ...?	
	kwan·to ko·bran por ...	

day	día	*dee*·a
game	partida	par·*tee*·da
hour	hora	*o*·ra
visit	visita	vee·*see*·ta

Can I hire a ...?	¿Es posible alquilar una ...?	
	es po·*see*·ble al·kee·*lar* oo·na ...	

ball	pelota	pe·*lo*·ta
bicycle	bicicleta	bee·thee·*kle*·ta
court	cancha	*kan*·cha
racquet	raqueta	ra·*ke*·ta

What a goal/pass!	¡Qué gol/pase!	
	ke gol/*pa*·se	
Your/My point.	Tu/Mi punto.	
	too/mee *poon*·to	
Kick it to me!	¡Pásamelo!	
	pa·sa·me·lo	

SOCIAL SPORTS

🔊 LISTEN FOR

fuera de juego	*fwe*·ra de *khwe*·go	offside
penalty m	pe·*nal*·tee	penalty
portero m	por·*te*·ro	goalkeeper
saque m **de esquina**	*sa*·ke de es·*kee*·na	corner
tiro m **libre**	*tee*·ro *lee*·bre	free kick

You're a good player.	Juegas bien. *khwe*·gas byen
Thanks for the game.	Gracias por el partido. *gra*·thyas por el par·*tee*·do

Soccer/Football

Who plays for (Real Madrid)?	¿Quién juega en el (Real Madrid)? kyen *khwe*·ga en el (re·*al* ma·*dreeth*)
What a terrible team!	¡Qué equipo más espantoso! ke e·*kee*·po mas es·pan·*to*·so
He's a great player.	Es un gran jugador. es oon gran khoo·ga·*dor*
He played brilliantly in the match against (Italy).	Jugó de fenomenal en el partido contra (Italia). khoo·*go* de fe·no·me·*nal* en el par·*tee*·do *kon*·tra (ee·*ta*·lya)
Which team is at the top of the league?	¿Qué equipo está en primera posición en la liga? ke e·*kee*·po es·*ta* en pree·*me*·ra po·see·*thyon* en la *lee*·ga

Outdoors

KEY PHRASES

Do we need a guide?	¿Se necesita un guía?	se ne·the·*see*·ta oon *gee*·a
I'm lost.	Estoy perdido/a. m/f	es·*toy* per·*dee*·do/a
What's the weather like?	¿Qué tiempo hace?	ke *tyem*·po *a*·the

Hiking

There's plenty of walking, hiking and mountaineering to do in Spain. A recognised cross-country walking trail is known as *Gran Recorrido (GR)* gran re·ko·*ree*·do, while the shorter walking paths scattered throughout the country are called *Pequeños Recorridos (PR)* pe·*ke*·nyos re·ko·*ree*·dos.

Where can I find out about hiking trails?	¿Dónde hay información sobre caminos rurales de la zona? *don*·de ai een·for·ma·*thyon so*·bre ka·*mee*·nos roo·*ra*·les de la *tho*·na
Do we need a guide?	¿Se necesita un guía? se ne·the·*see*·ta oon *gee*·a
Are there guided treks?	¿Se organizan excursiones guiadas? se or·ga·*nee*·than eks·koor·*syo*·nes gee·*a*·das

Where can I ...?	¿Dónde puedo ...?	
	don·de *pwe*·do ...	

buy supplies	comprar víveres	kom·*prar* *vee*·ver·es
find someone who knows this area	encontrar a alguien que conozca el área	en·kon·*trar* a *al*·gyen ke ko·*noth*·ka el *a*·re·a
get a map	obtener un mapa	ob·te·*ner* oon *ma*·pa
hire hiking gear	alquilar un equipo para ir de excursion	al·kee·*lar* oon e·*kee*·po *pa*·ra eer de eks·koor·*syon*

How long is the trail?	¿Cuántos kilómetros tiene el camino? *kwan*·tos kee·*lo*·me·tros *tye*·ne el ka·*mee*·no
How high is the climb?	¿A qué altura se escala? a ke al·*too*·ra se es·*ka*·la
Do we need to take bedding?	¿Se necesita llevar algo en qué dormir? se ne·the·*see*·ta lye·*var al*·go en ke dor·*meer*
Do we need to take food/water?	¿Se necesita llevar comida/agua? se ne·the·*see*·ta lye·*var* ko·*mee*·da/*a*·gwa
Is the track (well-)marked?	¿Es (bien) marcado el sendero? es (byen) mar·*ka*·do el sen·*de*·ro
Is the track open?	¿Es abierto el sendero? es a·*byer*·to el sen·*de*·ro

🔍 LOOK FOR

Por Aquí a ...	por a·*kee* a ...	This Way To ...
Prohibido Acampar	pro·ee·*bee*·do a·kam·*par*	No Camping
Terreno de Cámping	te·*re*·no de *kam*·peen	Camping Ground

Is the track scenic?	¿Es pintoresco el sendero? es peen·to·*res*·ko el sen·*de*·ro
Which is the easiest/ shortest route?	¿Cuál es el camino más fácil/corto? kwal es el ka·*mee*·no mas *fa*·theel/*kor*·to
Which is the most interesting route?	¿Cuál es el camino más interesante? kwal es el ka·*mee*·no mas een·te·re·*san*·te
Where's a/the ...?	¿Dónde hay ...? *don*·de ai ...

camping site	un cámping	oon *kam*·peen
village	un pueblo	oon *pwe*·blo
showers	duchas	*doo*·chas
toilets	servicios	ser·*vee*·thyos

Where have you come from?	¿De dónde vienes? de *don*·de *vye*·nes
How long did it take?	¿Cuánto ha tardado? *kwan*·to a tar·*da*·do
Does this path go to ...?	¿Este camino va a ...? *es*·te ka·*mee*·no va a ...
Can we go through here?	¿Se puede pasar por aquí? se *pwe*·de pa·*sar* por a·*kee*

SOCIAL OUTDOORS

¡Prohibido Nadar! pro·ee·*bee*·do na·*dar*	No Swimming!

Is the water OK to drink?	¿Se puede beber el agua? se *pwe*·de be·*ber* el *a*·gwa
Is it safe?	¿Es seguro? es se·*goo*·ro
Is there a hut there?	¿Hay una cabaña allí? ai *oo*·na ka·*ba*·nya a·*lyee*
When does it get dark?	¿A qué hora oscurece? a ke *o*·ra os·koo·*re*·the
I'm lost.	Estoy perdido/a. m/f es·*toy* per·*dee*·do/a

At the Beach

Where's the best beach?	¿Dónde está la playa mejor? *don*·de es·*ta* la *pla*·ya me·*khor*
Where's the nearest beach?	¿Dónde está la playa más cercana? *don*·de es·*ta* la *pla*·ya mas ther·*ka*·na
Is it safe to dive/swim here?	¿Es seguro bucear/nadar aquí? es se·*goo*·ro boo·the·*ar*/na·*dar* a·*kee*
What time is high/low tide?	¿A qué hora es la marea alta/baja? a ke *o*·ra es la ma·*re*·a *al*·ta/*ba*·kha
How much to rent a chair?	¿Cuánto por alquilar una silla? *kwan*·to por al·kee·*lar* *oo*·na *see*·lya

| How much to rent an umbrella? (for sun) | ¿Cuánto por alquilar un parasol? |
| | *kwan·to por al·kee·lar oon pa·ra·sol* |

Weather

| **Q** What's the weather like? | ¿Qué tiempo hace? |
| | *ke tyem·po a·the* |

| **A** Today it's ... | Hoy hace ... |
| | *oy a·the ...* |

cold	frío	*free·o*
freezing	un frío que pela	oon *free·o ke pe·la*
hot	mucho calor	*moo·cho ka·lor*
sunny	sol	sol
warm	calor	*ka·lor*
windy	viento	*vyen·to*

| **A** (Today) It's raining. | (Hoy) Está lloviendo. |
| | (oy) es·*ta* lyo·*vyen*·do |

| **A** (Today) It's snowing. | (Hoy) Está nevando. |
| | (oy) es·*ta* ne·*van*·do |

| **Q** What's the weather forecast? | ¿Cuál es el pronóstico del tiempo? |
| | kwal es el pro·*nos*·tee·ko del *tyem*·po |

| **A** (Tomorrow) It will be raining. | (Mañana) Lloverá. |
| | (ma·*nya*·na) lyo·ve·*ra* |

| Where can I buy a rain jacket? | ¿Dónde puedo comprar un impermeable? |
| | *don*·de *pwe*·do kom·*prar* oon eem·per·me·*a*·ble |

Where can I buy sunblock?	¿Dónde puedo comprar crema solar? *don*·de *pwe*·do kom·*prar* *kre*·ma so·*lar*
Where can I buy an umbrella? (for rain)	¿Dónde puedo comprar un paraguas? *don*·de *pwe*·do kom·*prar* oon pa·*ra*·gwas
hail	granizo m gra·*nee*·tho
storm	tormenta f tor·*men*·ta
sun	sol m sol

Flora & Fauna

What ... is that?	¿Qué ... es ése/ésa? m/f ke ... es *e*·se/*e*·sa

animal	animal m	a·nee·*mal*
bird	pájaro m	*pa*·kha·ro
flower	flor f	flor
plant	planta f	*plan*·ta
tree	árbol m	*ar*·bol

Can you eat the fruit?	¿Se puede comer la fruta? se *pwe*·de ko·*mer* la *froo*·ta
Is it endangered?	¿Está en peligro de extinción? es·*ta* en pe·*lee*·gro de eks·teen·*thyon*
Is it common?	¿Es común? es ko·*moon*

For geographical and agricultural terms, and names of animals and plants, see the **dictionary**.

Safe Travel

Emergencies

KEY PHRASES

Help!	¡Socorro!	so·*ko*·ro
There's been an accident.	Ha habido un accidente.	a a·*bee*·do oon ak·thee·*den*·te
It's an emergency!	¡Es una emergencia!	es *oo*·na e·mer·*khen*·thee·ya

Help!	¡Socorro! so·*ko*·ro
Stop!	¡Pare! *pa*·re
Go away!	¡Váyase! *va*·ya·se
Leave me alone!	¡Déjame en paz! *de*·kha·me en path
Thief!	¡Ladrón! lad·*ron*
Fire!	¡Fuego! *fwe*·go
It's an emergency!	¡Es una emergencia! es *oo*·na e·mer·*khen*·thee·ya
There's been an accident.	Ha habido un accidente. a a·*bee*·do oon ak·thee·*den*·te
Do you have a first-aid kit?	¿Tiene un botiquín de primeros auxilios? *tye*·ne oon bo·tee·*keen* de pree·*me*·ros owk·*see*·lyos

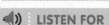
LISTEN FOR

¡Es peligroso!	es pe·lee·*gro*·so	It's dangerous!

Call the police!	¡Llame a la policía! *lya*·me a la po·lee·*thee*·a
Call a doctor!	¡Llame a un médico! *lya*·me a oon *me*·dee·ko
Call an ambulance!	¡Llame a una ambulancia! *lya*·me a *oo*·na am·boo·*lan*·thya
Could you help me, please?	¿Me puede ayudar, por favor? me *pwe*·de a·yoo·*dar* por fa·*vor*
I have to use the telephone.	Necesito usar el teléfono. ne·the·*see*·to oo·*sar* el te·*le*·fo·no
I'm lost.	Estoy perdido/a. m/f es·*toy* per·*dee*·do/a
Where are the toilets?	¿Dónde están los servicios? *don*·de es·*tan* los ser·*vee*·thyos

Police

KEY PHRASES

Where's the police station?	¿Dónde está la comisaría?	*don*·de es·*ta* la ko·mee·sa·*ree*·a
I want to contact my embassy/ consulate.	Quiero ponerme en contacto con mi embajada/ consulado.	*kye*·ro po·*ner*·me en kon·*tak*·to kon mee em·ba·*kha*·da/ kon·soo·*la*·do
My bag was stolen.	Mi bolso fue robado.	mee *bol*·so fwe ro·*ba*·do

In an emergency, call the police. They will then put you through to other emergency services (fire brigade and ambulance). For more on making a call, see **communications** (p85).

Where's the police station?	¿Dónde está la comisaría? *don*·de es·*ta* la ko·mee·sa·*ree*·a
I want to report an offence.	Quiero denunciar un delito. *kye*·ro de·noon·*thyar* oon de·*lee*·to
I've been robbed.	Me han robado. me an ro·*ba*·do
I've been raped.	He sido violado/a. **m/f** e *see*·do vee·o·*la*·do/a
It was him/her.	Fue él/ella. fwe el/*e*·lya
My (money) was stolen.	Mi (dinero) fue robado. mee (dee·*ne*·ro) fwe ro·*ba*·do
My (bag/handbag) was stolen.	Mi (bolso) fue robado. mee (*bol*·so) fwe ro·*ba*·do

My (bags/suitcases) were stolen.	Mis (maletas) fueron robadas. mee (ma·le·tas) fwe·ron ro·ba·das
I've lost (my passport).	He perdido (mi pasaporte). e per·dee·do (mee pa·sa·por·te)
What am I accused of?	¿De qué me acusan? de ke me a·ku·san
I didn't realise I was doing anything wrong.	No sabía que estaba haciendo algo mal. no sa·bee·a ke es·ta·ba a·thyen·do al·go mal
I'm innocent.	Soy inocente. soy ee·no·then·te
I want to contact my embassy/consulate.	Quiero ponerme en contacto con mi embajada/consulado. kye·ro po·ner·me en kon·tak·to kon mee em·ba·kha·da/kon·soo·la·do
Can I call a lawyer?	¿Puedo llamar a un abogado? pwe·do lya·mar a oon a·bo·ga·do
I need a lawyer who speaks (English).	Necesito un abogado que hable (inglés). ne·the·see·to oon a·bo·ga·do ke a·ble (een·gles)
Can I have a copy, please?	¿Puede darme una copia, por favor? pwe·de dar·me oo·na ko·pya por fa·vor
This drug is for personal use.	Esta droga es para uso personal. es·ta dro·ga es pa·ra oo·so per·so·nal
I have a prescription for this drug.	Tengo receta para esta droga. ten·go re·the·ta pa·ra es·ta dro·ga

Health

KEY PHRASES

Where's the nearest hospital?	¿Dónde está el hospital más cercano?	*don*·de es·*ta* el os·*pee*·tal mas ther·*ka*·no
I'm sick.	Estoy enfermo/a. m/f	es·*toy* en·*fer*·mo/a
I need a doctor.	Necesito un doctor.	ne·the·*see*·to oon dok·*tor*
I'm on regular medication for ...	Estoy bajo medicación para ...	es·*toy ba*·kho me·dee·ka·*thyon pa*·ra ...
I'm allergic to ...	Soy alérgico/a a... m/f	soy a·*ler*·khee·ko/a a ...

Doctor

Where's the nearest ...? ¿Dónde está ... más cercano/a? m/f
don·de es·*ta* ... mas ther·*ka*·no/a

chemist	la farmacia f	la far·*ma*·thya
dentist	el dentista m	el den·*tees*·ta
doctor	el médico m	el *me*·dee·ko
hospital	el hospital m	el os·pee·*tal*
medical centre	el consultorio m	el kon·sool·*to*·ryo
optometrist	el oculista m	el o·koo·*lees*·ta

CULTURE TIP — **Etiquette Tip**
A polite way to respond to someone sneezing is by
saying *¡Salud!* sa·*loo* (health) or *¡Jesús!* khe·*soos*
(lit: 'Jesus').

I need a doctor (who speaks English).	Necesito un doctor (que hable inglés). ne·the·*see*·to oon dok·*tor* (ke *a*·ble een·*gles*)
Could I see a female doctor?	¿Puede examinarme una doctora? *pwe*·de ek·sa·mee·*nar*·me oo·na dok·*to*·ra
I've run out of my medication.	Se me terminaron los medicamentos. se me ter·mee·*na*·ron los me·dee·ka·*men*·tos
This is my usual medicine.	Éste es mi medicamento habitual. *es*·te es mee me·dee·ka·*men*·to a·bee·too·*al*
I don't want a blood transfusion.	No quiero que me hagan una transfusión de sangre. no *kye*·ro ke me *a*·gan oo·na trans·foo·*syon* de *san*·gre
Please use a new syringe.	Por favor, use una jeringa nueva. por fa·*vor* oo·se oo·na khe·*reen*·ga *nwe*·va
I need new contact lenses.	Necesito lentes de contacto nuevas. ne·the·*see*·to *len*·tes de kon·*tak*·to *nwe*·vas
I need new glasses.	Necesito gafas nuevas. ne·the·*see*·to *ga*·fas *nwe*·vas

I've been vaccinated for ...	Estoy vacunado/a contra ... m/f es·*toy* va·koo·*na*·do/a *kon*·tra ...
He's/She's been vaccinated for ...	Está vacunado/a contra ... m/f es·*ta* va·koo·*na*·do/a *kon*·tra ...

tetanus	el tétano	el *te*·ta·no
typhoid	la tifus	la *tee*·foos
hepatitis A/B/C	la hepatitis A/B/C	la e·pa·*tee*·tees a/be/the
... fever	la fiebre ...	la *fye*·bre ...

For women's medical issues, see **women's health** (p162).

Symptoms & Conditions

I'm sick.	Estoy enfermo/a. m/f es·*toy* en·*fer*·mo/a
I have ...	Tengo ... *ten*·go ...
I've recently had ...	Hace poco he tenido ... a·the po·ko e te·*nee*·do ...
I'm on regular medication for ...	Estoy bajo medicación para ... es·*toy* ba·kho me·dee·ka·*thyon* pa·ra ...
It hurts here.	Me duele aquí. me *dwe*·le a·*kee*
I've been injured.	He sido herido/a. m/f e *see*·do e·*ree*·do/a
I've been vomiting.	He estado vomitando. e es·*ta*·do vo·mee·*tan*·do

🔊 LISTEN FOR

¿Qué le pasa?	ke le *pa*·sa	
	What's the problem?	
¿Dónde le duele?	*don*·de le *dwe*·le	
	Where does it hurt?	
¿Tiene fiebre?	*tye*·ne *fye*·bre	
	Do you have a temperature?	
¿Desde cuándo se siente así?	*des*·de *kwan*·do se *syen*·te a·*see*	
	How long have you been like this?	
¿Ha tenido esto antes?	a te·*nee*·do *es*·to *an*·tes	
	Have you had this before?	

I can't sleep.	No puedo dormir.
	no *pwe*·do dor·*meer*

I have a rash.	Tengo una erupción cutánea.
	ten·go *oo*·na e·roop·*thyon* koo·*ta*·ne·a

I have an infection.	Tengo una infección.
	ten·go *oo*·na in·fek·*thyon*

I feel ...	Me siento ...
	me *syen*·to ...

better	mejor m&f	me·*khor*
depressed	deprimido/a m/f	de·pree·*mee*·do/a
dizzy	mareado/a m/f	ma·re·*a*·do/a
shivery	destemplado/a m/f	des·tem·*pla*·do/a
weak	débil m&f	*de*·beel
worse	peor m&f	pe·*or*

asthma	asma m *as*·ma
diarrhoea	diarrea f dee·a·*re*·a
fever	fiebre f *fye*·bre
headache	dolor m de cabeza do·*lor* de ka·*be*·tha
sprain	torcedura f tor·the·*doo*·ra

For more symptoms & conditions, see the **dictionary**.

Women's Health

(I think) I'm pregnant.	(Creo que) Estoy embarazada. (*kre*·o ke) es·*toy* em·ba·ra·*tha*·da
I haven't had my period for ... weeks.	Hace ... semanas que no me viene la regla. *a*·the ... se·*ma*·nas ke no me *vye*·ne la *reg*·la
I'm on the Pill.	Tomo la píldora. *to*·mo la *peel*·do·ra
I've noticed a lump here.	He notado un bulto aquí. e no·*ta*·do oon *bool*·to a·*kee*
I have period pain.	Tengo dolor menstrual. *ten*·go do·*lor* mens·troo·*al*
contraception	anticonceptivos m pl an·tee·kon·thep·*tee*·vos
pregnancy test	prueba f de embarazo *prwe*·ba de em·ba·*ra*·tho
the morning-after pill	píldora f del día siguiente *peel*·do·ra del *dee*·a see·*gyen*·te

🔊 LISTEN FOR

¿Usted bebe?	oos·*te be*·be	Do you drink?
¿Usted fuma?	oos·*te foo*·ma	Do you smoke?
¿Usted toma drogas?	oos·*te to*·ma *dro*·gas	Do you take drugs?
¿Tiene Usted alergias?	*tye*·ne oos·*te* a·*ler*·khyas	Are you allergic to anything?
¿Se encuentra bajo medicación?	se en·*kwen*·tra *ba*·kho me·dee·ka·*thyon*	Are you on medication?

Allergies

I'm allergic to ...	Soy alérgico/a ... **m/f** soy a·*ler*·khee·ko/a ...
He/She is allergic to ...	Es alérgico/a ... **m/f** es a·*ler*·khee·ko/a ...

antibiotics	a los antibióticos	a los an·tee·*byo*·tee·kos
anti-inflammatories	a los anti-inflamatorios	a los an·tee· een·fla·ma·*to*·ryos
aspirin	a la aspirina	a la as·pee·*ree*·na
bees	a las abejas	a las a·*be*·khas
codeine	a la codeina	a la ko·de·*ee*·na
penicillin	a la penicilina	a la pe·nee·thee·*lee*·na
pollen	al polen	al *po*·len

I have a skin allergy.	Tengo una alergia en la piel. *ten*·go *oo*·na a·*ler*·khya en la pyel

head
cabeza f
ka·be·tha

eye
ojo m
o·kho

nose
nariz f
na·reeth

ear
oreja f
o·re·kha

mouth
boca f
bo·ka

arm
brazo m
bra·tho

chest
pecho m
pe·cho

hand
mano f
ma·no

stomach
estómago m
es·to·ma·go

bum
culo m
koo·lo

leg
pierna f
pyer·na

foot
pie m
pee·e

I'm on a special diet.	Estoy a régimen especial. es·*toy* a re·*khee*·men es·pe·*thyal*
antihistamines	antihistamínicos **m pl** an·tee·ees·ta·*mee*·nee·kos
inhaler	inhalador **m** een·a·la·*dor*
sulphur-based drugs	drogas con base de azufre **f pl** *dro*·gas kon *ba*·se de a·*thoo*·fre

For food-related allergies, see **vegetarian & special meals** (p187).

Parts of the Body

My ... hurts.	Me duele ... me *dwe*·le ...
I can't move my ...	No puedo mover ... no *pwe*·do mo·*ver* ...
I have a cramp in my ...	Tengo calambres en ... *ten*·go ka·*lam*·bres en ...
My ... is swollen.	Mi ... está hinchado. mee ... es·*ta* een·*cha*·do

For more parts of the body, see the **dictionary**.

Chemist

I need something for ...	Necesito algo para ... ne·the·*see*·to *al*·go *pa*·ra ...
I have a prescription.	Tengo receta médica. *ten*·go re·*the*·ta *me*·dee·ka
Do I need a prescription for ...?	¿Necesito receta para ...? ne·the·*see*·to re·*the*·ta *pa*·ra ...
How many times a day?	¿Cuántas veces al día? *kwan*·tas *ve*·thes al *dee*·a

For pharmaceutical items, see the **dictionary**.

LISTEN FOR

¿Ha tomado esto antes?	a to·*ma*·do *es*·to *an*·tes Have you taken this before?
Dos veces al día (con la comida).	dos *ve*·thes al *dee*·a (kon la ko·*mee*·da) Twice a day (with food).

🔊 LISTEN FOR

Abra.	*a*·bra	Open wide.
No se mueva.	no se *mwe*·va	Don't move.
¡Enjuague!	en·*khwa*·ge	Rinse!

Dentist

I have a broken tooth.	Se me ha roto un diente. se me a *ro*·to oon *dyen*·te
I have a toothache.	Me duele una muela. me *dwe*·le oo·na *mwe*·la
I've lost a filling.	Se me ha caído un empaste. se me a ka·*ee*·do oon em·*pas*·te
My orthodontic braces broke/fell off.	Se me rompió/cayó el aparato dental. se me rom·*pyo*/ka·*yo* el a·pa·*ra*·to den·*tal*
My gums hurt.	Me duelen las encías. me *dwe*·len las en·*thee*·as
I don't want it extracted.	No quiero que me lo saquen. no *kye*·ro ke me lo *sa*·ken
I need an anaesthetic.	Necesito una anestesia. ne·the·*see*·to oo·ne a·nes·*te*·sya
I need a filling.	Necesito un empaste ne·the·*see*·to oon em·*pas*·te

Food

Eating Out

KEY PHRASES

Can you recommend a restaurant?	¿Puede recomendar un restaurante?	*pwe·*de re·ko·men·*dar* oon res·tow·*ran*·te
I'd like a table for two, please.	Quisiera una mesa para dos, por favor.	kee·*sye*·ra oo·na me·sa pa·ra dos por fa·*vor*
I'd like the menu, please.	Quisiera el menú, por favor.	kee·*sye*·ra el me·*noo* por fa·*vor*
I'd like ...	Quisiera ...	kee·*sye*·ra ...
Please bring the bill.	Por favor nos trae la cuenta.	por fa·*vor* nos *tra*·e la *kwen*·ta

Basics

The main meal in Spain, 'lunchtime' is called *la hora de comer* la o·ra de ko·*mer*. It's served between 1.30pm and 4.30pm.

breakfast	desayuno m de·sa·*yoo*·no
lunch	comida f ko·*mee*·da
dinner	cena f *the*·na
snack	tentempié m ten·tem·*pye*
eat/drink	comer/beber ko·*mer*/be·*ber*

I'd like ...	Quisiera ...
	kee·*sye*·ra ...
I'm starving!	¡Estoy hambriento/a! m/f
	es·*toy* am·*bryen*·to/a
Enjoy your meal!	¡Buen provecho!
	bwen pro·*ve*·cho

Finding a Place to Eat

Can you recommend a ...?	¿Puede recomendar
	un/una ...? m/f
	pwe·de re·ko·men·*dar*
	oon/*oo*·na ...

bar	bar m	bar
cafe	café m	ka·*fe*
coffee bar	cafetería f	ka·fe·te·*ree*·a
restaurant	restaurante m	res·tow·*ran*·te

Are you still serving food?	¿Siguen sirviendo
	comida?
	see·gen seer·*vyen*·do
	ko·*mee*·da
How long is the wait?	¿Cuánto hay que esperar?
	kwan·to ai ke es·pe·*rar*
Where would you go for a cheap meal?	¿Adónde se va para comer barato?
	a·*don*·de se va *pa*·ra ko·*mer* ba·*ra*·to
Where would you go for local specialities?	¿Adónde se va para comer comida típica?
	a·*don*·de se va *pa*·ra ko·*mer* ko·*mee*·da *tee*·pee·ka

◀)) LISTEN FOR

Lo siento, hemos cerrado.	lo *syen*·to e·mos the·*ra*·do Sorry, we're closed.
No tenemos mesa.	no te·*ne*·mos *me*·sa We have no free tables.
Un momento.	oon mo·*men*·to One moment.

I'd like to reserve a table for (two) people.	Quisiera reservar una mesa para (dos) personas. kee·*sye*·ra re·ser·*var* oo·na *me*·sa *pa*·ra (dos) per·*so*·nas
I'd like to reserve a table for (eight) o'clock.	Quisiera reservar una mesa para las (ocho). kee·*sye*·ra re·ser·*var* oo·na *me*·sa *pa*·ra las (o·cho)

At the Restaurant

I'd like the (non)smoking section, please.	Quisiera el área de (no) fumadores, por favor. kee·*sye*·ra el *a*·re·a de (no) foo·ma·*do*·res por fa·*vor*
I'd like a table for (two), please.	Quisiera una mesa para (dos), por favor. kee·*sye*·ra oo·na *me*·sa *pa*·ra (dos) por fa·*vor*
✂ **For two, please.**	Para dos, por favor. *pa*·ra dos por fa·*vor*
I'd like the drink list, please.	Quisiera la lista de bebidas, por favor. kee·*sye*·ra la *lees*·ta de be·*bee*·das por fa·*vor*

Eating Out

Can I see the menu, please?
¿Puedo ver el menú, por favor?
pwe·do ver el me·noo por fa·vor

What would you recommend for ...?
¿Qué me recomendaría para ...?
ke me re·ko·men·da·ree·a pa·ra ...

 the main meal
el plato principal
el pla·to preen·thee·pal

 dessert
postre
pos·tre

 drinks
bebidas
be·bee·das

Can you bring me some ..., please?
Por favor me trae ...
por fa·vor me tra·e ...

 BILL / TOTAL \$\$

I'd like the bill, please.
Quisiera la cuenta, por favor.
kee·sye·ra la kwen·ta por fa·vor

FOOD EATING OUT

I'd like the menu, please.	Quisiera el menú, por favor.
	kee·*sye*·ra el me·*noo* por fa·*vor*

✂ The menu, please.	El menú, por favor.	el me·*noo* por fa·*vor*

Do you have children's meals?	¿Tienen comidas para niños?
	tye·nen ko·*mee*·das *pa*·ra *nee*·nyos

Do you have a menu in English?	¿Tienen un menú en inglés?
	tye·nen oon me·*noo* en een·*gles*

Is service included in the bill?	¿La cuenta incluye servicio?
	la *kwen*·ta een·*kloo*·ye ser·*vee*·thyo

What would you recommend?	¿Qué recomienda?
	ke re·ko·*myen*·da

Can you tell me which traditional foods I should try?	¿Que platos típicos debería probar?
	ke *pla*·tos *tee*·pee·kos de·be·*ree*·a pro·*bar*

🔊 LISTEN FOR

¿Le gusta ...?	le *goos*·ta ... Do you like ...?
Recomiendo ...	re·ko·*myen*·do ... I suggest the ...
¿Cómo lo quiere preparado?	*ko*·mo lo *kye*·re pre·pa·*ra*·do How would you like that cooked?

I'll have what they're having.	Tomaré lo mismo que ellos. *to·ma·re lo mees·mo ke e·lyos*
Does it take long to prepare?	¿Tarda mucho en prepararse? *tar·da moo·cho en pre·pa·rar·se*
What's in that dish?	¿Que lleva ese plato? *ke lye·va e·se pla·to*
Are these complimentary?	¿Éstos son gratis? *es·tos son gra·tees*
We're just having drinks.	Sólo queremos tomar algo. *so·lo ke·re·mos to·mar al·go*
✂ **Just drinks.**	Sólo bebidas. *so·lo be·bee·das*

spoon
cuchara f
koo·cha·ra

wineglass
copa de vino m
ko·pa de vee·no

glass
vaso m
va·so

fork
tenedor m
te·ne·dor

plate
plato m
pla·to

table
mesa f
me·sa

knife
cuchillo m
koo·chee·lyo

Requests

Please bring a glass.	Por favor nos trae un vaso. por fa·*vor* nos *tra*·e oon *va*·so
Please bring a serviette.	Por favor nos trae una servilleta. por fa·*vor* nos *tra*·e *oo*·na ser·vee·*lye*·ta
I'd like it ...	Lo quiero ... lo *kye*·ro ...
I don't want it ...	No lo quiero ... no lo *kye*·ro ...

deep fried	frito en aceite abundante	*free*·to en a·*they*·te a·boon·*dan*·te
medium	no muy hecho	no mooy e·cho
rare	vuelta y vuelta	*vwel*·ta ee *vwel*·ta
re-heated	recalentado	re·ka·len·*ta*·do
steamed	al vapor	al va·*por*
well-done	muy hecho	mooy e·cho
with the dressing on the side	con el aliño aparte	kon el a·*lee*·nyo a·*par*·te
without ...	sin ...	seen ...

For other specific meal requests, see **vegetarian & special meals** (p187).

Compliments & Complaints

I love this dish.	Me encanta este plato. me en·*kan*·ta *es*·te *pla*·to
I didn't order this.	Yo no he pedido esto. yo no e pe·*dee*·do *es*·to

🔍 LOOK FOR

Aperitivos	a·pe·ree·*tee*·vos	Appetisers
Cervezas	ther·*ve*·thas	Beers
Caldos	*kal*·dos	Soups
De Entrada	de en·*tra*·da	Entrees
Ensaladas	en·sa·*la*·das	Salads
Postres	*pos*·tres	Desserts
Refrescos	re·*fres*·kos	Soft Drinks
Segundos Platos	se·*goon*·dos *pla*·tos	Main Courses

That was delicious!	¡Estaba buenísimo! es·*ta*·ba bwe·*nee*·see·mo
My compliments to the chef.	Mi enhorabuena al cocinero. mee en·o·ra·*bwe*·na al ko·thee·*ne*·ro
I'm full.	Estoy lleno/a. m/f es·*toy* lye·no/a
This is burnt.	Esto está quemado. es·to es·*ta* ke·*ma*·do
This is (too) cold.	Esto está (demasiado) frío. es·to es·*ta* (de·ma·*sya*·do) *free*·o
This is superb.	Esto está exquisito. es·to es·*ta* eks·kee·*see*·to
We love the local cuisine.	Nos encanta la comida típica de la zona. nos en·*kan*·ta la ko·*mee*·da *tee*·pee·ka de la *tho*·na

Paying the Bill

Please bring the bill.	Por favor nos trae la cuenta. por fa·*vor* nos *tra*·e la *kwen*·ta
✂ **Bill, please.**	La cuenta, por favor. la *kwen*·ta por fa·*vor*
There's a mistake in the bill.	Hay un error en la cuenta. ai oon e·*ror* en la *kwen*·ta

For methods of payment, see **money & banking** (p91).

Nonalcoholic Drinks

I don't drink alcohol.	No bebo alcohol. no *be*·bo al·*kol*
(cup of) coffee ...	(taza de) café ... (*ta*·tha de) ka·*fe* ...
(cup of) tea ...	(taza de) té ... (*ta*·tha de) te ...
with milk	con leche kon *le*·che
without sugar	sin azúcar seen a·*thoo*·kar
soft drink	refresco m re·*fres*·ko
(boiled) water	agua (hervida) *a*·gwa (er·*vee*·da)
(sparkling) mineral water	agua mineral (con gas) *a*·gwa mee·ne·*ral* (kon gas)

Alcoholic Drinks

... beer		cerveza f ... ther·*ve*·tha ...
draught	de barril	de ba·*ril*
dark	negra	*neg*·ra
light	rubia	*roo*·bee·a
nonalcoholic	sin alcohol	sin al·*kol*

small bottle of beer (250 ml)	botellín m bo·te·*lyin*
litre bottle of beer	litrona f lee·*tro*·na
bottle of beer (300 ml)	mediana f me·*dya*·na

What would you recommend?
ke re·ko·*myen*·da

¿Qué recomienda?

a glass/pint of beer	una caña/pinta de cerveza *oo*·na *ka*·nya/*peen*·ta de ther·*ve*·tha
a jug of beer	una jarra de cerveza *oo*·na *kha*·ra de ther·*ve*·tha
brandy	coñac m *ko*·nyak
Champagne	champán m cham·*pan*
cocktail	combinado m kom·bee·*na*·do
sangria (red-wine punch)	sangría f san·*gree*·a
a shot of (rum)	un chupito de (ron) oon choo·*pee*·to de (ron)
a shot of (gin)	un chupito de (ginebra) oon choo·*pee*·to de (khee·*ne*·bra)
a shot of (whisky)	un chupito de (güisqui) oon choo·*pee*·to de (*gwees*·kee)
a bottle/glass of ... wine	una botella/copa de vino ... *oo*·na bo·*te*·lya/*ko*·pa de *vee*·no ...

dessert	dulce	*dool*·the
red	tinto	*teen*·to
rose	rosado	ro·*sa*·do
sparkling	espumoso	es·poo·*mo*·so
white	blanco	*blan*·ko

CULTURE TIP	**Tapas**	

Tapas are scrumptious cooked bar snacks, available pretty much around the clock at bars and some clubs. You'll find they're free in some places, laid out in the bar for you to choose from. Other venues will rotate the dishes.

banderilla f / **moruno** m / **pinchito** m	ban·de·*ree*·lya / mo·*roo*·no / peen·*chee*·to	small tapa serving on bread or a toothpick
ración f	ra·*thyon*	large tapa serving
montadito m	mon·ta·*dee*·to	bread-topped tapa
pan tumaca m	pan too·*ma*·ka	tapa of toasted bread rubbed with tomatoes and garlic, served with oil
queso m **en aceite**	*ke*·so en a·*they*·te	cheese in olive oil, served as a tapa

In the Bar

Excuse me!	¡Oiga! *oy*·ga
I'm next.	Ahora voy yo. a·o·ra voy yo
Q What would you like?	¿Qué quieres tomar? ke *kye*·res to·*mar*
A I'll have ...	Para mí ... *pa*·ra mee ...
Same again, please.	Otra de lo mismo. *o*·tra de lo *mees*·mo
No ice, thanks.	Sin hielo, gracias. seen *ye*·lo *gra*·thyas
I'll buy you a drink.	Te invito a una copa. te een·*vee*·to a *oo*·na *ko*·pa

FOOD EATING OUT

¿Dónde le gustaría sentarse?	*don*·de le gus·ta·*ree*·a sen·*tar*·se Where would you like to sit?
¿En qué le puedo servir?	en ke le *pwe*·do ser·*veer* What can I get for you?
¡Aquí tiene!	a·*kee tye*·ne Here you go!

It's my round.	Es mi ronda. es mee *ron*·da
You can get the next one.	La próxima la pagas tú. la *prok*·see·ma la *pa*·gas too
Do you serve meals here?	¿Sirven comidas aquí? *seer*·ven ko·*mee*·das a·*kee*

Drinking Up

Cheers!	¡Salud! sa·*loo*
Thanks, but I don't feel like it.	Lo siento, pero no me apetece. lo *syen*·to *pe*·ro no me a·pe·te·the
No thanks, I'm driving.	No gracias, tengo que conducir. no *gra*·thyas *ten*·go ke kon·doo·*theer*
This is hitting the spot.	Me lo estoy pasando muy bien. me lo es·*toy* pa·*san*·do mooy byen

CULTURE TIP

Minis

Many Spanish bars provide massive plastic beakers of beer to cater for young revellers. It's cut with water and average tasting – but cheap and free flowing! These fountains of froth are called *minis*.

I feel fantastic!	¡Me siento fenomenal! me *syen*·to fe·no·me·*nal*
I'm feeling drunk.	Esto me está subiendo mucho. *es*·to me es·*ta* soo·*byen*·do *moo*·cho
I think I've had one too many.	Creo que he tomado demasiado. *kre*·o ke e to·*ma*·do de·ma·*sya*·do
I'm tired, I'd better go home.	Estoy cansado/a, mejor me voy a casa. m/f es·*toy* kan·*sa*·do/a me·*khor* me voy a *ka*·sa
I don't think you should drive.	No creo que deberías conducir. no *kre*·o ke de·be·*ree*·as kon·doo·*theer*
Can you call a taxi for me?	¿Me puedes pedir un taxi? me *pwe*·des pe·*deer* oon *tak*·see

Self-Catering

KEY PHRASES

What's the local speciality?	¿Cuál es la especialidad de la zona?	kwal es la es·pe·thya·lee·da de la tho·na
Where can I find the ... section?	¿Dónde está la sección de ...?	don·de es·ta la sek·thyon de ...
I'd like ...	Póngame ...	pon·ga·me ...

Buying Food

Where can I find the ... section?	¿Dónde está la sección de ...? don·de es·ta la sek·thyon de ...

dairy	productos lácteos	pro·dook·tos lak·te·os
frozen goods	productos congelados	pro·dook·tos kon·khe·la·dos
fruit and vegetable	frutas y verduras	froo·tas ee ver·doo·ras
meat	carne	kar·ne

Where's the health-food section/store?	¿Dónde esta la sección/ tienda de comida dietética? don·de es·ta la sek·thyon/ tyen·da de ko·mee·da dye·te·tee·ka
What's that?	¿Qué es eso? ke es e·so

🔊 LISTEN FOR

¿En qué le puedo servir?	en ke le *pwe*·do ser·*veer* Can I help you?
¿Qué querías?	ke ke·*ree*·as What would you like?
No tengo.	no *ten*·go I don't have any.
No queda más.	no *ke*·da mas There's none left.

Can I taste it?	¿Puedo probarlo/a? m/f *pwe*·do pro·*bar*·lo/a
What's the local speciality?	¿Cuál es la especialidad de la zona? kwal es la es·pe·thya·lee·*da* de la *tho*·na
How much?	¿Cuánto? *kwan*·to
How many?	¿Cuántos/as? m/f *kwan*·tos/as
How much is (a kilo of cheese)?	¿Cuánto vale (un kilo de queso)? *kwan*·to *va*·le (oon *kee*·lo de *ke*·so)
Do you have anything cheaper?	¿Tiene algo más barato? *tye*·ne *al*·go mas ba·*ra*·to
Do you have any other kinds?	¿Tiene otros tipos? *tye*·ne *ot*·ros *tee*·pos
Do you sell locally produced food?	¿Se venden comestibles de la zona? se *ven*·den ko·mes·*tee*·bles de la *tho*·na

FOOD

SELF-CATERING

Do you sell organic produce?	¿Se venden productos agrícolas biológicos? se *ven*·den pro·*dook*·tos a·*gree*·ko·las bee·o·lo·khee·kos
I'd like ...	Póngame ... *pon*·ga·me ...

(three) pieces	(tres) piezas	(tres) *pye*·thas
(six) slices	(seis) lonchas	(seys) *lon*·chas
(two) kilos	(dos) kilos	(dos) *kee*·los
(200) grams	(doscientos) gramos	(dos·*thyen*·tos) *gra*·mos

half a dozen	una media docena oo·na *me*·dya do·*the*·na
half a kilo	un medio kilo oon *me*·dyo *kee*·lo
a kilo	un kilo oon *kee*·lo
a bottle (of ...)	una botella (de ...) oo·na bo·*te*·lya (de ...)
a jar	una jarra oo·na *kha*·ra
a packet	un paquete oon pa·*ke*·te
(just) a little	(sólo) un poquito (*so*·lo) oon po·*kee*·to
many	muchos/as m/f *moo*·chos/as
(a bit) more	(un poco) más (oon *po*·ko) mas
some	algunos/as m/f al·*goo*·nos/as

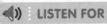

LISTEN FOR

Eso es (un manchego).	*e·*so es (oon man·*che·*go)
	That's (a manchego).
Eso es (cinco euros).	*e·*so es (*theen·*ko e·oo·ros)
	That's (five euros).
¿Algo más?	*al·*go mas
	Anything else?

less	menos
	*me·*nos
that one	ése
	*e·*se
this	esto
	*es·*to
Enough!	¡Basta!
	*ba·*sta

For food items, see the **menu decoder** (p190) and the **dictionary**.

Cooking

cooked	cocido/a m/f
	ko·*thee·*do/a
dried	seco/a m/f
	*se·*ko/a
fresh	fresco/a m/f
	*fres·*ko/a
frozen	congelado/a m/f
	kon·khe·*la·*do/a
raw	crudo/a m/f
	*kroo·*do/a
smoked	ahumado/a m/f
	a·oo·*ma·*do/a

FOOD SELF-CATERING

Could I please borrow a/an ...?	¿Me puede prestar un/una ...? m/f	me *pwe*·de pres·*tar* oon/*oo*·na ...
Where's a/an ...?	¿Dónde hay un/una ...? m/f	*don*·de ai oon/*oo*·na ...

bottle opener	abrebotellas m	a·bre·bo·*te*·lyas
can opener	abrelatas m	a·bre·*la*·tas
chopping board	tabla f para cortar	*tab*·la pa·ra kor·*tar*
corkscrew	sacacorchos m	sa·ka·*kor*·chos
cup	taza f	*ta*·tha
fork	tenedor m	te·ne·*dor*
frying pan	sartén f	sar·*ten*
glass	vaso m	*va*·so
knife	cuchillo m	koo·*chee*·lyo
plate	plato m	*pla*·to
saucepan	cazo m	*ka*·tho
spoon	cuchara f	koo·*cha*·ra
toaster	tostadora f	tos·ta·*do*·ra

For more cooking terminology, see the **dictionary**.

Vegetarian & Special Meals

KEY PHRASES

Do you have vegetarian food?	¿Tienen comida vegetariana?	tye·nen ko·mee·da ve·khe·ta·rya·na
Could you prepare a meal without ...?	¿Me puede preparar una comida sin ...?	me pwe·de pre·pa·rar oo·na ko·mee·da seen ...
I'm allergic to ...	Soy alérgico/a a ... m/f	soy a·ler·khee·ko/a a ...

Special Diets & Allergies

I'm vegetarian.	Soy vegetariano/a. m/f soy ve·khe·ta·rya·no/a
I'm on a special diet.	Estoy a régimen especial. es·toy a re·khee·men es·pe·thyal
I'm allergic to ...	Soy alérgico/a ... m/f soy a·ler·khee·ko/a ...

dairy produce	a los productos lácteos	a los pro·dook·tos lak·te·os
honey	al miel	al myel
MSG	al glutamato monosódico	al gloo·ta·ma·to mo·no·so·dee·ko
nuts	a las nueces	a las nwe·thes
seafood	a los mariscos	a los ma·rees·kos
shellfish	a los crustáceos	a los kroos·ta·thyos

Ordering Food

Is there a (vegetarian) restaurant near here?	¿Hay un restaurante (vegetariano) por aquí? *ai oon res·tow·ran·te (ve·khe·ta·rya·no) por a·kee*
Do you have vegetarian food?	¿Tienen comida vegetariana? *tye·nen ko·mee·da ve·khe·ta·rya·na*
Do you have halal food?	¿Tienen comida halal? *tye·nen ko·mee·da a·lal*
Do you have kosher food?	¿Tienen comida kosher? *tye·nen ko·mee·da ko·sher*
Do you have vegan food?	¿Tienen comida vegetariana estricta? *tye·nen ko·mee·da ve·khe·ta·rya·na es·trik·ta*
I don't eat red meat.	No como carne roja. *no ko·mo kar·ne ro·kha*
Is it cooked in/with butter?	¿Esta cocinado en/con mantequilla? *es·ta ko·thee·na·do en/kon man·te·kee·lya*
Could you prepare a meal without ...?	¿Me puede preparar una comida sin ...? *me pwe·de pre·pa·rar oo·na ko·mee·da seen ...*

eggs	huevo	*we·vo*
fish	pescado	*pes·ka·do*
meat/fish stock	caldo de carne/ pescado	*kal·do de kar·ne/ pes·ka·do*
pork	cerdo	*ther·do*
poultry	aves	*a·ves*

🔊 LISTEN FOR

¿Puede comer ...?	*pwe*·de ko·*mer* ... Can you eat ...?
Le preguntaré al cocinero.	le pre·goon·ta·*re* al ko·thee·*ne*·ro I'll check with the cook.
Todo lleva (carne).	*to*·do *lye*·va (*kar*·ne) It all has (meat) in it.

Is this ...?	¿Esto es ...? *es*·to es ...
free of animal produce	sin productos de animales	seen pro·*dook*·tos de a·nee·*ma*·les
free-range	de corral	de ko·*ral*
genetically modified	transgénico	trans·*khe*·nee·ko
gluten-free	sin gluten	seen *gloo*·ten
low in sugar	bajo en azúcar	*ba*·kho en a·*thoo*·kar
low-fat	bajo en grasas	*ba*·kho en *gra*·sas
organic	orgánico	or·*ga*·nee·ko
salt-free	sin sal	seen sal

A

Menu
~ DECODER ~
léxico culinario

This miniguide to Spanish cuisine lists dishes and ingredients in Spanish alphabetical order (see **alphabet**, p12). Spanish nouns have their gender indicated by ⓜ or ⓕ. If it's a plural noun, you'll also see pl.

~ A ~

acebuche ⓜ a·the·*boo*·che wild olive

acedía ⓕ a·the·*dee*·a plaice/flounder

aceite ⓜ a·*they*·te oil

— de girasol de khee·ra·*sol* sunflower oil

— de oliva de o·*lee*·va olive oil

— de oliva virgen extra de o·*lee*·va veer·khen eks·tra extra virgin olive oil

aceituna ⓕ a·*they*·*too*·na olive

— negra ne·gra black olive

— verde ver·de green olive

ácido/a ⓜ/ⓕ a·*thee*·do/a tart (flavour)

adobo ⓜ a·*do*·bo marinade

agrios ⓜ pl a·gryos citrus fruits

aguacate ⓜ a·gwa·*ka*·te avocado

aguaturma ⓕ a·gwa·*toor*·ma Jerusalem artichoke

ajiaco ⓜ a·*khya*·ko spicy potato dish

ajoaceite ⓜ a·kho·a·*they*·te garlic & oil sauce • garlic mayonnaise

ajoharina ⓕ a·kho·a·*ree*·na potatoes stewed in garlic sauce

(al) ajoarriero (al) a·kho·a·*rye*·ro 'mule-driver's garlic' – anything cooked in a sauce of onions, garlic & chilli

ala ⓕ a·la (chicken) wing

alajú ⓜ a·la·*khoo* honey & almond cake

albaricoque ⓜ al·ba·ree·*ko*·ke apricot

— seco se·ko dried apricot

albóndigas ⓕ pl al·*bon*·dee·gas meatballs

— de pescado de pes·*ka*·do fish balls

alcachofas ⓕ pl al·ka·*cho*·fas artichokes

— guisadas a la española gee·*sa*·das a la es·pa·*nyo*·la artichokes in wine

— rellenas re·*lye*·nas stuffed artichokes

alcaparra ⓕ al·ka·*pa*·ra caper

alioli ⓜ a·lee·o·lee garlic mayonnaise

almejas ⓕ pl al·*me*·khas clams – superb eaten raw

— a la marinera a la ma·ree·*ne*·ra clams in white wine

— al horno al or·no baked clams

almendrado ⓜ al·men·*dra*·do almond cake or biscuit • chocolate covered ice cream bar

almendras ⓕ pl al·*men*·dras almond

alubia ⓕ a·*loo*·bya haricot bean

nacardo ⓜ a·na·*kar*·do cashew nut

nchoas ⓕ pl an·*cho*·as anchovies –
mostly eaten fresh, grilled or fried

ngelote ⓜ an·khe·*lo*·te monkfish

nguila ⓕ an·*gee*·la adult eel

ngulas ⓕ pl an·*goo*·las baby eels –
prized as a delicacy, they resemble
vermicelli

— en all i pebre en al ee *pe*·bre baby
eels with pepper & garlic

pio ⓜ a·*pyo* celery

rándano ⓜ a·*ran*·da·no blueberry

renque ⓜ a·*ren*·ke herring

— ahumado a·oo·*ma*·do kipper

rroz ⓜ a·*roth* rice

— a la Alcireña a la al·thee·*re*·nya
baked rice dish

— abanda (de València) a·*ban*·da
de va·*len*·thya) fish paella

— con leche kon *le*·che rice pudding

— con pollo kon *po*·lyo chicken
& rice

— integral een·te·*gral* brown rice

— marinera ma·ree·*ne*·ra seafood
& rice

— salvaje sal·*va*·khe wild rice

sadillo ⓜ a·sa·*dee*·lyo roasted red
capsicums

sados ⓜ pl a·*sa*·dos roast meats

tún ⓜ a·*toon* tuna – often served
marinated & raw

— al horno al or·no baked tuna

vellana ⓕ a·ve·*lya*·na hazelnut

ves ⓕ pl a·*ves* poultry

zúcar ⓜ a·*thoo*·kar sugar

~ B ~

acalao ⓜ ba·ka·*low* cod – usually
salted & dried

— a la vizcaína a la veeth·ka·ee·na
cod with chillies & capsicums

— del convento del kon·*ven*·to cod
with potatoes & spinach in broth

acón ⓜ ba·*kon* bacon

arbo ⓜ *bar*·bo red mullet

barra ⓕ *ba*·ra long stick of bread

batata ⓕ ba·*ta*·ta sweet potato

beicon ⓜ *bey*·kon streaky bacon
rashers

berberechos ⓜ pl ber·be·*re*·chos
cockles

— en vinagre en vee·*na*·gre cockles
in vinegar

berenjenas ⓕ pl be·ren·*khe*·nas
eggplants

— a la mallorquina a la
ma·lyor·*kee*·na eggplants with garlic
mayonnaise

— con setas kon *se*·tas eggplants
with mushrooms

berza ⓕ *ber*·tha cabbage

— a la andaluza a la an·da·*loo*·tha
cabbage & meat hotpot

besugo ⓜ be·*soo*·go red bream

— a la Donostiarra a la do·nos·*tya*·ra
barbecued red bream with garlic &
paprika

— estilo San Sebastián es·*tee*·lo
san se·bas·*tyan* barbecued red
bream with garlic & paprika

bienmesabe ⓜ byen·me·*sa*·be sponge
cake, egg & almond confection

bisbe ⓜ *bees*·be black & white blood
sausage

bistec ⓜ *bees*·tek steak

— con patatas kon pa·*ta*·tas steak
with chips

bizcocha ⓕ **manchega** beeth·*ko*·cha
man·*che*·ga cake soaked in milk,
sugar, vanilla & cinnamon

bizcocho ⓜ beeth·*ko*·cho sponge
cake

— de almendra de al·*men*·dra
almond cake

— de avellana de a·ve·*lya*·na
hazelnut cake

bizcochos ⓜ pl **borrachos**
beeth·*ko*·chos bo·*ra*·chos cake
soaked in liqueur

bocadillo ⓜ bo·ka·*dee*·lyo bread roll
with a filling

C

bocas ① pl **de la isla** bo·kas de la ees·la large crab claws

bogavante ⓜ bo·ga·van·te lobster

bollo ⓜ bo·lyo crusty bread roll

bonito ⓜ bo·nee·to white fleshy tuna

boquerón ⓜ bo·ke·ron whitebait

boquerones ⓜ pl bo·ke·ro·nes anchovies marinated in wine vinegar

— fritos free·tos fried anchovies

brama ① bra·ma sea bream

bróculi ⓜ bro·ko·lee broccoli

budín ⓜ **de atún** boo·deen de a·toon baked tuna pudding

bull ⓜ **de atún** bool de a·toon rabbit with garlic & tuna boiled with potatoes

buñuelitos ⓜ pl boo·nywe·lee·tos small cheese or ham fritters

— de San José de san kho·se lemon & vanilla crepes

buñuelo ⓜ boo·nywe·lo fried pastry

burrida ① **de ratjada** boo·ree·da de rat·kha·da fish soup with almonds

butifarra ① **(blanca)** boo·tee·fa·ra (blan·ka) cured pork sausage

— con setas kon se·tas Catalan sausage with mushrooms

~ **C** ~

caballa ① ka·ba·lya mackerel

cabra ① ka·bra goat

cabracho ⓜ ka·bra·cho scorpion fish • mullet

cacahuete ⓜ ka·ka·we·te peanut

cachelos ⓜ pl ka·che·los potatoes with spicy sausage & pork

cádiz ⓜ ka·deeth fresh goats' milk cheese

calabacín ⓜ ka·la·ba·theen zucchini

calabaza ① ka·la·ba·tha pumpkin

calamares ⓜ pl ka·la·ma·res calamari – popular fried or stuffed

— fritos a la romana free·tos a la ro·ma·na squid rings fried in batter

— rellenos re·lye·nos stuffed squid

calçots ⓜ pl kal·sots spring onion-like vegetables chargrilled and eaten with a **romesco** dipping sauce

caldeirada ① kal·dey·ra·da salted cod & potatoes in a paprika sauce • fish soup

caldereta ① kal·de·re·ta stew

— asturiana as·too·rya·na fish stew

— de cordero de kor·de·ro lamb stew

caldillo ⓜ **de perro** kal·dee·lyo de pe·ro 'puppy dog soup' – stew of onions, fresh fish & orange juice

caldo ⓜ kal·do broth • clear soup • stock

— al estilo del Mar Menor al es·tee·lo del mar me·nor fish stew from the Mar Menor

— gallego ga·lye·go broth with haricot beans, ham & sausage

callos ⓜ pl ka·lyos tripe

camarones fritos ⓜ pl ka·ma·ro·nes free·tos deep-fried prawns

canagroc ka·na·grok mushroom

cañaillas ① pl **de la Isla** ka·nyay·lyas de la ees·la boiled sea snails

canelones ⓜ pl ka·na·lo·nes square of pasta for making cannelloni

— con espinaca kon es·pee·na·ka cannelloni with spinach, anchovies & bechamel

— con pescado kon pes·ka·do cannelloni with cod, eggs & mushrooms

canapés ⓜ pl **de fiambres** ka·na·pes de fee·am·bres mini hors d'oeuvres with ham, anchovies or cheese

cangrejo ⓜ kan·gre·kho large-clawed crab usually eaten steamed or boiled

cantalupo ⓜ kan·ta·loo·po cantaloupe

canutillos ⓜ pl ka·noo·tee·lyos cream biscuits

apones ⓜ pl **de Villalba** ka·po·nes e vee·lyal·ba Christmas dish of hicken marinated in brandy

aracoles ⓜ ka·ra·ko·les snails

aramelos ⓜ pl ka·ra·me·los aramels • confection

ardos ⓜ pl **fritos** kar·dos free·tos ied thistles

arne ⓕ kar·ne meat

- de membrillo de mem·bree·lyo uince 'cheese'

- molida mo·lee·da minced meat

assolada ⓕ ka·so·la·da potato & egetable stew with bacon & ribs

astaña ⓕ kas·ta·nya chestnut

aviar ⓜ ka·vyar caviar

aza ⓕ ka·tha game

azón ⓜ ka·thon dogfish or shark ith a sweet scallop-like flavour

azuelitas ⓕ pl **de langostinos an Rafael** ka·thwe·lee·tas de an·gos·tee·nos san ra·fa·el baked rice ith seafood

ebolla ⓕ the·bo·lya onion

ecina ⓕ the·thee·na cured meat

erdo ⓜ ther·do pork

ereales ⓜ pl the·re·a·les cereal

ereza ⓕ the·re·tha cherry

- silvestre seel·ves·tre wild cherry

iervo ⓜ thyer·vo deer

igala ⓕ thee·ga·la crayfish

iruela ⓕ thee·rwe·la plum

- pasa pa·sa prune

ivet ⓜ **de llebre** see·vet de le·bre are stew

halote ⓜ cha·lo·te shallot

hampiñones ⓜ pl cham·pee·nyo·nes cultivated white ushrooms

hanquetes ⓜ pl chan·ke·tes hitebait • baby anchovies

al) chilindrón (al) chee·leen·dron ooked in a tomato & red pepper auce

hipirón ⓜ chee·pee·ron baby quid – very popular in the Basque Country

chocolate ⓜ cho·ko·la·te chocolate

— caliente ka·lee·en·te thick hot chocolate

chocos ⓜ pl cho·kos squid

chorizo ⓜ cho·ree·tho spicy red cooked sausage, similar to salami

— de Pamplona de pam·plo·na fine-textured, hard chorizo

— de Salamanca de sa·la·man·ka chunky chorizo from Salamanca

chuletas ⓕ pl choo·le·tas chops • cutlets

— al sarmiento al sar·myen·to chops prepared over wood from vines

— de buey de bwey ox chops

— de cerdo a la aragonesa de ther·do a la a·ra·go·ne·sa baked pork chops with wine & onion

churros ⓜ choo·ros fried doughnut strips bought from street-sellers or in cafes

cochifrito ⓜ **de cordero** ko·chee·free·to de kor·de·ro lamb fried with garlic & lemon

cochinillo ⓜ ko·chee·nee·lyo suckling pig

— asado a·sa·do roast suckling pig

— de pelotas de pe·lo·tas meatball stew

coco ⓜ ko·ko coconut

codornices ⓕ pl **a la plancha** ko·dor·nee·thes a la plan·cha grilled quail

codorniz ⓕ ko·dor·neeth quail

— con pimientos kon pee·myen·tos capsicums stuffed with quail

col ⓕ kol cabbage

— lombarda lom·bar·da red cabbage

coles ⓕ pl **de bruselas** ko·les de broo·se·las Brussels sprouts

coliflor ⓕ ko·lee·flor cauliflower

conejo ⓜ ko·ne·kho rabbit

— de monte de mon·te wild rabbit

coquina ⓕ ko·kee·na large clam

C

D

corazón ⓜ ko·ra·*thon* heart

cordero ⓜ kor·de·ro lamb

— al chilindrón al che·leen·*dron* lamb in tomato & capsicum sauce

— con almendras kon al·*men*·dras lamb in almond sauce

costillas ⓕ pl kos·*tee*·lyas ribs

crema ⓕ *kre*·ma cream

— catalana ka·ta·*la*·na creme brulee

— de espinacas de es·pee·*na*·kas cream of spinach soup

— de naranja de na·*ran*·kha orange cream dessert

— de San José de san kho·*se* egg custard flavoured with cinnamon

— de verduras de ver·*doo*·ras cream of vegetable soup

crocante ⓜ kro·*kan*·te ice cream with chopped nuts & chocolate

~ D ~

de soja de so·kha of/with soya

despojos ⓜ pl des·*po*·khos offal

dorada ⓕ **a la sal** do·*ra*·da a la sal salted sea bream

dulce ⓜ *dool*·the sweet

— de batata de ba·*ta*·ta sweet potato pudding from Málaga

dulces ⓜ pl *dool*·thes sweets

— de las monjas *dool*·thes de las *mon*·khas confectionery made by nuns & sold in convents or cake shops

~ E ~

embutidos ⓜ pl em·boo·*tee*·dos generic name for cured sausages

empanada ⓕ em·pa·*na*·da savoury pie

— de carne de *kar*·ne spicy meat pie

— de espinaca de es·pee·*na*·ka spinach pie

empanadilla ⓕ em·pa·na·*dee*·lya small pie, either sweet or savoury

empanado ⓜ em·pa·*na*·do coated bread crumbs

emparedado ⓜ em·pa·re·*da*·do sandwich

— de jamón y espárragos de kha·*mon* ee es·*pa*·ra·gos fried ham & asparagus rolls

empiñonado ⓜ em·pee·nyo·*na*·do small marzipan-filled pastry with pinenuts

en salsa verde en *sal*·sa ver·de in a parsley & garlic sauce

encurtidos ⓜ pl en·koor·*tee*·dos pickles

ensaimada ⓕ **mallorquina** en·sai·*ma*·da ma·lyor·*kee*·na spiral-shaped bun made with lard

ensalada ⓕ en·sa·*la*·da salad

— de frutas de *froo*·tas fruit salad

— de patatas de pa·*ta*·tas potato salad

— del tiempo del *tyem*·po seasonal salad

— mixta *meeks*·ta mixed salad

escaldadillas ⓕ pl es·kal·da·*dee*·lyas dough soaked in orange juice & fried

escalivada ⓕ es·ka·lee·*va*·da roasted red capsicums in olive oil

escalopes ⓜ pl **de ternera rellenos** es·ka·*lo*·pes de ter·*ne*·ra re·*lye*·nos deep fried veal cutlets stuffed with egg & cheese

espaguetis ⓜ pl es·pa·*ge*·tees spaghetti

espárragos ⓜ pl es·*pa*·ra·gos asparagus

— con dos salsas kon dos *sal*·sas asparagus & tomato or paprika mayonnaise

— en vinagreta en vee·na·*gre*·ta asparagus in vinaigrette

espinacas ⓕ pl es·pee·*na*·kas spinach

— a la catalana a la ka·ta·*la*·na spinach with pinenuts & raisins

squeixada ⓕ es·kee·*sha*·da cod ressed with olives, tomato & onion
txeko kopa e·*che*·ko *ko*·pa ice ream dessert

~ F ~

abada ⓕ **asturiana** fa·*ba*·da s·too·*rya*·na stew made with pork, lood sausage & white beans
aisán ⓜ fai·*san* pheasant
aves ⓕ pl **a la catalana** *fa*·ves a la a·ta·*la*·na broad beans with ham
ambres ⓜ pl fee·*am*·bres cold heats
— surtidos soor·*tee*·dos selection of old meats
deos ⓜ pl fee·*de*·os pasta noodles
deua ⓕ fee·*de*·wa rice or noodles with fish & shellfish
deus ⓜ pl **a la cassola** fee·*de*·oos a la ka·*so*·la Catalan noodle dish
lete ⓜ fee·*le*·te steak • any oneless slice of meat
— a la parrilla a la pa·*ree*·lya grilled eef steak
— de ternera de ter·*ne*·ra veal steak
lloas ⓕ pl fee·*lyo*·as Galician ancakes filled with cream
an ⓜ flan creme caramel
aó ⓕ *fla*·o sweet cheese flan
or manchega ⓜ flor man·*che*·ga eep-fried sweet wafers
rambuesa ⓕ fram·*bwe*·sa rasp-erry
angellos ⓜ pl fran·*khe*·lyos sweet nade from cornmeal, milk & honey
resa ⓕ *fre*·sa strawberry
ricandó ⓜ **de langostinos** ee·kan·*do* de lan·gos·*tee*·nos shrimp almond sauce
rite ⓜ *free*·te lamb stew, served on estive occasions
ritos ⓜ pl *free*·tos fritters
— con miel kon myel honey-roasted ritters

fritura ⓕ free·*too*·ra mixed fried fish
fruta ⓕ *froo*·ta fruit
— variada va·*ree*·a·da selection of fresh fruit
frutas ⓕ pl **en almibar** *froo*·tas en al·*mee*·bar fruit in syrup
frutos ⓜ pl **secos** *froo*·tos *se*·kos nuts & dried fruit
fuet ⓕ foo·*et* thin pork sausage

~ G ~

gachas ⓕ pl **manchegas** *ga*·chas man·*che*·gas flavoured porridge
galleta ⓕ ga·*lye*·ta biscuit
gambas ⓕ pl *gam*·bas prawns
— a la plancha a la *plan*·cha grilled prawns
— en gabardina en ga·bar·*dee*·na prawns in batter
Gamonedo ⓜ ga·mo·*ne*·do sharp- tasting cheese, smoked & cured
garbanzos ⓜ pl gar·*ban*·thos chickpeas
— con cebolla kon the·*bo*·lya chickpeas in onion sauce
— tostados tos·*ta*·dos roasted chickpeas (sold as a snack)
garbure ⓕ gar·*boo*·re green vegetable soup • pork & ham dish
garúm ⓜ ga·*room* olive & anchovy dip
Gata-Hurdes ga·ta·*oor*·des cheese
gazpacho ⓜ gath·*pa*·cho cold tomato soup
— andaluz an·da·*looz* cold tomato soup with chopped salad vegetables
— pastoril pas·to·*reel* rabbit stew with tomato & garlic
gazpachos ⓜ pl **manchegos** gath·*pa*·chos man·*che*·gos game & vegetable hotpot
Gaztazarra ⓜ gath·ta·*tha*·ra cheese
gitano ⓜ khee·*ta*·no Andalusian chickpea & tripe stew

gofio ⓜ *go*-fyo toasted cornmeal or barley

granadilla ⓕ gra-na-*dee*-lya passion fruit

grano ⓜ *gra*-no grain
— largo *lar*-go long-grain (rice)

gratinado ⓜ **de berenjenas** gra-tee-*na*-do de be-ren-*khe*-nas eggplant gratin

Grazalema ⓕ gra-tha-*le*-ma semi-cured sheep's milk cheese

guindilla ⓕ geen-*dee*-lya mild green chilli

guisado ⓜ gee-*sa*-do stew
— de cordero de kor-*de*-ro lamb ragout
— de ternera de ter-*ne*-ra veal ragout

guisante ⓜ gee-*san*-te pea
— seco *se*-ko split pea
— mollar mo-*lyar* snow pea

guisantes ⓜ pl **con jamón a la española** gee-*san*-tes kon kha-*mon* a la es-*pa*-nyo-la pea & ham dish

guisat ⓜ **de marisco** gee-*sat* de ma-*rees*-ko stew made with seafood

guiso ⓜ **de conejo estilo canario** *gee*-so de ko-*ne*-kho es-*tee*-lo ka-*na*-ryo rabbit stew

guiso ⓜ **de rabo de toro** *gee*-so de *ra*-bo de *to*-ro stewed bull's tail with potatoes

~ **H** ~

habas ⓕ pl *a*-bas broad beans
— a la granadina a la gra-na-*dee*-na broad beans with eggs & ham
— fritas *free*-tas fried broad beans (sold as a snack)

habichuela ⓕ a-bee-*chwe*-la white bean

hamburguesa ⓕ am-boor-*ge*-sa hamburger

harina ⓕ a-*ree*-na flour
— integral een-te-*gral* wholemeal flour

helado ⓜ e-*la*-do ice cream

hígado ⓜ *ee*-ga-do liver

higo ⓜ *ee*-go fig
— seco *se*-ko dried fig

hogaza ⓕ o-*ga*-tha dense, thick-crusted bread

hoja ⓕ **de parra** *o*-kha de *pa*-ra vine leaf

hojaldres ⓜ pl o-*khal*-dres small flaky pastries covered in sugar

hojas ⓕ pl **verdes** *o*-khas *ver*-des green vegetables

hornazo ⓜ or-*na*-tho bread stuffed with sausage

hortalizas ⓕ pl or-ta-*lee*-thas vegetables

huevo ⓜ *we*-vo egg
— cocido ko-*thee*-do boiled egg
— de chocolate de cho-ko-*la*-te chocolate egg
— frito *free*-to fried egg

huevos ⓜ pl *we*-vos egg dishes
— a la flamenca a la fla-*men*-ka baked vegetables with egg & ham
— al estilo Sóller al es-*tee*-lo so-*lyer* fried eggs served with a milk & vegetable sauce
— en salsa agria en *sal*-sa a-*grya* boiled eggs in wine & vinegar
— escalfados es-kal-*fa*-dos poached eggs
— revueltos re-*vwel*-tos scrambled eggs

~ **J** ~

jabalí ⓜ kha-ba-*lee* wild boar
— con salsa de castaños kon *sal*-sa de kas-*ta*-nyos wild boar in chestnut sauce

jamón ⓜ kha-*mon* ham
— cocido ko-*thee*-do cooked ham
— ibérico ee-*ber*-ik-o ham from the Iberian pig, said to be the best in Spain
— serrano se-*ra*-no cured mountain ham

K

ngibre ⓜ khen·*gee*·bre ginger
rez (al) khe·*reth* (al) in a sherry
auce
día ⓕ khoo·*dee*·a fresh green
ean • dried kidney bean
días ⓕ pl **del tío Lucas**
hoo·*dee*·as del *tee*·o *loo*·kas bean
tew with garlic & bacon
días ⓕ pl **verdes a la castellana**
hoo·*dee*·as ver·des a la kas·te·*lya*·na
ied capsicums, garlic & green beans
diones ⓜ pl **de la granja**
ho·dee·o·nes de la *gran*·kha pork &
ean stew

~ K ~

skilla kees·*kee*·lya shrimp (also
pelled **quisquilla**)

~ L ~

ngosta ⓕ lan·gos·ta lobster
• **a la ibicenca** a la ee·bee·*then*·ka
bster with stuffed squid
ngostinos ⓜ pl lan·gos·*tee*·nos
ng prawns
• **a la plancha** a la *plan*·cha grilled
ng prawns
vanco ⓜ la·*van*·ko wild duck
chuga ⓕ le·*choo*·ga lettuce
gumbres ⓕ pl le·*goom*·bres
ulses • vegetables • vegetable
shes
• **secas** se·kas dried pulses
guminosas ⓕ pl
goo·mee·*no*·sas legumes
ngua ⓕ *len*·gwa tongue
• **a la aragonesa** a la a·ra·go·*ne*·sa
ngue in tomato & capsicum sauce
nguado ⓜ len·*gwa*·do sole
• **al chacolí con hongos** al
ha·ko·*lee* kon *on*·gos sole with white
ine & mushrooms
nguados ⓜ pl **al plato**
n·gwa·dos al *pla*·to sole &
ushroom casserole

lenguas ⓕ pl **con salsa de
almendras** *len*·gwas kon *sal*·sa de
al·*men*·dras tongue in almond sauce
lentejas ⓕ pl len·*te*·khas lentils
liebre ⓕ *lye*·bre hare
— con castañas kon kas·*ta*·nyas
hare with chestnuts
— estofada es·to·*fa*·da stewed hare
lima ⓕ *lee*·ma lime
limón ⓜ lee·*mon* lemon
llagostí ⓜ **a l'allioli** lyan·gos·*tee* a
la·lyee·o·lee grilled prawns in garlic
mayonnaise
llenguado ⓜ **a la nyoca** lyen·*gwa*·do
a la *nyo*·ka sole with pine nuts & raisins
lomo ⓜ *lo*·mo fillet • loin • sirloin
— curado koo·*ra*·do cured pork
sausage
— de cerdo de *ther*·do loin of pork
longaniza ⓕ lon·ga·*nee*·tha chorizo,
long & skinny sausage
lubina ⓕ loo·*bee*·na sea bass
— a la marinera a la ma·ree·*ne*·ra
sea bass in parsley sauce
lucio ⓜ *loo*·thyo pike

~ M ~

macedonia ⓕ **de frutas**
ma·the·*do*·nya de *froo*·tas fruit salad
macedonia ⓕ **de verduras**
ma·the·*do*·nya de ver·*doo*·ras mixed
vegetables
magdalena ⓕ ma·da·*le*·na small
fairy cake to dunk in coffee
magras ⓕ pl *ma*·gras fried eggs,
ham, cheese & tomato
maíz ⓜ ma·*eeth* maize • corn
— tierno *tyer*·no sweetcorn
mandarina ⓕ man·da·*ree*·na
tangerine • mandarin
mango ⓜ *man*·go mango
manitas ⓕ pl **de cerdo** ma·*nee*·tas
de *ther*·do pig's trotters

M

manitas ① pl **de cordero** ma·nee·tas de kor·de·ro leg of lamb

manteca ① man·te·ka lard

mantecado ⓜ man·te·ka·do a soft lard biscuit • dairy ice cream

mantequilla ① man·te·kee·lya butter

— sin sal seen sal unsalted butter

manzana ① man·tha·na apple

manzanas asadas man·tha·nas a·sa·das baked apples

margarina ① mar·ga·ree·na margarine

marinera (a la) ma·ree·ne·ra (a la) cooked or served in a white wine sauce

mariscos ⓜ ma·rees·kos shellfish • seafood

marmitako mar·mee·ta·ko fresh tuna & potato casserole

marrano ⓜ ma·ra·no pork

mar y cel ⓜ mar ee sel dish of sausages, rabbit, shrimp & angler fish

masa ① ma·sa pastry (dough)

mayonesa ① ma·yo·ne·sa mayonnaise

medallones ⓜ pl **de merluza** me·da·lyo·nes de mer·loo·tha hake steaks

mejillones ⓜ pl me·khee·lyo·nes mussels

— al vino blanco al vee·no blan·ko mussels in white wine

— con salsa kon sal·sa mussels with tomato sauce

mel ① **i mató** mel ee ma·to dessert of curd cheese with honey

melocotón ⓜ me·lo·ko·ton peach

melocotones ⓜ pl **al vino** me·lo·ko·to·nes al vee·no peaches in red wine

melón ⓜ me·lon melon

membrillo ⓜ mem·bree·lyo quince

menestra ① me·nes·tra mixed vegetable stew

— de pollo de po·lyo chicken & vegetable stew

merengue ⓜ me·ren·ge meringue

merluza ① mer·loo·tha hake

mermelada ① mer·me·la·da marmalade

mero ⓜ me·ro halibut • grouper • sea bass

miel ① myel honey

— de azahar de a·tha·ar orange blossom honey

— de caña de ka·nya treacle

migas ① pl mee·gas fried cubes of bread with capsicums

— a la aragonesa a la a·ra·go·ne·sa fried bread with bacon rashers in tomato sauce

— mulatas moo·la·tas cubes of bread soaked in chocolate & fried

mojarra ⓜ mo·kha·ra type of sea bream

moje ⓜ **manchego** mo·khe man·che·go cold broth with black olives

mojete ⓜ mo·khe·te dipping sauce for bread, made from potatoes, garlic, tomatoes & paprika

— murciano moor·thya·no fish & capsicum dish

mojo ⓜ mo·kho spicy capsicum sauce

mollejas ① pl mo·lye·khas sweetbreads

mollete ⓜ mo·lye·te soft round bap roll

monas ① pl **de pascua** mo·nas de pas·kwa Easter cakes • figures made of chocolate

mongetes ① pl **seques i butifarra** mon·zhe·tes se·kes ee boo·tee·fa·ra haricot beans with roasted pork sausage

mora ① mo·ra blackberry

moraga ① **de sardina** mo·ra·ga de sar·dee·na fresh anchovies on a spit

morcilla ① mor·thee·lya black pudding, often stewed with beans & vegetables

mortadela ① mor·ta·de·la mortadella sausage

morteruelo ⑩ mor·te·rwe·lo pate dish containing offal, game & spices

mostachones ⑩ pl mos·ta·cho·nes small cakes for dipping in coffee or hot chocolate (also spelled **mostatxones**)

mostaza ① mos·ta·tha mustard
— **en grano** en gra·no mustard seed

múgil ⑩ moo·kheel grey mullet

mujol ⑩ **guisado** moo·khol gee·sa·do red mullet

mus ⑩ **de chocolate** moos de cho·ko·la·te chocolate mousse

muslo ⑩ moos·lo (chicken) leg & thigh

N

nabo ⑩ na·bo root vegetable · turnip

naranja ① na·ran·kha orange

nata ① na·ta cream
— **agria** a·grya sour cream
— **montada** mon·ta·da whipped cream

natillas ① pl na·tee·lyas creamy custard dessert
— **de chocolate** de cho·ko·la·te chocolate custard

navaja ① na·va·kha razor clam

nécora ① ne·ko·ra small crab

nueces ① pl new·thes nuts

nuez ① nweth nut
— **de América** de a·me·ree·ka pecan nut
— **de nogal** de no·gal walnut

~ Ñ ~

ñora ① nyo·ra sweet red capsicum (usually dried)

~ O ~

oca ① o·ka goose

olla ① o·lya meat & vegetable stew · cooking pot

oreja ① **de mar** o·re·kha de mar abalone

ostiones ⑩ pl **a la gaditana** os·tyo·nes a la ga·dee·ta·na Cádiz oysters with garlic, parsley & bread crumbs

ostra ① os·tra oyster

oveja ① o·ve·kha mutton

~ P ~

pá ⑩ **amb oli** pa amb o·lee toasted bread with garlic & olive oil

pacana ① pa·ka·na pecan

paella ① pa·e·lya rice dish which has many regional variations
— **marinera** ma·ree·ne·ra paella with fish & seafood
— **zamorana** tha·mo·ra·na paella with meat

palitos ⑩ pl **de queso** pa·lee·tos de ke·so cheese straws

palmera ① pal·me·ra leaf-shaped flaky pastry, often coated in chocolate

palomitas ① pl pa·lo·mee·tas popcorn

pan ⑩ pan bread
— **aceite** a·they·te flat round bread
— **árabe** a·ra·be pita bread
— **de Alá** de a·la 'Allah's Bread' – dessert
— **de boda** de bo·da sculpted bread traditionally made for weddings
— **de centeno** de then·te·no rye bread
— **duro** doo·ro stale bread, used for toasting & eating with olive oil
— **integral** een·te·gral wholemeal bread

panaché ⑩ pa·na·che mixed vegetable stew

panallets ⑩ pl pa·na·lyets marzipan sweets

panceta ① pan·the·ta salt-cured, streaky bacon

panchineta ① pan·chee·*ne*·ta almond tart

panecillo ⑩ pa·ne·*thee*·lyo small bread roll

panojas ① pl **malagueñas** pa·*no*·khas ma·la·*ge*·nyas sardine dish

papas ① pl **arrugadas** *pa*·pas a·roo·*ga*·das potatoes boiled in their jackets

pargo ⑩ *par*·go sea bream

parrillada ① pa·ree·*lya*·da grilled meat

— de mariscos de ma·*rees*·kos seafood grill

pastel ⑩ pas·*tel* cake

— de boda de *bo*·da wedding cake

— de chocolate de cho·ko·*la*·te chocolate cake

— de cierva de *thyer*·va meat pie

— de cumpleaños de koom·ple·a·*nyos* birthday cake

pastelitos ⑩ pl **de miel** pas·te·*lee*·tos de myel honey fritters

pataco ⑩ pa·*ta*·ko tuna & potato stew

patatas ① pl pa·*ta*·tas potatoes

— a la riojana a la ree·o·*kha*·na potatoes with chorizo & paprika

— alioli a·lee·o·lee potatoes in garlic mayonnaise

— bravas *bra*·vas potatoes in spicy tomato sauce

— con chorizo kon cho·*ree*·tho potatoes with chorizo

— estofadas es·to·*fa*·das boiled potatoes

pato ⑩ *pa*·to duck

— a la sevillana a la se·vee·*lya*·na duck with orange sauce

— alcaparrada al·ka·pa·*ra*·da duck with capers & almonds

pavo ⑩ *pa*·vo turkey

pececillos ⑩ pl pe·pe·the·*thee*·lyos small fish

pechina ① pe·*chee*·na scallop

pecho ⑩ *pe*·cho breast of lamb

pechuga ① pe·*choo*·ga breast of poultry

pepinillo ⑩ pe·pee·*nee*·lyo gherkin

pepino ⑩ pe·*pee*·no cucumber

pepitoria ① pe·pee·*to*·rya sauce made with egg & almond

pepitos ⑩ pl pe·*pee*·tos chocolate eclair cakes filled with custard

pera ① *pe*·ra pear

La Peral ① la pe·*ral* soft cheese

perca ① *per*·ka perch

perdices ① pl per·*dee*·thes partridges

— a la manchega a la man·*che*·ga partridge in red wine & capsicums

— con chocolate kon cho·ko·*la*·te partridge with chocolate

perdiz ① per·*deeth* partridge

peregrina ① pe·re·*gree*·na scallop

pericana ① pe·ree·*ka*·na dish of olives, cod oil, capsicums & garlic

perrito ⑩ **caliente** pe·*ree*·to ka·lee·*en*·te hot dog

pescada ① **á galega** pes·*ka*·da a ga·*le*·ga hake fried in olive oil & served with garlic & paprika sauce

pescadilla ① pes·ka·*dee*·lya whiting · young hake

pescaditos ⑩ pl **rebozados** pes·ka·*dee*·tos re·bo·*tha*·dos small fish fried in batter

pescado ⑩ pes·*ka*·do fish

— a l'all cremat a lal kre·*mat* fish in burnt garlic

pescaíto ① **frito** pes·ka·*ee*·to *free*·to tiny fried fish

pestiños ⑩ pl pes·*tee*·nyos honey-coated aniseed pastries, fried with filling

pez ① **espada** peth es·*pa*·da swordfish

— frito *free*·to fried swordfish steaks on a skewer

picada ① pee·*ka*·da mixture of garlic, parsley, toasted almonds & nuts, often used to thicken sauces

P

icadillo ⓜ pee·ka·dee·lyo salad consisting of diced vegetables
— **de atún** de a·toon salad made with diced tuna & capsicums
— **de ternera** de ter·ne·ra minced veal
ichón ⓜ pee·chon pigeon
ichones ⓜ pl **asados** pee·cho·nes a·sa·dos roast pigeons
ilotes ① pl pee·lo·tes Catalan meatballs
imiento ⓜ pee·myen·to capsicum
— **amarillo** a·ma·ree·lyo yellow capsicum
— **rojo** ro·kho red capsicum
— **verde** ver·de green capsicum
imientos ⓜ pl pee·myen·tos capsicums (the ones from El Bierzo are especially good)
— **a la riojana** a la ree·o·kha·na roast red capsicum fried in oil & garlic
— **al chilindrón** al chee·leen·dron capsicum casserole
oiña ① pee·nya pineapple
inchito ⓜ **moruno** peen·chee·to mo·roo·no lamb & chicken kebabs
oiñón ⓜ pee·nyon pinenut
inta ① peen·ta pinto bean
intada ① peen·ta·da guinea fowl
iquillo ⓜ pee·kee·lyo sweet & spicy capsicums
istacho ⓜ pees·ta·cho pistachio nut
isto ⓜ **manchego** pees·to man·che·go zucchini with capsicum & tomato, fried or stewed
látano ⓜ pla·ta·no banana
ochas ① pl po·chas beans
— **a la riojana** a la ree·o·kha·na beans with chorizo in spicy paprika sauce
— **con almejas** kon al·me·khas beans with clams
ollo ⓜ po·lyo chicken
— **asado** a·sa·do roast chicken
— **con samfaina** kon sam·fai·na chicken with mixed vegetables

— **en escabeche** en es·ka·be·che marinated chicken
— **en salsa de ajo** en sal·sa de a·kho chicken in garlic sauce
— **granadina** gra·na·dee·na chicken with wine & ham
— **y langosta** ee lan·gos·ta chicken with crayfish
polvorón ⓜ pol·vo·ron almond shortbread, often eaten at Christmas
pomelo ⓜ po·me·lo grapefruit
postre ⓜ pos·tre dessert
— **de naranja** de na·ran·kha cream-filled oranges
potaje ⓜ po·ta·khe broth
— **castellano** kas·te·lya·no broth with beans & sausages
— **de garbanzos** de gar·ban·thos broth with chickpeas
— **de lentejas** de len·te·khas lentil broth
pote ⓜ **gallego** po·te ga·lye·go stew
potito ⓜ po·tee·to jar of baby food
pringada ① preen·ga·da bread dipped in sauce • a marinated sandwich
productos ⓜ pl **biológicos** pro·dook·tos bee·o·lo·khee·kos organic produce
productos ⓜ pl **del mar** pro·dook·tos del mar seafood products
productos ⓜ pl **lácteos** pro·dook·tos lak·te·os dairy products
puchero ⓜ poo·che·ro casserole
pudín ⓜ poo·din pudding
puerco ⓜ pwer·ko pork
puerro ⓜ pwe·ro leek
pulpo ⓜ pool·po octopus
— ⓜ **a feira** pool·po a fey·ra spicy boiled octopus
punta ① **de diamante** poon·ta de dya·man·te confection from Valencia
porrusalda ① po·roo·sal·da cod & potato stew

Q

~ Q ~

queso ⓜ *ke·so* cheese
— azul *a·thool* blue cheese
— crema *kre·ma* cream cheese
quisquilla ⓕ *kees·kee·lya* shrimp (also spelled **kiskilla**)

~ R ~

rábano ⓜ *ra·ba·no* radish
rabas ⓕ **en salsa verde** *ra·bas en sal·sa ver·de* squid in green sauce
rabassola ⓕ *ra·ba·so·la* mushroom
rape ⓜ *ra·pe* monkfish
— a la gallega a la *ga·lye·ga* monkfish with potatoes & garlic sauce
— a la Monistrol a la mo·nees·*trol* monkfish with bechamel sauce
redondo ⓜ *re·don·do* round (of beef)
— al horno al *or·no* roast beef
regañaos ⓜ pl *re·ga·nya·os* pastry stuffed with sardines & red capsicum
relleno ⓜ *re·lye·no* stuffing
remolacha ⓕ *re·mo·la·cha* beetroot
reo ⓜ *re·o* sea trout
repollo ⓜ *re·po·lyo* cabbage
repostería ⓕ *re·pos·te·ree·a* confectionery
requesón ⓜ *re·ke·son* cottage cheese
riñón ⓜ *ree·nyon* kidney
róbalo ⓜ *ro·ba·lo* haddock • sea bass
rodaballo ⓜ *ro·da·ba·lyo* turbot • brill
romero ⓜ *ro·me·ro* rosemary
romesco ⓜ *ro·mes·ko* sweet red capsicum, almond & garlic sauce
rosca ⓕ **de carne** *ros·ka* de *kar·ne* meatloaf wrapped in bacon
rosco ⓜ *ros·ko* small sweet bun
rossejat ⓜ *ro·se·dyat* rice with fish & shellfish

rovellons ⓜ pl **a la plancha** *ro·ve·lyons* a la *plan·cha* garlic mushrooms
ruibarbo ⓜ *roo·ee·bar·bo* rhubarb

~ S ~

salchicha ⓕ *sal·chee·cha* pork sausage
salchichón ⓜ *sal·chee·chon* cured & peppery white sausage
salmón ⓜ *sal·mon* salmon
— a la ribereña a la *ree·be·re·nya* salmon in a cider sauce
— ahumado *a·oo·ma·do* smoked salmon
salmonete ⓜ *sal·mo·ne·te* red mullet
salmorejo ⓜ *sal·mo·re·kho* thick gazpacho soup made from tomato, bread, olive oil, vinegar, garlic & green capsicum
— de Córdoba de *kor·do·ba* gazpacho soup made with more vinegar than usual
salpicón ⓜ *sal·pee·kon* fish or meat salad
salsa ⓕ *sal·sa* sauce
— alioli *a·lee·o·lee* garlic & olive oil vinaigrette • garlic mayonnaise
— de holandesa de *o·lan·de·sa* hollandaise sauce
— de mayonesa de *ma·yo·ne·sa* mayonnaise sauce
— de tomate de to·*ma·te* tomato sauce
— inglesa een·*gle·*sa Worcestershire sauce
— tártara *tar·ta·ra* tartar sauce
— verde *ver·de* parsley & garlic sauce
samfaina ⓕ *sam·fai·na* grilled vegetable sauce
sancocho ⓜ *san·ko·cho* fish dish served with potatoes
sandía ⓕ *san·dee·a* watermelon

sándwich ⓜ *san*·weech sandwich
— mixto *meeks*·to toasted ham & cheese sandwich
sanocho ⓜ **canario** sa·*no*·cho ka·*na*·ryo baked monkfish with potatoes
sardinas ⓕ sar·*dee*·nas sardines
— a la parrilla a la pa·*ree*·lya sardines grilled
— en cazuela en ka·*thwe*·la sardines served in a clay pot
sargo ⓜ *sar*·go bream
sepia ⓕ *se*·pya cuttlefish
sesos ⓜ pl *se*·sos brains
setas ⓕ pl *se*·tas wild mushrooms
— a la kashera a la ka·*she*·ra sauteed wild mushrooms
— rellenas re·*lye*·nas mushrooms stuffed
sofrit pagés ⓜ so·*freet* pa·*zhes* vegetable stew
sofrito ⓜ so·*free*·to fried tomato sauce
soja ⓕ *so*·kha soya bean
soldaditos ⓜ pl **de Pavía** sol·da·*dee*·tos de pa·*vee*·a cod fritters
solomillo ⓜ so·lo·*mee*·lyo fillet
sopa ⓕ *so*·pa soup
— del día del *dee*·a soup of the day
sopas ⓕ pl **de leche** *so*·pas de *le*·che pieces of bread soaked in milk & cinnamon
sopas ⓕ pl **engañadas** *so*·pas en·ga·*nya*·das soup made from capsicum, onion shoots, vinegar, figs & grapes
sorbete ⓜ sor·*be*·te sorbet
sorroputún ⓜ so·ro·poo·*toon* tuna casserole
suizo ⓜ *swee*·tho sugared bun
sukaldi soo·*kal*·dee beef stew
suquet ⓜ soo·*ket* clams in almond sauce
suquet de peix ⓜ soo·*ket* de peysh fish stew

suspiros ⓜ pl **de monja** soos·*pee*·ros de *mon*·kha 'nun's sighs' – custard sweets

tallarines ⓜ pl ta·lya·*ree*·nes pasta noodles
tarta ⓕ *tar*·ta cake • tart
— de almendra de al·*men*·dra almond tart
— de manzana de man·*tha*·na apple tart
tartaleta ⓕ tar·ta·*le*·ta tartlet
tartaletas ⓕ pl **de huevos revueltos** tar·ta·*le*·tas de *we*·vos re·*vwel*·tos scrambled egg tartlets
ternera ⓕ ter·*ne*·ra veal
— a la sevillana a la se·vee·*lya*·na veal served with wine & olives
— en cazuela con berenjenas en ka·*thwe*·la kon be·ren·*khe*·nas veal & eggplant casserole
tocino ⓜ to·*thee*·no salted pork • bacon
— del cielo del *thye*·lo creamy dessert made with egg yolk & sugar, with a caramel topping
tocrudo ⓜ to·*kroo*·do 'everything raw' – salad of meat, garlic, onion & green capsicum
tomate ⓜ to·*ma*·te tomatoes
— (de) pera (de) *pe*·ra plum tomato
— frito *free*·to tinned tomato sauce
tomates ⓜ pl to·*ma*·tes
— enteros y pelados en·*te*·ros ee pe·*la*·dos tinned whole tomatoes
— rellenos de atún re·*lye*·nos de a·*toon* tomatoes stuffed with tuna
toro ⓜ *to*·ro bull meat
torrefacto ⓜ to·re·*fak*·to dark-roasted coffee beans
torrija ⓕ to·*ree*·kha French toast
torta ⓕ *tor*·ta pie • tart • flat bread
— de aceite de a·*they*·te sweet, flat cake or biscuit made with oil

— pascualina pas·kwa·*lee*·na spinach & egg pie, eaten at Easter

tortilla ① tor·*tee*·lya omelette

— española es·pa·*nyo*·la potato & onion omelette

— francesa fran·*the*·sa plain omelette

tortillas ① pl **de camarones** tor·*tee*·lyas de ka·ma·*ro*·nes shrimp fritters

tortita ① tor·*tee*·ta waffle

tostada ① tos·*ta*·da toasted bread

tocino ⑩ to·*thee*·no bacon

tripas ① pl *tree*·pas intestines • guts

trucha ① *troo*·cha trout

— a la marinera a la ma·ree·*ne*·ra trout in a white wine sauce

truchas ① pl *troo*·chas trout

— a la navarra a la na·*va*·ra trout with ham

— con vino y romero kon *vee*·no ee ro·*me*·ro trout with red wine & rosemary

trufa ① *troo*·fa truffle

— tarta *tar*·ta chocolate truffle cake

tumbet (de peix) ⑩ toom·*bet* (de peysh) vegetable souffle, sometimes containing fish

turrón ⑩ too·*ron* Spanish nougat

~ U ~

uva ① *oo*·va grape

— de corinto de ko·*reen*·to currant

— pasa *pa*·sa raisin

— sultana sool·*ta*·na sultana

~ V ~

vacuno ⑩ va·*koo*·no beef

venado ⑩ ve·*na*·do venison

verduras ① ver·*doo*·ras vegetables

vieira ① vee·*ey*·ra scallop

villagodio ⑩ vee·lya·*go*·dyo large steak

vinagre ① vee·*na*·gre vinegar

visita ① vee·*see*·ta almond cake

~ Y ~

yemas ① pl *ye*·mas small round cakes • egg whites

yogur ⑩ yo·*goor* yoghurt

~ Z ~

zanahoria ① tha·na·o·rya carrot

zarangollo ⑩ tha·ran·*go*·lyo fried zucchini

zarzamora ① thar·tha·*mo*·ra blackberry

zarzuela ① **de mariscos** thar·*thwe*·la de ma·*rees*·kos spicy shellfish stew

zarzuela ① **de pescado** thar·*thwe*·la de pes·*ka*·do fish in almond sauce

zurrukutano ⑩ thoo·roo·koo·*ta*·no cod & green capsicum soup

A

Dictionary

ENGLISH *to* SPANISH

inglés–español

Nouns in the dictionary have their gender indicated by ⓜ or ⓕ. If it's a plural noun, you'll also see pl. Where a word that could be either a noun or a verb has no gender indicated, it's a verb.

A

(to be) able poder po·*der*
aboard a bordo a bor·do
abortion aborto ⓜ a·*bor*·to
about sobre *so*·bre
above arriba a·*ree*·ba
abroad en el extranjero en el eks·tran·*khe*·ro
accept aceptar a·thep·*tar*
accident accidente ⓜ ak·thee·*den*·te
accommodation alojamiento ⓜ ·lo·kha·*myen*·to
across a través a tra·ves
activist activista ⓜ&ⓕ ak·tee·vees·ta
acupuncture acupuntura ⓕ ·koo·poon·*too*·ra
adaptor adaptador ⓜ a·dap·ta·*dor*
address dirección ⓕ dee·rek·*thyon*
administration administración ⓕ d·mee·nees·tra·*thyon*
admission price precio ⓜ de entrada ·re·thyo de en·*tra*·da
admit admitir ad·mee·*teer*
adult adulto ⓜ a·*dool*·to
advertisement anuncio ⓜ ·*noon*·thyo
advice consejo ⓜ kon·se·kho
aerobics aeróbic ⓜ ai·ro·beek

Africa África ⓕ a·*free*·ka
after después de des·*pwes* de
aftershave bálsamo de aftershave bal·sa·mo de ahf·ter·sha·eev
again otra vez o·tra veth
age edad ⓕ e·*da*
aggressive agresivo/a ⓜ/ⓕ a·gre·see·vo/a
agree estar de acuerdo es·*tar* de a·*kwer*·do
agriculture agricultura ⓕ a·gree·kul·*too*·ra
AIDS SIDA ⓜ see·da
air aire ⓜ ai·re
air mail por vía aérea por vee·a a·e·re·a
air-conditioned con aire acondicionado kon ai·re a·kon·dee·thyo·na·do
air-conditioning aire ⓜ acondicionado ai·re a·kon·dee·thyo·na·do
airline aerolínea ⓕ ai·ro·lee·nya
airport aeropuerto ⓜ ai·ro·pwer·to
airport tax tasa ⓕ del aeropuerto ta·sa del ai·ro·pwer·to
alarm clock despertador ⓜ des·per·ta·dor
alcohol alcohol ⓜ al·kol
all todo to·do
allergy alergia ⓕ a·ler·khya

B

allow permitir per·*mee·teer*
almonds almendras ① pl al·*men*·dras
almost casi *ka·*see
alone solo/a ⓜ/① *so·*lo/a
already ya ya
also también tam·*byen*
altar altar ⓜ al·*tar*
altitude altura ① al·*too·*ra
always siempre *syem·*pre
amateur amateur ⓜ&① a·ma·*ter*
ambassador embajador/embajadora ⓜ/① em·ba·kha·*dor*/em·ba·kha·*do·*ra
among entre *en·*tre
anarchist anarquista ⓜ&① a·nar·*kees·*ta
ancient antiguo/a ⓜ/① an·*tee·*gwo/a
and y ee
angry enfadado/a ⓜ/① en·fa·*da·*do/a
animal animal ⓜ a·nee·*mal*
ankle tobillo ⓜ to·*bee·*lyo
answer respuesta ① res·*pwes·*ta
answering machine contestador ⓜ automático kon·tes·ta·*dor* ow·to·*ma·*tee·ko
ant hormiga ① or·*mee·*ga
anthology antología ① an·to·lo·*khee·*a
antibiotics antibióticos ⓜ pl an·tee·*byo·*tee·kos
antinuclear antinuclear an·tee·noo·kle·*ar*
antique antigüedad ① an·tee·gwe·*da*
antiseptic antiséptico ⓜ an·tee·*sep·*tee·ko
any alguno/a ⓜ/① al·*goo·*no/a
appendix apéndice ⓜ a·*pen·*dee·the
apple manzana ① man·*tha·*na
appointment cita ① *thee·*ta
apricot albaricoque ⓜ al·ba·ree·*ko·*ke
archaeological arqueológico/a ⓜ/① ar·keo·*lo·*khee·ko/a
architect arquitecto/a ⓜ/① ar·kee·*tek·*to/a
architecture arquitectura ① ar·kee·tek·*too·*ra
argue discutir dees·koo·*teer*

arm brazo ⓜ *bra·*tho
army ejército ⓜ e·*kher·*thee·to
arrest detener de·te·*ner*
arrivals llegadas ① pl lye·*ga·*das
arrive llegar lye·*gar*
art arte ⓜ *ar·*te
art gallery museo ⓜ de arte moo·*se·*o de *ar·*te
artichoke alcachofa ① al·ka·*cho·*fa
artist artista ⓜ&① ar·*tees·*ta
ashtray cenicero ⓜ the·nee·*the·*ro
Asia Asia ① *a·*sya
ask (a question) preguntar pre·goon·*tar*
ask (for something) pedir pe·*deer*
aspirin aspirina ① as·pee·*ree·*na
assault asalto ⓜ a·*sal·*to
asthma asma ⓜ *as·*ma
athletics atletismo ⓜ at·le·*tees·*mo
atmosphere atmósfera ① at·*mos·*fe·ra
aubergine berenjena ① be·ren·*khe·*r
aunt tía ① *tee·*a
Australia Australia ① ow·*stra·*lya
Australian Rules football fútbol ⓜ australiano *foot*·bol ow·stra·*lya·*no
automatic teller machine cajero ⓜ automático ka·*khe·*ro ow·to·*ma·*tee·k(
autumn otoño ⓜ o·*to·*nyo
avenue avenida ① a·ve·*nee·*da
avocado aguacate ⓜ a·gwa·*ka·*te

B

B&W (film) blanco y negro *blan·*ko ee *ne·*gro
baby bebé ⓜ be·*be*
baby food comida ① de bebé ko·*mee·*da de be·*be*
baby powder talco ⓜ *tal·*ko
babysitter canguro ⓜ kan·*goo·*ro
back (of body) espalda ① es·*pal·*da
back (of chair) respaldo ⓜ res·*pal·*d(
backpack mochila ① mo·*chee·*la
bacon tocino ⓜ to·*thee·*no
bad malo/a ⓜ/① *ma·*lo/a
bag bolso ⓜ *bol·*so

ggage equipaje ⓜ e·kee·*pa*·khe

ggage allowance ⓜ límite de equi·je *lee*·mee·te de e·kee·*pa*·khe

ggage claim recogida ⓕ de equi·ajes re·ko·*khee*·da de e·kee·*pa*·khes

akery panadería ⓕ pa·na·de·*ree*·a

alance (account) saldo ⓜ *sal*·do

alcony balcón ⓜ bal·*kon*

all pelota ⓕ pe·*lo*·ta

allet ballet ⓜ ba·*le*

anana plátano ⓜ *pla*·ta·no

and grupo ⓜ *groo*·po

andage vendaje ⓜ ven·*da*·khe

and-aids tiritas ⓕ pl tee·*ree*·tas

ank banco ⓜ *ban*·ko

ank account cuenta ⓕ bancaria *kwen*·ta ban·*ka*·rya

anknotes billetes ⓜ pl (de banco) ee·*lye*·tes (de *ban*·ko)

aptism bautizo ⓜ bow·*tee*·tho

ar bar ⓜ bar

ar (with music) pub ⓜ poob

ar work trabajo ⓜ de camarero/a ⓜ/ⓕ tra·*ba*·kho de ka·ma·*re*·ro/a

asket canasta ⓕ ka·*nas*·ta

asketball baloncesto ⓜ a·lon·*thes*·to

ath bañera ⓕ ba·*nye*·ra

athing suit bañador ⓜ ba·nya·*dor*

athroom baño ⓜ *ba*·nyo

attery (car) batería ⓕ ba·te·*ree*·a

attery (small) pila ⓕ *pee*·la

e ser ser · estar es·*tar*

each playa ⓕ *pla*·ya

ean sprouts brotes ⓜ pl de soja *ro*·tes de *so*·kha

eans judías khoo·*dee*·as

eautiful hermoso/a ⓜ/ⓕ r·*mo*·so/a

eauty salon salón ⓜ de belleza a·*lon* de be·*lye*·tha

ecause porque *por*·ke

ed cama ⓕ *ka*·ma

edding ropa ⓕ de cama *ro*·pa de *a*·ma

edroom habitación ⓕ a·bee·ta·*thyon*

bee abeja ⓕ a·*be*·kha

beef carne ⓕ de vaca *kar*·ne de *va*·ka

beer cerveza ⓕ ther·*ve*·tha

beetroot remolacha ⓕ re·mo·*la*·cha

before antes *an*·tes

beggar mendigo/a ⓜ/ⓕ men·*dee*·go/a

begin comenzar ko·men·*thar*

behind detrás de de·*tras* de

Belgium Bélgica ⓕ *bel*·khee·ka

below abajo a·*ba*·kho

best lo mejor lo me·*khor*

bet apuesta ⓕ a·*pwes*·ta

better mejor me·*khor*

between entre *en*·tre

bible biblia ⓕ *bee*·blya

bicycle bicicleta ⓕ bee·thee·*kle*·ta

big grande *gran*·de

bike bici ⓕ *bee*·thee

bike chain cadena ⓕ de bici ka·*de*·na de *bee*·thee

bike path camino ⓜ de bici ka·*mee*·no de *bee*·thee

bill cuenta ⓕ *kwen*·ta

biodegradable biodegradable bee·o·de·gra·*da*·ble

biography biografía ⓕ bee·o·gra·*fee*·a

bird pájaro ⓜ *pa*·kha·ro

birth certificate partida ⓕ de nacimiento par·*tee*·da de na·thee·*myen*·to

birthday cumpleaños ⓜ koom·ple·*a*·nyos

birthday cake pastel ⓜ de cumpleaños pas·*tel* de koom·ple·*a*·nyos

biscuit ⓕ galleta ga·*lye*·ta

bite (dog) mordedura ⓕ mor·de·*doo*·ra

bite (food) bocado ⓜ bo·*ka*·do

bite (insect) picadura ⓕ pee·ka·*doo*·ra

black negro/a ⓜ/ⓕ *ne*·gro/a

blanket manta ⓕ *man*·ta

bleed sangrar san·*grar*

blind ciego/a ⓜ/ⓕ *thye*·go/a

B

blister ampolla ⓕ am·po·lya
blocked atascado/a ⓜ/ⓕ a·tas·ka·do/a
blood sangre ⓕ san·gre
blood group grupo ⓜ sanguíneo groo·po san·gee·neo
blood pressure presión ⓕ arterial pre·syon ar·te·ryal
blood test análisis ⓜ de sangre a·na·lee·sees de san·gre
blue azul a·thool
board (ship, etc) embarcarse em·bar·kar·se
boarding house pensión ⓕ pen·syon
boarding pass tarjeta ⓕ de embarque tar·khe·ta de em·bar·ke
bone hueso ⓜ we·so
book libro ⓜ lee·bro
book (make a reservation) reservar re·ser·var
booked out lleno/a ⓜ/ⓕ lye·no/a
bookshop librería ⓕ lee·bre·ree·a
boots botas ⓕ pl bo·tas
border frontera ⓕ fron·te·ra
boring aburrido/a ⓜ/ⓕ a·boo·ree·do/a
botanic garden jardín ⓜ botánico khar·deen bo·ta·nee·ko
both ambos/as ⓜ/ⓕ pl am·bos/bas
bottle botella ⓕ bo·te·lya
bottle opener abrebotellas ⓜ a·bre·bo·te·lyas
bowl bol ⓜ bol
box caja ⓕ ka·kha
boxer shorts calzones ⓜ pl kal·tho·nes
boxing boxeo ⓜ bo·se·o
boy chico ⓜ chee·ko
boyfriend novio ⓜ no·vyo
bra sujetador ⓜ soo·khe·ta·dor
brakes frenos ⓜ pl fre·nos
branch (office) sucursal ⓕ soo·koor·sal
brandy coñac ⓜ ko·nyak

brave valiente va·lyen·te
bread pan ⓜ pan
bread (brown) pan moreno pan mo·re·no
bread rolls bollos bo·lyos
bread (rye) pan de centeno pan de then·te·no
bread (sourdough) pan de masa fermentada pan de ma·sa fer·men·ta·da
bread (white) pan blanco pan blan·k
bread (wholemeal) pan integral pan een·te·gral
break romper rom·per
break down descomponerse des·kom·po·ner·se
breakfast desayuno ⓜ des·a·yoo·no
breasts senos ⓜ pl se·nos
breathe respirar res·pee·rar
brewery fábrica ⓕ de cerveza fab·ree·ka de ther·ve·tha
bribe soborno ⓜ so·bor·no
bribe sobornar so·bor·nar
bridge puente ⓜ pwen·te
briefcase maletín ⓜ ma·le·teen
brilliant cojonudo/a ⓜ/ⓕ ko·kho·noo·do/a
bring traer tra·er
brochure folleto ⓜ fo·lye·to
broken roto/a ⓜ/ⓕ ro·to/a
bronchitis bronquitis ⓕ bron·kee·tees
brother hermano ⓜ er·ma·no
brown marrón ma·ron
bruise cardenal ⓜ kar·de·nal
brussels sprouts coles ⓜ pl de Bruselas ko·les de broo·se·las
bucket cubo ⓜ koo·bo
Buddhist budista ⓜ&ⓕ boo·dees·ta
buffet buffet ⓜ boo·fe
bug bicho ⓜ bee·cho
build construir kons·troo·eer
building edificio ⓜ e·dee·fee·thyo
bull toro ⓜ to·ro
bullfight corrida ⓕ ko·ree·da
bullring plaza ⓕ de toros pla·tha de to·ros
bum (of body) culo ⓜ koo·lo

burn quemadura ⓕ ke·ma·doo·ra

bus autobús ⓜ ow·to·*boos*

bus (intercity) autocar ⓜ ow·to·*kar*

bus station estación de auto-
uses/autocares ⓕ es·ta·*thyon* de
w·to·*boo*·ses/ow·to·ka·res

bus stop parada ⓕ de autobús
a·ra·da de ow·to·*boos*

business negocios ⓜ pl ne·go·thyos

business class clase ⓕ preferente
la·se pre·fe·*ren*·te

business person comerciante ⓜ&ⓕ
o·mer·*thyan*·te

busker artista callejero/a ⓜ/ⓕ
r·tees·ta ka·lye·*khe*·ro/a

busy ocupado/a ⓜ/ⓕ o·koo·*pa*·do/a

but pero *pe*·ro

butcher's shop carnicería ⓕ
ar·nee·the·*ree*·a

butter mantequilla ⓕ man·te·*kee*·lya

butterfly mariposa ⓕ ma·ree·po·sa

buttons botones ⓜ pl bo·to·nes

buy comprar kom·*prar*

C

cabbage col kol

cable cable ⓜ *ka*·ble

cable car teleférico ⓜ te·le·fe·ree·ko

cafe café ⓜ ka·*fe*

cake pastel ⓜ pas·*tel*

cake shop pastelería ⓕ
as·te·le·*ree*·a

calculator calculadora ⓕ
al·koo·la·do·ra

calendar calendario ⓜ ka·len·da·ryo

calf ternero ⓜ ter·ne·ro

camera cámara ⓕ (fotográfica)
ka·ma·ra (fo·to·gra·fee·ka)

camera shop tienda ⓕ de fotografía
ryen·da de fo·to·gra·*fee*·a

camp acampar a·kam·*par*

camping store tienda ⓕ de cámping
ryen·da de kam·peen

campsite cámping ⓜ *kam*·peen

can lata ⓕ *la*·ta

can (be able) poder po·*der*

can opener abrelatas ⓜ a·bre·*la*·tas

Canada Canadá ⓕ ka·na·*da*

cancel cancelar kan·the·*lar*

cancer cáncer ⓜ *kan*·ther

candle vela ⓕ *ve*·la

cantaloupe cantalupo ⓜ
kan·ta·*loo*·po

capsicum (red/green) pimiento ⓜ
rojo/verde pee·*myen*·to ro·kho/*ver*·de

car coche ⓜ *ko*·che

car hire alquiler ⓜ de coche al·kee·*ler*
de *ko*·che

car owner's title papeles ⓜ pl del
coche pa·*pe*·les del *ko*·che

car registration matrícula ⓕ
ma·*tree*·koo·la

caravan caravana ⓕ ka·ra·va·na

cards cartas ⓕ pl *kar*·tas

care (about something) preocuparse
por pre·o·koo·*par*·se por

care (for someone) cuidar de
kwee·*dar* de

caring bondadoso/a ⓜ/ⓕ
bon·da·do·so/a

carpark aparcamiento ⓜ
a·par·ka·*myen*·to

carpenter carpintero/a ⓜ/ⓕ
kar·peen·*te*·ro/a

carrot zanahoria ⓕ tha·na·o·rya

carry llevar lye·*var*

carton cartón ⓜ kar·*ton*

cash dinero ⓜ en efectivo dee·*ne*·ro
en e·fek·*tee*·vo

cash (a cheque) cambiar (un
cheque) kam·*byar* (oon *che*·ke)

cash register caja ⓕ registradora
ka·kha re·khees·tra·do·ra

cashew nut anacardo ⓜ a·na·*kar*·do

cashier caja ⓕ *ka*·kha

casino casino ⓜ ka·see·no

cassette casete ⓜ ka·se·te

castle castillo ⓜ kas·tee·lyo

casual work trabajo ⓜ eventual
tra·ba·kho e·ven·*twal*

cat gato/a ⓜ/ⓕ ga·to/a

cathedral catedral ⓕ ka·te·*dral*

C

Catholic católico/a ⓜ/ⓕ ka·to·lee·ko/a
cauliflower coliflor ⓕ ko·lee·*flor*
caves cuevas ⓕ pl *kwe*·vas
CD cómpact ⓜ *kom*·pakt
celebrate (an event) celebrar the·le·*brar*
celebration celebración ⓕ the·le·bra·*thyon*
cemetery cementerio ⓜ the·men·*te*·ryo
cent centavo ⓜ then·*ta*·vo
centimetre centímetro ⓜ then·*tee*·me·tro
central heating calefacción ⓕ central ka·le·fak·*thyon* then·*tral*
centre centro ⓜ *then*·tro
ceramic cerámica ⓕ the·*ra*·mee·ka
cereal cereales ⓜ pl the·re·*a*·les
certificate certificado ⓜ ther·tee·fee·*ka*·do
chair silla ⓕ *see*·lya
champagne champán ⓜ cham·*pan*
chance oportunidad ⓕ o·por·too·nee·*da*
change (money) cambio ⓜ *kam*·byo
change cambiar kam·*byar*
changing rooms vestuarios ⓜ pl ves·*twa*·ryos
charming encantador/encantadora ⓜ/ⓕ en·kan·ta·*dor*/en·kan·ta·*do*·ra
chat up ligar lee·*gar*
cheap barato/a ⓜ/ⓕ ba·*ra*·to/a
cheat tramposo/a ⓜ/ⓕ tram·*po*·so/a
check revisar re·vee·*sar*
check (bank) cheque ⓜ *che*·ke
check-in facturación ⓕ de equipajes fak·too·ra·*thyon* de e·kee·*pa*·khes
checkpoint control ⓜ kon·*trol*
cheese queso ⓜ *ke*·so
chef cocinero ⓜ ko·thee·*ne*·ro
chemist (person) farmacéutico/a ⓜ/ⓕ far·ma·the·oo·ti·ko/a
chemist (shop) farmacia ⓕ far·*ma*·thya
chess ajedrez ⓜ a·khe·*dreth*
chess board tablero ⓜ de ajedrez ta·*ble*·ro de a·khe·*dreth*

chest pecho ⓜ *pe*·cho
chewing gum chicle ⓜ *chee*·kle
chicken pollo ⓜ *po*·lyo
chicken breast pechuga ⓕ pe·*choo*·ga
chickpeas garbanzos ⓜ pl gar·*ban*·thos
child niño/a ⓜ/ⓕ *nee*·nyo/a
child seat asiento ⓜ de seguridad para bebés a·*syen*·to de se·goo·ree·*da* *pa*·ra be·*bes*
childminding service guardería ⓕ gwar·de·*ree*·a
children hijos ⓜ pl ee·khos
chilli guindilla ⓕ geen·*dee*·lya
chilli sauce salsa ⓕ de guindilla *sal*·sa de geen·*dee*·lya
chocolate chocolate ⓜ cho·ko·*la*·te
choose escoger es·ko·*kher*
Christian cristiano/a ⓜ/ⓕ krees·*tya*·no/a
Christian name nombre ⓜ de pila *nom*·bre de *pee*·la
Christmas Navidad ⓕ na·vee·*da*
Christmas Eve Nochebuena ⓕ no·che·*bwe*·na
church iglesia ⓕ ee·*gle*·sya
cider sidra ⓕ *see*·dra
cigar cigarro ⓜ thee·*ga*·ro
cigarette cigarrillo ⓜ thee·ga·*ree*·lyo
cigarette lighter mechero ⓜ me·*che*·ro
cigarette machine máquina ⓕ de tabaco *ma*·kee·na de ta·*ba*·ko
cigarette paper papel ⓜ de fumar pa·*pel* de foo·*mar*
cinema cine ⓜ *thee*·ne
circus circo ⓜ *theer*·ko
citizenship ciudadanía ⓕ thyu·da·da·*nee*·a
city ciudad ⓕ thyu·*da*
city centre centro ⓜ de la ciudad *then*·tro de la thyu·*da*
city walls murallas ⓕ pl moo·*ra*·lyas
civil rights derechos civiles ⓜ pl de·*re*·chos thee·*vee*·les
classical clásico/a ⓜ/ⓕ *kla*·see·ko/a

C

ean limpio/a ⓜ/ⓕ *leem·pyo/a*
eaning limpieza ⓕ *leem·pye·tha*
ient cliente/a ⓜ/ⓕ *klee·en·te/a*
iff acantilado ⓜ *a·kan·tee·la·do*
imb subir *soo·beer*
oak capote ⓜ *ka·po·te*
oakroom guardarropa ⓜ *gwar·da·ro·pa*
ock reloj ⓜ *re·lokh*
ose cerrar *the·rar*
osed cerrado/a ⓜ/ⓕ *the·ra·do/a*
othes line cuerda ⓕ para tender la ropa *kwer·da pa·ra ten·der la ro·pa*
othing ropa ⓕ *ro·pa*
othing store tienda ⓕ de ropa *tyen·da de ro·pa*
oud nube ⓕ *noo·be*
oudy nublado *noo·bla·do*
ove (garlic) diente ⓜ (de ajo) *dyen·te (de a·kho)*
oves clavos ⓜ pl *kla·vos*
utch embrague ⓜ *em·bra·ge*
oach entrenador/entrenadora ⓜ/ⓕ *en·tre·na·dor/en·tre·na·do·ra*
oast costa ⓕ *kos·ta*
ocaine cocaína ⓕ *ko·ka·ee·na*
ockroach cucaracha ⓕ *koo·ka·ra·cha*
ocoa cacao ⓜ *ka·kow*
oconut coco ⓜ *ko·ko*
odeine codeína ⓕ *ko·de·ee·na*
offee café ⓜ *ka·fe*
oins monedas ⓕ pl *mo·ne·das*
old frío/a ⓜ/ⓕ *free·o/a*
old (illness) resfriado ⓜ *es·free·a·do*
olleague colega ⓜ&ⓕ *ko·le·ga*
ollect call llamada ⓕ a cobro revertido *lya·ma·da a ko·bro re·ver·tee·do*
ollege residencia ⓕ de estudiantes *re·see·den·thya de es·too·dyan·tes*
olour color ⓜ *ko·lor*
olour (film) película ⓕ en color *pe·lee·koo·la en ko·lor*
omb peine ⓜ *pey·ne*
ome venir *ve·neer*
ome (arrive) llegar *lye·gar*

comedy comedia ⓕ *ko·me·dya*
comfortable cómodo/a ⓜ/ⓕ *ko·mo·do/a*
communion comunión ⓕ *ko·moo·nyon*
communist comunista ⓜ&ⓕ *ko·moo·nees·ta*
companion compañero/a ⓜ/ⓕ *kom·pa·nye·ro/a*
company compañía ⓕ *kom·pa·nyee·a*
compass brújula ⓕ *broo·khoo·la*
complain quejarse *ke·khar·se*
computer ordenador ⓜ *or·de·na·dor*
computer game juegos ⓜ pl de ordenador *khwe·gos de or·de·na·dor*
concert concierto ⓜ *kon·thyer·to*
conditioner acondicionador ⓜ *a·kon·dee·thyo·na·dor*
condoms condones ⓜ pl *kon·do·nes*
confession confesión ⓕ *kon·fe·syon*
confirm confirmar *kon·feer·mar*
connection conexión ⓕ *ko·ne·ksyon*
conservative conservador/conservadora ⓜ/ⓕ *kon·ser·va·dor/kon·ser·va·do·ra*
constipation estreñimiento ⓜ *es·tre·nyee·myen·to*
consulate consulado ⓜ *kon·soo·la·do*
contact lenses lentes ⓜ pl de contacto *len·tes de kon·tak·to*
contraceptives anticonceptivos ⓜ pl *an·tee·kon·thep·tee·vos*
contract contrato ⓜ *kon·tra·to*
convenience store negocio ⓜ de artículos básicos *ne·go·thyo de ar·tee·koo·los ba·see·kos*
convent convento ⓜ *kon·ven·to*
cook cocinero ⓜ *ko·thee·ne·ro*
cook cocinar *ko·thee·nar*
cookie galleta ⓕ *ga·lye·ta*
corn maíz ⓜ *ma·eeth*
corn flakes copos ⓜ pl de maíz *ko·pos de ma·eeth*
corner esquina ⓕ *es·kee·na*
corrupt corrupto/a ⓜ/ⓕ *ko·roop·to/a*
cost costar *kos·tar*

ENGLISH *to* **SPANISH**

D

cottage cheese requesón ⓜ re·ke·son
cotton algodón ⓜ al·go·don
cotton balls bolas ⓕ pl de algodón bo·las de al·go·don
cough tos ⓕ tos
cough medicine jarabe ⓜ kha·ra·be
count contar kon·tar
counter mostrador ⓜ mos·tra·dor
country país ⓜ pa·ees
countryside campo ⓜ kam·po
coupon cupón ⓜ koo·pon
courgette calabacín ⓕ ka·la·ba·theen
court (tennis) pista ⓕ pees·ta
cous cous cus cus ⓜ koos koos
cover charge precio ⓜ del cubierto pre·thyo del koo·byer·to
cow vaca ⓕ va·ka
crab cangrejo ⓜ kan·gre·kho
crackers galletas ⓕ pl saladas ga·lye·tas sa·la·das
crafts artesanía ⓕ ar·te·sa·nee·a
crash choque ⓜ cho·ke
crazy loco/a ⓜ/ⓕ lo·ko/a
cream (food) crema kre·ma
cream (moisturising) crema ⓕ hidratante kre·ma ee·dra·tan·te
cream cheese queso ⓜ crema ke·so kre·ma
creche guardería ⓕ gwar·de·ree·a
credit card tarjeta ⓕ de crédito tar·khe·ta de kre·dee·to
cricket críquet ⓜ kree·ket
crop cosecha ⓕ ko·se·cha
crowded abarrotado/a ⓜ/ⓕ a·ba·ro·ta·do/a
cucumber pepino ⓜ pe·pee·no
cuddle abrazo ⓜ a·bra·tho
cup taza ⓕ ta·tha
cupboard armario ⓜ ar·ma·ryo
currency exchange cambio ⓜ (de dinero) kam·byo (de dee·ne·ro)
current (electricity) corriente ⓕ ko·ryen·te
current affairs informativo ⓜ een·for·ma·tee·vo
curry curry ⓜ koo·ree

curry powder curry ⓜ en polvo koo·ree en pol·vo
customs aduana ⓕ a·dwa·na
cut cortar kor·tar
cutlery cubiertos ⓜ pl koo·byer·tos
CV historial ⓜ profesional ees·to·ry·al pro·fe·syo·nal
cycle andar en bicicleta an·dar en bee·thee·kle·ta
cycling ciclismo ⓜ thee·klees·mo
cyclist ciclista ⓜ&ⓕ thee·klees·ta
cystitis cistitis ⓕ thees·tee·tees

D

dad papá ⓜ pa·pa
daily diariamente dya·rya·men·te
dance bailar bai·lar
dancing bailar ⓜ bai·lar
dangerous peligroso/a ⓜ/ⓕ pe·lee·gro·so/a
dark oscuro/a ⓜ/ⓕ os·koo·ro/a
date citarse thee·tar·se
date (a person) salir con sa·leer kon
date (time) fecha ⓕ fe·cha
date of birth fecha ⓕ de nacimiento fe·cha de na·thee·myen·to
daughter hija ⓕ ee·kha
dawn alba ⓕ al·ba
day día ⓜ dee·a
day after tomorrow pasado mañana pa·sa·do ma·nya·na
day before yesterday anteayer an·te·a·yer
dead muerto/a ⓜ/ⓕ mwer·to/a
deaf sordo/a ⓜ/ⓕ sor·do/a
deal (cards) repartir re·par·teer
decide decidir de·thee·deer
deep profundo/a ⓜ/ⓕ pro·foon·do/a
deforestation deforestación ⓕ de·fo·res·ta·thyon
degree título ⓜ tee·too·lo
delay demora ⓕ de·mo·ra
delirious delirante de·lee·ran·te
deliver entregar en·tre·gar
democracy democracia ⓕ de·mo·kra·thya

demonstration manifestación ⓕ
ma·ne·fes·ta·*thyon*

Denmark Dinamarca ⓕ
dee·na·*mar*·ka

dental floss hilo ⓜ dental *ee*·lo
en·*tal*

dentist dentista ⓜ&ⓕ den·*tees*·ta

deny negar ne·*gar*

deodorant desodorante ⓜ
e·so·do·*ran*·te

depart salir de sa·*leer* de

department store grande almacen ⓜ
ⓜ *gran*·de al·ma·*then*

departure salida ⓕ sa·*lee*·da

deposit depósito ⓜ de·*po*·see·to

descendant descendiente ⓜ
es·then·*dyen*·te

desert desierto ⓜ de·*syer*·to

design diseño ⓜ dee·*se*·nyo

destination destino ⓜ des·*tee*·no

destroy destruir des·troo·*eer*

detail detalle ⓜ de·*ta*·lye

diabetes diabetes ⓕ dee·a·*be*·tes

diaper pañal ⓜ pa·*nyal*

diaphragm diafragma ⓜ
dee·a·*frag*·ma

diarrhoea diarrea ⓕ dee·a·*re*·a

diary agenda ⓕ a·*khen*·da

dice (die) dados ⓜ pl *da*·dos

dictionary diccionario ⓜ
deek·*thyo*·na·ryo

die morir mo·*reer*

diet régimen ⓜ *re*·khee·men

different diferente ⓜ/ⓕ dee·fe·*ren*·te

difficult difícil ⓜ/ⓕ dee·*fee*·theel

dining car vagón ⓜ restaurante
a·*gon* res·tow·*ran*·te

dinner cena ⓕ *the*·na

direct directo/a ⓜ/ⓕ dee·*rek*·to/a

direct-dial marcar directo mar·*kar*
ee·*rek*·to

director director/directora ⓜ/ⓕ
ee·*rek*·tor/dee·rek·*to*·ra

dirty sucio/a ⓜ/ⓕ *soo*·thyo/a

disabled minusválido/a ⓜ/ⓕ
ee·noos·*va*·lee·do/a

disco discoteca ⓕ dees·ko·*te*·ka

discount descuento ⓜ des·*kwen*·to

discover descubrir des·koo·*breer*

discrimination discriminación ⓕ
dees·kree·mee·na·*thyon*

disease enfermedad ⓕ en·fer·me·*da*

disk disco ⓜ *dees*·ko

dive bucear boo·the·*ar*

diving submarinismo ⓜ
soob·ma·ree·*nees*·mo

diving equipment equipo ⓜ de
inmersión ⓜ e·*kee*·po de een·mer·*syon*

dizzy mareado/a ⓜ/ⓕ ma·re·a·*do*/a

do hacer a·*ther*

doctor doctor/doctora ⓜ/ⓕ dok·*tor*/
dok·*to*·ra

documentary documental ⓜ
do·koo·men·*tal*

dog perro/a ⓜ/ⓕ *pe*·rro/a

dole paro ⓜ *pa*·ro

doll muñeca ⓕ moo·*nye*·ka

domestic flight vuelo ⓜ doméstico
vwe·lo do·mes·tee·ko

donkey burro ⓜ *boo*·ro

door puerta ⓕ *pwer*·ta

dope droga ⓕ *dro*·ga

double doble ⓜ/ⓕ *do*·ble

double bed cama ⓕ de matrimonio
ka·ma de ma·*tree*·mo·nyo

double room habitación ⓕ doble
a·bee·ta·*thyon* *do*·ble

down abajo a·*ba*·kho

downhill cuesta abajo kwes·ta a·*ba*·kho

dozen docena ⓕ do·*the*·na

draw dibujar dee·boo·*khar*

dream soñar so·*nyar*

dress vestido ⓜ ves·*tee*·do

dried fruit fruto ⓜ seco *froo*·to se·ko

drink bebida ⓕ be·*bee*·da

drink beber be·*ber*

drive conducir kon·doo·*theer*

drivers licence carnet ⓜ de conducir
kar·ne de kon·doo·*theer*

drug droga ⓕ *dro*·ga

drug addiction drogadicción ⓕ
dro·ga·deek·*thyon*

E

drug dealer traficante ⓜ de drogas tra·fee·*kan*·te de *dro*·gas

drums batería ⓕ ba·te·*ree*·a

drumstick (chicken) muslo ⓜ *mus*·lo

drunk borracho/a ⓜ/ⓕ bo·*ra*·cho/a

dry secar se·*kar*

duck pato ⓜ *pa*·to

dummy (pacifier) chupete ⓜ choo·*pe*·te

E

each cada *ka*·da

ear oreja ⓕ o·*re*·kha

early temprano tem·*pra*·no

earplugs tapones ⓜ pl para los oídos ta·*po*·nes *pa*·ra los o·*ee*·dos

earn ganar ga·*nar*

earrings pendientes ⓜ pl pen·*dyen*·tes

Earth Tierra ⓕ *tye*·ra

earthquake terremoto ⓜ te·re·*mo*·to

east este *es*·te

Easter Pascua ⓕ *pas*·kwa

Easter Week Semana ⓕ Santa se·*ma*·na *san*·ta

easy fácil *fa*·theel

eat comer ko·*mer*

economy class clase ⓕ turística *kla*·se too·*rees*·tee·ka

eczema eczema ⓕ ek·*the*·ma

editor editor/editora ⓜ/ⓕ e·dee·*tor*/e·dee·*to*·ra

education educación ⓕ e·doo·ka·*thyon*

eggplant berenjenas ⓕ pl be·ren·*khe*·nas

egg huevo ⓜ *we*·vo

elections elecciones ⓕ pl e·lek·*thyo*·nes

electrical store tienda ⓕ de productos eléctricos *tyen*·da de pro·*dook*·tos e·*lek*·tree·kos

electricity electricidad ⓕ e·lek·tree·thee·*da*

elevator ascensor ⓜ as·then·*sor*

embarrassed avergonzado/a ⓜ/ⓕ a·ver·gon·*tha*·do/a

embassy embajada ⓕ em·ba·*kha*·da

emergency emergencia ⓕ e·mer·*khen*·thya

emotional emocional e·mo·thyo·*nal*

employee empleado/a ⓜ/ⓕ em·ple·a·do/a

employer jefe/a ⓜ/ⓕ *khe*·fe/a

empty vacío/a ⓜ/ⓕ va·*thee*·o/a

end fin ⓜ feen

end acabar a·ka·*bar*

endangered species especies ⓕ pl en peligro de extinción es·*pe*·thyes en pe·*lee*·gro de eks·teen·*thyon*

engagement compromiso ⓜ kom·pro·*mee*·so

engine motor ⓜ mo·*tor*

engineer ingeniero/a ⓜ/ⓕ een·khe·*nye*·ro/a

engineering ingeniería ⓕ een·khe·nye·*ree*·a

England Inglaterra ⓕ een·gla·*te*·ra

English inglés ⓜ een·*gles*

enjoy (oneself) divertirse dee·ver·*teer*·se

enough suficiente ⓜ/ⓕ soo·fee·*thyen*·te

enter entrar en·*trar*

entertainment guide guía ⓕ del ocio *gee*·a del o·thyo

envelope sobre ⓜ *so*·bre

environment medio ⓜ ambiente *me*·dyo am·*byen*·te

epilepsy epilepsia ⓕ e·pee·*lep*·sya

equal opportunity igualdad ⓕ de oportunidades ee·gwal·*da* de o·por·too·nee·*da*·des

equality igualdad ⓕ ee·gwal·*da*

equipment equipo ⓜ e·*kee*·po

escalator escaleras ⓕ pl mecánicas es·ka·*le*·ras me·*ka*·nee·kas

euro euro ⓜ *e*·oo·ro

Europe Europa ⓕ e·oo·*ro*·pa

euthanasia eutanasia ⓕ e·oo·ta·*na*·sya

evening noche ⓕ *no*·che

everything todo *to*·do

ample ejemplo ⓜ e·*khem*·plo

cellent excelente ⓜ/ⓕ
s·the·*len*·te

change cambio ⓜ *kam*·byo

change (money) cambiar kam·*byar*

change rate tipo ⓜ de cambio
e·po de *kam*·byo

change (give gifts) regalar
·ga·*lar*

cluded no incluido no
n·kloo·ee·do

haust tubo ⓜ de escape *too*·bo de
·*ka*·pe

hibit exponer eks·po·*ner*

hibition exposición ⓕ
s·po·see·*thyon*

it salida ⓕ sa·*lee*·da

pensive caro/a ⓜ/ⓕ *ka*·ro/a

perience experiencia ⓕ
s·pe·*ryen*·thya

press expreso/a ⓜ/ⓕ eks·*pre*·so/a

press mail correo ⓜ urgente
·re·o oor·*khen*·te

tension (visa) prolongación ⓕ
·o·lon·ga·*thyon*

e ojo ⓜ o·kho

e drops gotas ⓕ pl para los ojos
·tas *pa*·ra los o·*khos*

bric tela ⓕ *te*·la

ce cara ⓕ *ka*·ra

ce cloth toallita ⓕ to·a·*lyee*·ta

ctory fábrica ⓕ *fa*·bree·ka

ctory worker obrero/a ⓜ/ⓕ
·*bre*·ro/a

ll caída ⓕ ka·*ee*·da

mily familia ⓕ fa·*mee*·lya

mily name apellido ⓜ a·pe·*lyee*·do

mous famoso/a ⓜ/ⓕ fa·*mo*·so/a

n (hand held) abanico ⓜ
·ba·*nee*·ko

n (electric) ventilador ⓜ
·n·tee·la·*dor*

nbelt correa ⓕ del ventilador
·*re*·a del ven·tee·la·*dor*

far lejos *le*·khos

farm granja ⓕ *gran*·kha

farmer agricultor/agricultora ⓜ/ⓕ
a·gree·kool·*tor*/a·gree·kool·*to*·ra

fast rápido/a ⓜ/ⓕ *ra*·pee·do/a

fat gordo/a ⓜ/ⓕ *gor*·do/a

father padre ⓜ *pa*·dre

father-in-law suegro ⓜ *swe*·gro

fault falta ⓕ *fal*·ta

faulty defectuoso/a ⓜ/ⓕ
de·fek·*two*·so/a

feed dar de comer dar de ko·*mer*

feel sentir sen·*teer*

feelings sentimientos ⓜ pl
sen·tee·*myen*·tos

fence cerca ⓕ *ther*·ka

fencing esgrima ⓕ es·*gree*·ma

festival festival ⓜ fes·tee·*val*

fever fiebre ⓕ *fye*·bre

few pocos/as ⓜ/ⓕ *po*·kos/as

fiance prometido ⓜ pro·me·*tee*·do

fiancee prometida ⓕ pro·me·*tee*·da

fiction ficción ⓕ feek·*thyon*

field campo ⓜ *kam*·po

fig higo ⓜ *ee*·go

fight pelea ⓕ pe·*le*·a

fight luchar loo·*char*

fill llenar lye·*nar*

fillet filete ⓜ fee·*le*·te

film película ⓕ pe·*lee*·koo·la

film speed sensibilidad ⓕ
sen·see·bee·lee·*da*

filtered con filtro kon *feel*·tro

find encontrar en·kon·*trar*

fine multa ⓕ *mool*·ta

finger dedo ⓜ *de*·do

finish terminar ter·mee·*nar*

fire fuego ⓜ *fwe*·go

firewood leña ⓕ *le*·nya

first primero/a ⓜ/ⓕ pree·*me*·ro/a

first class primera clase pree·*me*·ra
kla·se

first-aid kit maletín ⓜ de primeros
auxilios ma·le·*teen* de pree·*me*·ros
ow·*ksee*·lyos

fish pez ⓜ peth

G

fish (as food) pescado ⓜ pes·*ka*·do
fish shop pescadería ⓕ pes·ka·de·*ree*·a
fishing pesca ⓕ *pes*·ka
flag bandera ⓕ ban·*de*·ra
flannel franela ⓕ fra·*ne*·la
flashlight linterna ⓕ leen·*ter*·na
flat llano/a ⓜ/ⓕ *lya*·no/a
flea pulga ⓕ *pool*·ga
flooding inundación ⓕ ee·noon·da·*thyon*
floor suelo ⓜ *swe*·lo
florist florista ⓜ&ⓕ flo·*rees*·ta
flour harina ⓕ a·*ree*·na
flower flor ⓕ flor
flower seller vendedor/vendedora ⓜ/ⓕ de flores ven·de·*dor*/ven·de·*do*·ra de *flo*·res
fly volar vo·*lar*
follow seguir se·*geer*
food comida ⓕ ko·*mee*·da
food supplies víveres ⓜ pl *vee*·ve·res
foot pie ⓜ pye
football fútbol ⓜ *foot*·bol
footpath acera ⓕ a·*the*·ra
foreign extranjero/a ⓜ/ⓕ eks·tran·*khe*·ro/a
forest bosque ⓜ *bos*·ke
forever para siempre *pa*·ra syem·pre
forget olvidar ol·vee·*dar*
forgive perdonar per·do·*nar*
fork tenedor ⓜ te·ne·*dor*
fortnight quincena ⓕ keen·*the*·na
foul sucio/a ⓜ/ⓕ *soo*·thyo/a
foyer vestíbulo ⓜ ves·*tee*·boo·lo
fragile frágil *fra*·kheel
France Francia ⓕ *fran*·thya
free (not bound) libre *lee*·bre
free (of charge) gratis *gra*·tees
freeze helarse e·*lar*·se
friend amigo/a ⓜ/ⓕ a·*mee*·go/a
frost escarcha ⓕ es·*kar*·cha
frozen foods productos congelados ⓜ pl pro·*dook*·tos kon·khe·*la*·dos
fruit fruta ⓕ *froo*·ta

fruit picking recolección ⓕ de fruta re·ko·lek·*thyon* de *froo*·ta
fry freír fre·*eer*
frying pan sartén ⓕ sar·*ten*
full lleno/a ⓜ/ⓕ *lye*·no/a
full-time a tiempo completo a *tyem*·po kom·*ple*·to
fun diversión ⓕ dee·ver·*syon*
funeral funeral ⓜ foo·ne·*ral*
funny gracioso/a ⓜ/ⓕ gra·*thyo*·so/a
furniture muebles ⓜ pl *mwe*·bles
future futuro ⓜ foo·*too*·ro

G

gay gay gai
general general khe·ne·*ral*
Germany Alemania ⓕ a·le·*ma*·nya
gift regalo ⓜ re·*ga*·lo
gig bolo ⓜ *bo*·lo
gin ginebra ⓕ khee·*ne*·bra
ginger jengibre ⓜ khen·*khee*·bre
girl chica ⓕ *chee*·ka
girlfriend novia ⓕ *no*·vya
give dar dar
glandular fever fiebre ⓕ glandular *fye*·bre glan·doo·*lar*
glass (material) vidrio ⓜ *vee*·dryo
glass (drinking) vaso ⓜ *va*·so
glasses gafas ⓕ pl *ga*·fas
gloves guantes ⓜ pl *gwan*·tes
go ir eer
go out with salir con sa·*leer* kon
go shopping ir de compras eer de *kom*·pras
goal gol ⓜ gol
goalkeeper portero/a ⓜ/ⓕ por·*te*·ro/a
goat cabra ⓕ *ka*·bra
goat's cheese queso ⓜ de cabra *ke*·so de *ka*·bra
god Dios ⓜ dyos
goggles gafas ⓕ pl de submarinismo *ga*·fas de soob·ma·ree·*nees*·mo
golf ball pelota ⓕ de golf pe·*lo*·ta de golf
golf course campo ⓜ de golf *kam*·po de golf

ood bueno/a ⓜ/ⓕ *bwe*·no/a
overnment gobierno ⓜ ·*byer*·no
am gramo ⓜ *gra*·mo
andchild nieto/a ⓜ/ⓕ *nye*·to/a
andfather abuelo ⓜ a·*bwe*·lo
andmother abuela ⓕ a·*bwe*·la
apefruit pomelo ⓜ po·*me*·lo
apes uvas ⓕ pl *oo*·vas
aphic art arte ⓜ gráfico *ar*·te ·a·*fee*·ko
ass hierba ⓕ *yer*·ba
ave tumba ⓕ *toom*·ba
ay gris grees
eat fantástico/a ⓜ/ⓕ n·*tas*·tee·ko/a
een verde *ver*·de
eengrocery (shop) verdulería ⓕ r·doo·le·*ree*·a
ocer (shopkeeper) verdulero/a ·ⓜ/ⓕ ver·doo·*le*·ro/a
ey gris grees
ocery tienda ⓕ de comestibles ·*en*·da de ko·mes·*tee*·bles
ow crecer kre·*ther*
string tanga ⓕ *tan*·ga
ess adivinar a·dee·vee·*nar*
ide (audio) guía ⓕ audio *gee*·a v·dyo
ide (person) guía ⓜ&ⓕ *gee*·a
ide dog perro lazarillo ⓜ *pe*·ro tha·*ree*·lyo
idebook guía ⓕ *gee*·a
ided tour recorrido ⓜ guiado ·ko·*ree*·do gee·a·do
ilty culpable kool·*pa*·ble
itar guitarra ⓕ gee·*ta*·ra
um chicle ⓜ *chee*·kle
ymnastics gimnasia ⓕ rítmica eem·*na*·sya *reet*·mee·ka
ynaecologist ginecólogo ⓜ ·ee·ne·*ko*·lo·go

I

air pelo ⓜ *pe*·lo
airbrush cepillo ⓜ the·*pee*·lyo

hairdresser peluquero/a ⓜ/ⓕ pe·loo·*ke*·ro/a
halal halal a·*lal*
half medio/a ⓜ/ⓕ *me*·dyo/a
half a litre medio litro ⓜ *me*·dyo *lee*·tro
hallucinate alucinar a·loo·thee·*nar*
ham jamón ⓜ kha·*mon*
hammer martillo ⓜ mar·*tee*·lyo
hammock hamaca ⓕ a·*ma*·ka
hand mano ⓕ *ma*·no
handbag bolso ⓜ *bol*·so
handicrafts artesanía ⓕ ar·te·sa·*nee*·a
handlebar manillar ⓜ ma·nee·*lyar*
handmade hecho a mano e·cho a *ma*·no
handsome hermoso ⓜ er·*mo*·so
happy feliz fe·*leeth*
harassment acoso ⓜ a·*ko*·so
harbour puerto ⓜ *pwer*·to
hard duro/a ⓜ/ⓕ *doo*·ro/a
hardware store ferretería ⓕ fe·re·te·*ree*·a
hash hachís ⓜ a·*chees*
hat sombrero ⓜ som·*bre*·ro
have tener te·*ner*
have a cold estar constipado/a ⓜ/ⓕ es·*tar* kons·tee·*pa*·do/a
have fun divertirse dee·ver·*teer*·se
hay fever alergia ⓕ al polen a·*ler*·khya al *po*·len
he él el
head cabeza ⓕ ka·*be*·tha
headache dolor ⓜ de cabeza do·*lor* de ka·*be*·tha
headlights faros ⓜ pl *fa*·ros
health salud ⓕ sa·*loo*
hear oír o·*eer*
hearing aid audífono ⓜ ow·*dee*·fo·no
heart corazón ⓜ ko·ra·*thon*
heart condition condición ⓕ cardíaca kon·dee·*thyon* kar·*dee*·a·ka
heat calor ⓜ ka·*lor*
heater estufa ⓕ es·*too*·fa
heavy pesado/a ⓜ/ⓕ pe·*sa*·do/a

I

helmet casco ⓜ *kas*·ko
help ayudar a·yoo·*dar*
hepatitis hepatitis ⓕ e·pa·*tee*·tees
her su soo
herbalist herbolario/a ⓜ/ⓕ
er·bo·*la*·ree·o/a
herbs hierbas ⓕ pl *yer*·bas
here aquí a·*kee*
heroin heroína ⓕ e·ro·*ee*·na
herring arenque ⓜ a·*ren*·ke
high alto/a ⓜ/ⓕ *al*·to/a
high school instituto ⓜ
eens·tee·*too*·to
hike ir de excursión eer de
eks·koor·*syon*
hiking excursionismo ⓜ
eks·koor·syo·*nees*·mo
hiking boots botas ⓕ pl de montaña
bo·tas de mon·*ta*·nya
hiking routes caminos ⓜ pl rurales
ka·*mee*·nos roo·*ra*·les
hill colina ⓕ ko·*lee*·na
Hindu hindú ⓜ&ⓕ een·*doo*
hire alquilar al·kee·*lar*
his su soo
historical histórico/a ⓜ/ⓕ
ees·*to*·ree·ko/a
hitchhike hacer dedo a·*ther* de·do
HIV positive seropositivo/a ⓜ/ⓕ
se·ro·po·see·*tee*·vo/a
hockey hockey ⓜ *kho*·kee
holiday día festivo ⓜ *dee*·a fes·*tee*·vo
holidays vacaciones ⓕ pl
va·ka·*thyo*·nes
homeless sin hogar seen o·*gar*
homemaker ama ⓕ de casa *a*·ma
de *ka*·sa
homosexual homosexual ⓜ&ⓕ
o·mo·sek·*swal*
honey miel ⓕ myel
honeymoon luna ⓕ de miel *loo*·na
de myel
horoscope horóscopo ⓜ
o·*ros*·ko·po
horse caballo ⓜ ka·*ba*·lyo
horse riding equitación ⓕ
e·kee·ta·*thyon*

horseradish rábano ⓜ picante
ra·ba·no pee·*kan*·te
hospital hospital ⓜ os·pee·*tal*
hospitality hostelería ⓕ os·te·le·*ree*
hot caliente ka·*lyen*·te
hot water agua caliente ⓜ *a*·gwa
ka·*lyen*·te
hotel hotel ⓜ o·*tel*
house casa ⓕ *ka*·sa
housework trabajo ⓜ de casa
tra·*ba*·kho de *ka*·sa
how cómo *ko*·mo
how much cuánto *kwan*·to
hug abrazo ⓜ a·*bra*·tho
huge enorme e·*nor*·me
human rights derechos ⓜ pl humanos de·*re*·chos oo·*ma*·nos
humanities humanidades ⓕ pl
oo·ma·nee·da·des
hungry hambriento/a ⓜ/ⓕ
am·*bryen*·to/a
hungry tener hambre te·*ner* am·bre
hunting caza ⓕ *ka*·tha
hurt dañar da·*nyar*
husband marido ⓜ ma·*ree*·do

I

I yo yo
ice hielo ⓜ *ye*·lo
ice axe piolet ⓜ pyo·*le*
ice cream helado ⓜ e·*la*·do
ice cream parlour heladería ⓕ
e·la·de·*ree*·a
ice hockey hockey ⓜ sobre hielo
kho·kee *so*·bre *ye*·lo
identification identificación ⓕ
ee·den·tee·fee·ka·*thyon*
identification card carnet ⓜ de
identidad kar·*net* de ee·den·tee·*da*
idiot idiota ⓜ&ⓕ ee·*dyo*·ta
if si see
ill enfermo/a ⓜ/ⓕ en·*fer*·mo/a
immigration inmigración ⓕ
een·mee·gra·*thyon*
important importante eem·por·*tan*·te
in a hurry de prisa de *pree*·sa

 front of enfrente de en·*fren*·te de
cluded incluido een·kloo·ee·do
come tax impuesto ⓜ sobre la
 nta eem·*pwes*·to so·bre la *ren*·ta
 dia India ① *een*·dya
 dicator indicador ⓜ een·dee·ka·*dor*
 digestion indigestión ①
 en·fla·ma·*thyon*
 dustry industria ① een·*doos*·trya
 fection infección ① een·fek·*thyon*
 flammation inflamación ①
 en·fla·ma·*thyon*
 fluenza gripe ① *gree*·pe
 gredient ingrediente ⓜ
 en·gre·*dyen*·te
 ject inyectarse een·yek·*tar*·se
 njection inyección ① een·yek·*thyon*
 njury herida ① e·*ree*·da
 nnocent inocente ee·no·*then*·te
 nside adentro a·*den*·tro
 nstructor profesor/profesora ⓜ/①
 ·ro·fe·*sor*/pro·fe·*sor*·ra
 nsurance seguro ⓜ se·*goo*·ro
 nteresting interesante
 en·te·re·*san*·te
 ntermission descanso ⓜ
 ·les·*kan*·so
 nternational internacional
 en·ter·na·thyo·*nal*
 nternet internet een·ter·net
 nternet cafe cibercafé thee·ber·ka·*fe*
 nterpreter intérprete ⓜ&①
 en·*ter*·pre·te
 ntersection cruce ⓜ *croo*·the
 nterview entrevista ① en·tre·*vees*·ta
 nvite invitar een·vee·*tar*
 reland Irlanda ① eer·*lan*·da
 ron plancha ① *plan*·cha
 sland isla ① *ees*·la
 T informática ① een·for·*ma*·tee·ka
 taly Italia ① ee·*ta*·lya
 tch picazón ① pee·ka·*thon*
 temised detallado/a ⓜ/①
 ·e·ta·*lya*·do/a
 tinerary itinerario ① ee·tee·ne·*ra*·ryo
 UD DIU ⓜ de·ee·oo

J

jacket chaqueta ① cha·*ke*·ta
jail cárcel ① *kar*·thel
jam mermelada ① mer·me·*la*·da
Japan Japón ⓜ kha·*pon*
jar jarra ① *kha*·ra
jaw mandíbula ① man·*dee*·boo·la
jealous celoso/a ⓜ/① the·*lo*·so/a
jeans vaqueros ⓜ pl va·*ke*·ros
jeep yip ⓜ yeep
jet lag jet lag ⓜ dyet lag
jewellery shop joyería ① kho·ye·*ree*·a
Jewish judío/a ⓜ/① khoo·*dee*·o/a
job trabajo ⓜ tra·*ba*·kho
jockey jockey ⓜ *dyo*·kee
jogging footing ⓜ *foo*·teen
joke broma ① *bro*·ma
joke bromear bro·me·*ar*
journalist periodista ⓜ&①
pe·ryo·*dees*·ta
judge juez ⓜ&① khweth
juice jugo ⓜ *khoo*·go • zumo ⓜ
thoo·mo
jump saltar sal·*tar*
jumper (sweater) jersey ⓜ kher·say
jumper leads cables ⓜ pl de
arranque ka·bles de a·*ran*·ke

K

ketchup salsa ① de tomate *sal*·sa de
to·*ma*·te
key llave ① *lya*·ve
keyboard teclado ① te·*kla*·do
kick dar una patada dar oo·na pa·*ta*·da
kick (a goal) meter (un gol) me·*ter*
(oon gol)
kill matar ma·*tar*
kilogram kilogramo ⓜ kee·lo·*gra*·mo
kilometre kilómetro ① kee·*lo*·me·tro
kind amable a·*ma*·ble
kindergarten escuela ① de párvulos
es·*kwe*·la de *par*·voo·los
king rey ⓜ rey
kiss beso ⓜ *be*·so
kiss besar be·*sar*

L

kitchen cocina ① ko·*thee*·na
kitten gatito/a ⓜ/① ga·*tee*·to/a
kiwifruit kiwi ⓜ *kee*·wee
knapsack mochila ① mo·*chee*·la
knee rodilla ① ro·*dee*·lya
knife cuchillo ⓜ koo·*chee*·lyo
know (someone) conocer ko·no·*ther*
know (something) saber sa·*ber*
kosher kosher *ko*·sher

L

labourer obrero/a ⓜ/① o·*bre*·ro/a
lace encaje ⓜ en·*ka*·khe
lager cerveza ① rubia ther·*ve*·tha *roo*·bya
lake lago ⓜ *la*·go
lamb cordero ⓜ kor·*de*·ro
land tierra ① *tye*·ra
landlady propietaria ① pro·pye·*ta*·rya
landlord propietario ⓜ pro·pye·*ta*·ryo
languages idiomas ⓜ pl ee·*dyo*·mas
laptop ordenador ⓜ portátil or·de·na·*dor* por·*ta*·teel
lard manteca ① man·*te*·ka
large grande *gran*·de
late tarde *tar*·de
laugh reírse re·*eer*·se
laundrette lavandería ① la·van·de·*ree*·a
laundry lavadero ⓜ la·va·*de*·ro
law ley ① ley
lawyer abogado/a ⓜ/① a·bo·*ga*·do/a
leader líder ⓜ&① *lee*·der
leaf hoja ① *o*·kha
learn aprender a·pren·*der*
leather cuero ⓜ *kwe*·ro
leave dejar de·*khar*
leave (behind/over) quedar ke·*dar*
lecturer profesor/profesora ⓜ/① pro·fe·*sor*/pro·fe·*so*·ra
ledge saliente ⓜ sa·*lyen*·te
leek puerro ⓜ *pwe*·ro
left izquierda ① eeth·*kyer*·da
left luggage consigna ① kon·*seeg*·na
left-wing de izquierdas de eeth·*kyer*·das

leg pierna ① *pyer*·na
legal legal le·*gal*
legislation legislación ① le·khees·la·*thyon*
lemon limón ⓜ lee·*mon*
lemonade limonada ① lee·mo·*na*·da
lens objetivo ⓜ ob·khe·*tee*·vo
Lent Cuaresma ① kwa·*res*·ma
lentils lentejas ① pl len·*te*·khas
lesbian lesbiana ① les·bee·*a*·na
less menos *me*·nos
letter carta ① *kar*·ta
lettuce lechuga ① le·*choo*·ga
liar mentiroso/a ⓜ/① men·tee·ro·so/a
library biblioteca ① bee·blyo·*te*·ka
lice piojos ⓜ pl *pyo*·khos
license plate number matrícula ① ma·*tree*·koo·la
lie (not stand) tumbarse toom·*bar*·se
life vida ① *vee*·da
lifejacket chaleco ⓜ salvavidas cha·*le*·ko sal·va·*vee*·das
lift ascensor ⓜ as·then·*sor*
light (weight) leve *le*·ve
light luz ① looth
light bulb bombilla ① bom·*bee*·lya
light meter fotómetro ⓜ fo·*to*·me·tro
lighter encendedor ⓜ en·then·de·*dor*
like gustar(le) goos·*tar*(le)
lime lima ① *lee*·ma
line línea ① *lee*·ne·a
lip balm bálsamo ⓜ de labios *bal*·sa·mo de *la*·byos
lips labios ⓜ pl *la*·byos
lipstick pintalabios ⓜ peen·ta·la·byos
liquor store bodega ① bo·*de*·ga
listen escuchar es·koo·*char*
live (life) vivir vee·*veer*
live (somewhere) ocupar o·koo·*par*
liver hígado ⓜ ee·ga·do
lizard lagartija ① la·gar·*tee*·kha
local de cercanías de ther·ka·*nee*·as
lock cerradura ① la·ra·*doo*·ra
lock cerrar the·*rar*
locked cerrado/a ⓜ/① con llave the·*ra*·do/a kon *lya*·ve

llies caramelos ⓜ pl ka·ra·me·los
ng largo/a ⓜ/ⓕ lar·go/a
ng-distance a larga distancia a
··ga dees·tan·thya
ok mirar mee·rar
ok after cuidar kwee·dar
ok for buscar boos·kar
okout mirador ⓜ mee·ra·dor
se perder per·der
st perdido/a ⓜ/ⓕ per·dee·do/a
st property office oficina ⓕ de
·jetos perdidos o·fee·thee·na de
··khe·tos per·dee·dos
ud ruidoso/a ⓜ/ⓕ rwee·do·so/a
ve querer ke·rer
ver amante ⓜ&ⓕ a·man·te
w bajo/a ⓜ/ⓕ ba·kho/a
bricant lubricante ⓜ loo·bree·kan·te
ck suerte ⓕ swer·te
cky afortunado/a ⓜ/ⓕ
·for·too·na·do/a
ggage equipaje ⓜ e·kee·pa·khe
ggage lockers consigna ⓕ
·tomática kon·seeg·na
·w·to·ma·tee·ka
ggage tag etiqueta ⓕ de equipaje
·tee·ke·ta de e·kee·pa·khe
mp bulto ⓜ bool·to
nch almuerzo ⓜ al·mwer·tho
ngs pulmones ⓜ pl pool·mo·nes
xury lujo ⓜ loo·kho

M

achine máquina ⓕ ma·kee·na
ade of (cotton) hecho a de
·lgodón) e·cho a de (al·go·don)
agazine revista ⓕ re·vees·ta
agician mago/a ⓜ/ⓕ ma·go/a
ail correo ⓜ ko·re·o
ailbox buzón ⓜ boo·thon
ain principal preen·thee·pal
ake hacer a·ther
ake fun of burlarse de boor·lar·se de
ake-up maquillaje ⓜ ma·kee·lya·khe
ammogram mamograma ⓜ
·a·mo·gra·ma

man hombre ⓜ om·bre
manager gerente ⓜ&ⓕ khe·ren·te
mandarin mandarina ⓕ
man·da·ree·na
mango mango ⓜ man·go
manual worker obrero/a ⓜ/ⓕ
o·bre·ro/a
many muchos/as ⓜ/ⓕ pl moo·chos/
as
map mapa ⓜ ma·pa
margarine margarina ⓕ
mar·ga·ree·na
marijuana marihuana ⓕ
ma·ree·wa·na
marital status estado ⓜ civil
es·ta·do thee·veel
market mercado ⓜ mer·ka·do
marmalade mermelada ⓕ
mer·me·la·da
marriage matrimonio ⓜ
ma·tree·mo·nyo
marry casarse ka·sar·se
martial arts artes ⓜ pl marciales
ar·tes mar·thya·les
mass misa ⓕ mee·sa
massage masaje ⓜ ma·sa·khe
masseur/masseuse masajista ⓜ&ⓕ
ma·sa·khees·ta
mat esterilla ⓕ es·te·ree·lya
match partido ⓜ par·tee·do
matches cerillas ⓕ pl the·ree·lyas
mattress colchón ⓜ kol·chon
maybe quizás kee·thas
mayonnaise mayonesa ⓕ
ma·yo·ne·sa
mayor alcalde ⓜ&ⓕ al·kal·de
measles sarampión ⓜ sa·ram·pyon
meat carne ⓕ kar·ne
mechanic mecánico/a ⓜ/ⓕ
me·ka·nee·ko
media medios ⓜ pl de comunicación
me·dyos de ko·moo·nee·ka·thyon
medicine medicina ⓕ me·dee·thee·na
meditation meditación ⓕ
me·dee·ta·thyon
meet encontrar en·kon·trar

M

melon melón ⓜ me·*lon*

member miembro ⓜ *myem*·bro

menstruation menstruación ⓕ
mens·trwa·*thyon*

menu menú ⓜ me·*noo*

message mensaje ⓜ men·*sa*·khe

metal metal ⓜ me·*tal*

metre metro ⓜ *me*·tro

metro station estación ⓕ de metro
es·ta·*thyon* de *me*·tro

microwave microondas ⓜ
mee·kro·*on*·das

midnight medianoche ⓕ
me·dya·*no*·che

migraine migraña ⓕ mee·*gra*·nya

military service servicio ⓜ militar
ser·*vee*·thyo mee·lee·*tar*

milk leche ⓕ *le*·che

millimetre milímetro ⓜ mee·*lee*·me·tro

million millón ⓜ mee·*lyon*

mince (meat) carne ⓜ molida *kar*·ne
mo·*lee*·da

mind (object) cuidar kwee·*dar*

mineral water agua ⓜ mineral *a*·gwa
mee·ne·*ral*

mints pastillas ⓕ pl de menta
pas·*tee*·lyas de *men*·ta

minute minuto ⓜ mee·*noo*·to

mirror espejo ⓜ es·*pe*·kho

miscarriage aborto ⓜ natural
a·*bor*·to na·too·*ral*

miss (feel sad) echar de menos
e·*char* de *me*·nos

mistake error ⓜ e·*ror*

mix mezclar meth·*klar*

mobile phone teléfono ⓜ móvil
te·*le*·fo·no *mo*·veel

modem módem ⓜ *mo*·dem

moisturiser crema ⓕ hidratante
kre·ma ee·dra·*tan*·te

monastery monasterio ⓜ
mo·nas·*te*·ryo

money dinero ⓜ dee·*ne*·ro

month mes ⓜ mes

monument monumento ⓜ
mo·noo·*men*·to

(full) moon luna ⓕ (llena) *loo*·na
(*lye*·na)

morning (6am–1pm) mañana ⓕ
ma·*nya*·na

morning sickness náuseas ⓕ pl del
embarazo *now*·se·as del em·ba·*ra*·tho

mosque mezquita ⓕ meth·*kee*·ta

mosquito mosquito ⓜ mos·*kee*·to

mosquito coil rollo ⓜ repelente
contra mosquitos *ro*·lyo re·pe·*len*·te
kon·tra mos·*kee*·tos

mosquito net mosquitera ⓕ
mos·kee·*te*·ra

mother madre ⓕ *ma*·dre

mother-in-law suegra ⓕ *swe*·gra

motorboat motora ⓕ mo·*to*·ra

motorcycle motocicleta ⓕ
mo·to·thee·*kle*·ta

motorway autovía ⓕ ow·to·*vee*·a

mountain montaña ⓕ mon·*ta*·nya

mountain bike bicicleta ⓕ de
montaña bee·thee·*kle*·ta de
mon·*ta*·nya

mountain path sendero ⓜ sen·*de*·ro

mountain range cordillera ⓕ
kor·dee·*lye*·ra

mountaineering alpinismo ⓜ
al·pee·*nees*·mo

mouse ratón ⓜ ra·*ton*

mouth boca ⓕ *bo*·ka

movie película ⓕ pe·*lee*·koo·la

mud lodo ⓜ *lo*·do

muesli muesli ⓜ *mwes*·lee

mum mamá ⓕ ma·*ma*

muscle músculo ⓜ *moos*·koo·lo

museum museo ⓜ moo·*se*·o

mushroom ⓜ champiñón
cham·pee·*nyon*

music música ⓕ *moo*·see·ka

musician músico/a ⓜ/ⓕ
moo·see·ko/a

Muslim musulmán/musulmana ⓜ/ⓕ
moo·sool·*man*/moo·sool·*ma*·na

mussels mejillones ⓜ pl
me·khee·*lyo*·nes

mustard mostaza ⓕ mos·*ta*·tha

N

ute mudo/a ⓜ/ⓕ *moo*·do/a
y mi mee

ail clippers cortauñas ⓜ pl
or·ta·oo·nyas
ame nombre ⓜ *nom*·bre
apkin servilleta ⓕ ser·vee·*lye*·ta
appy pañal ⓜ pa·*nyal*
appy rash irritación ⓕ de pañal
e·ree·ta·*thyon* de pa·*nyal*
ational park parque ⓜ nacional
par·ke na·thyo·*nal*
ationality nacionalidad ⓕ
a·thyo·na·lee·*da*
ature naturaleza ⓕ na·too·ra·*le*·tha
aturopathy naturopatía ⓕ
a·too·ro·pa·*tya*
ausea náusea ⓕ *now*·se·a
ear cerca *ther*·ka
earby cerca *ther*·ka
earest más cercano/a ⓜ/ⓕ mas
her·*ka*·no/a
ecessary necesario/a ⓜ/ⓕ
e·the·*sa*·ryo/a
eck cuello ⓜ *kwe*·lyo
ecklace collar ⓜ ko·*lyar*
eed necesitar ne·the·see·*tar*
eedle (sewing) aguja ⓕ a·*goo*·kha
eedle (syringe) jeringa ⓕ
he·*reen*·ga
either tampoco tam·po·ko
et red ⓕ red
Netherlands Holanda ⓕ o·*lan*·da
ever nunca *noon*·ka
ew nuevo/a ⓜ/ⓕ *nwe*·vo/a
New Year Año Nuevo ⓜ a·nyo *nwe*·vo
New Year's Eve Nochevieja ⓕ
o·che·*vye*·kha
New Zealand Nueva Zelanda ⓕ
nwe·va the·*lan*·da
ews noticias ⓕ pl no·*tee*·thyas
ews stand quiosco ⓜ *kyos*·ko
ewsagency quiosco ⓜ *kyos*·ko
ewspaper periódico ⓜ
e·*ryo*·dee·ko

next (month) el próximo (mes) el
prok·see·mo (mes)
next to al lado de al *la*·do de
nice simpático/a ⓜ/ⓕ
seem·*pa*·tee·ko/a
nickname apodo ⓜ a·*po*·do
night noche ⓕ *no*·che
no no no
noisy ruidoso/a ⓜ/ⓕ rwee·*do*·so/a
none nada *na*·da
nonsmoking no fumadores no
foo·ma·*do*·res
noodles fideos ⓜ pl fee·*de*·os
noon mediodía ⓜ me·dyo·*dee*·a
north norte ⓜ *nor*·te
nose nariz ⓕ na·*reeth*
notebook cuaderno ⓜ kwa·*der*·no
nothing nada *na*·da
now ahora a·o·ra
nuclear energy energía ⓕ nuclear
e·ner·*khee*·a noo·kle·*ar*
nuclear testing pruebas ⓕ pl
nucleares *prwe*·bas noo·kle·*a*·res
nuclear waste desperdicios ⓜ
pl nucleares des·per·*dee*·thyos
noo·kle·*a*·res
number número ⓜ *noo*·me·ro
nun monja ⓕ *mon*·kha
nurse enfermero/a ⓜ/ⓕ
en·fer·*me*·ro/a
nuts nueces ⓕ *nwe*·thes
nuts (raw) nueces ⓕ pl (crudas)
nwe·thes (*kroo*·das)
nuts (roasted) nueces ⓕ pl
(tostadas) *nwe*·thes (tos·*ta*·das)

O

oats avena ⓕ a·*ve*·na
ocean océano ⓜ o·*the*·a·no
off (food) pasado/a ⓜ/ⓕ pa·*sa*·do/a
office oficina ⓕ o·fee·*thee*·na
office worker oficinista ⓜ&ⓕ
o·fee·thee·*nees*·ta
offside fuera de juego *fwe*·ra de *khwe*·go
often a menudo a me·*noo*·do
oil aceite ⓜ a·*they*·te

old viejo/a ⓜ/ⓕ *vye*·kho/a

olive oil aceite ⓜ de oliva a·*they*·te de o·*lee*·va

Olympic Games Juegos ⓜ pl Olímpicos *khwe*·gos o·*leem*·pee·kos

on en en

once vez ⓕ veth

one-way ticket billete ⓜ sencillo bee·*lye*·te sen·*thee*·lyo

onion ⓕ cebolla the·*bo*·lya

only sólo *so*·lo

open abierto/a ⓜ/ⓕ a·*byer*·to/a

open abrir a·*breer*

opening hours horas ⓕ pl de abrir o·ras de a·*breer*

opera ópera ⓕ o·pe·ra

opera house teatro ⓜ de la ópera te·a·tro de la o·pe·ra

operation operación ⓕ o·pe·ra·*thyon*

operator operador/operadora ⓜ/ⓕ o·pe·ra·*dor*/o·pe·ra·do·ra

opinion opinión ⓕ o·pee·*nyon*

opposite frente a *fren*·te a

or o o

orange (fruit) naranja ⓕ na·*ran*·kha

orange (colour) naranja na·*ran*·kha

orange juice zumo ⓜ de naranja *thoo*·mo de na·*ran*·kha

orchestra orquesta ⓕ or·*kes*·ta

order orden ⓜ *or*·den

order ordenar or·de·*nar*

ordinary corriente ko·*ryen*·te

orgasm orgasmo ⓜ or·*gas*·mo

original original o·ree·khee·*nal*

other otro/a o·tro/a

our nuestro/a ⓜ/ⓕ *nwes*·tro/a

outside exterior ⓜ eks·te·*ryor*

ovarian cyst quiste ⓜ ovárico *kees*·te o·va·ree·ko

oven horno ⓜ *or*·no

overcoat abrigo ⓜ a·*bree*·go

overdose sobredosis ⓕ so·bre·*do*·sees

owe deber de·*ber*

owner dueño/a ⓜ/ⓕ *dwe*·nyo/a

oxygen oxígeno ⓜ ok·*see*·khe·no

oyster ⓕ ostra *os*·tra

ozone layer capa ⓕ de ozono *ka*·pa de o·*tho*·no

P

pacemaker marcapasos ⓜ mar·ka·pa·sos

pacifier chupete ⓜ choo·pe·te

package paquete ⓜ pa·ke·te

packet paquete ⓜ pa·ke·te

padlock candado ⓜ kan·*da*·do

page página ⓕ *pa*·khee·na

pain dolor ⓜ do·*lor*

painful doloroso/a ⓜ/ⓕ do·lo·ro·so/a

painkillers analgésicos ⓜ pl a·nal·*khe*·see·kos

paint pintar peen·*tar*

painter pintor/pintora ⓜ/ⓕ peen·*tor*/ peen·*to*·ra

painting pintura ⓕ peen·*too*·ra

pair (couple) pareja ⓕ pa·re·kha

palace palacio ⓜ pa·la·thyo

pan cazuela ⓕ ka·*thwe*·la

pants pantalones ⓜ pl pan·ta·lo·nes

panty liners salvaeslips ⓜ pl sal·va·e·*sleeps*

pantyhose medias ⓕ pl *me*·dyas

pap smear citología ⓕ thee·to·lo·*khee*·a

paper papel ⓜ pa·*pel*

paperwork trabajo ⓜ administrativo tra·ba·kho ad·mee·nees·tra·*tee*·vo

paraplegic parapléjico/a ⓜ/ⓕ pa·ra·*ple*·khee·ko/a

parasailing esquí ⓜ acuático con paracaídas es·*kee* a·kwa·tee·ko kon pa·ra·ka·ee·das

parcel paquete ⓜ pa·ke·te

parents padres ⓜ pl *pa*·dres

park parque ⓜ *par*·ke

park (car) estacionar es·ta·thyo·*nar*

parliament parlamento ⓜ par·la·*men*·to

parsley perejil ⓜ pe·re·*kheel*

part parte ⓕ *par*·te

part-time a tiempo parcial a *tyem*·po par·*thyal*

rty fiesta ① *fyes*·ta
rty (political) partido ⓜ par·*tee*·do
ss pase ⓜ *pa*·se
ssenger pasajero/a ⓜ/①
·sa·*khe*·ro
ssport pasaporte ⓜ pa·sa·*por*·te
ssport number número ⓜ de
saporte *noo*·me·ro de pa·sa·*por*·te
st pasado ⓜ pa·*sa*·do
sta pasta ① *pas*·ta
te (food) paté ⓜ pa·*te*
y pagar pa·*gar*
ace paz ① *pas*
ach melocotón ⓜ me·lo·ko·*ton*
·ka·we·tes
ar pera ① *pe*·ra
as guisantes ⓜ pl gee·*san*·tes
dal pedal ⓜ pe·*dal*
destrian peatón ⓜ&① pe·a·*ton*
destrian crossing paso ⓜ de
bra pa·so de *the*·bra
en bolígrafo ⓜ bo·*lee*·gra·fo
ncil lápiz ⓜ *la*·peeth
nis pene ⓜ *pe*·ne
nknife navaja ① na·*va*·kha
nsioner pensionista ⓜ&①
·n·syo·*nees*·ta
ople gente ① *khen*·te
pper (vegetable) pimiento ⓜ
·e·*myen*·to
pper (spice) pimienta ①
·e·*myen*·ta
r (day) por (dia) por (*dee*·a)
ercent por ciento por *thyen*·to
erformance actuación ①
·twa·*thyon*
erfume perfume ⓜ per·*foo*·me
eriod pain dolor ⓜ menstrual do·*lor*
ens·*trwal*
ermission permiso ⓜ per·*mee*·so
ermit permiso ⓜ per·*mee*·so
ermit permitir per·mee·*teer*

person persona ① per·*so*·na
perspire sudar soo·*dar*
petition petición ① pe·tee·*thyon*
petrol gasolina ① ga·so·*lee*·na
pharmacy farmacia ① far·*ma*·thya
phone book guía ① telefónica *gee*·a
te·le·fo·*nee*·ka
phone box cabina ① telefónica
ka·*bee*·ka te·le·fo·*nee*·ka
phone card tarjeta ① de teléfono
tar·*khe*·ta de te·le·fo·no
photo foto ① *fo*·to
photographer fotógrafo/a ⓜ/①
fo·*to*·gra·fo/a
photography fotografía ①
fo·to·gra·*fee*·a
phrasebook libro ⓜ de frases *lee*·bro
de *fra*·ses
pick up ligar lee·*gar*
pickaxe piqueta ① pee·*ke*·ta
pickles encurtidos ⓜ pl
en·koor·*tee*·dos
picnic comida ① en el campo
ko·*mee*·da en el *kam*·po
pie pastel ⓜ pas·*tel*
piece pedazo ① pe·*da*·tho
pig cerdo ⓜ *ther*·do
pill pastilla ① pas·*tee*·lya
pill, the (contraceptive) píldora ①
peel·do·ra
pillow almohada ① al·*mwa*·da
pillowcase funda ① de almohada
foon·da de al·*mwa*·da
pineapple piña ① *pee*·nya
pink rosa *ro*·sa
pistachio pistacho ⓜ pees·*ta*·cho
place lugar ⓜ loo·*gar*
place of birth lugar ⓜ de nacimiento
loo·*gar* de na·thee·*myen*·to
plane avión ⓜ a·*vyon*
planet planeta ① pla·*ne*·ta
plant planta ① *plan*·ta
plant sembrar sem·*brar*
plastic plástico ⓜ *plas*·tee·ko
plate plato ⓜ *pla*·to
plateau meseta ① me·*se*·ta

P

platform plataforma ⨍ pla·ta·*for*·ma
play obra ⨍ *o*·bra
play (musical instrument) tocar to·*kar*
play (sport/games) jugar khoo·*gar*
plug tapar ta·*par*
plum ciruela thee·*rwe*·la
pocket bolsillo ⓜ bol·*see*·lyo
poetry poesía ⨍ po·e·*see*·a
point apuntar a·poon·*tar*
point (tip) punto ⓜ *poon*·to
poisonous venenoso/a ⓜ/⨍ ve·ne·*no*·so/a
poker póquer ⓜ *po*·ker
police policía ⨍ po·lee·*thee*·a
police station comisaría ⨍ ko·mee·sa·*ree*·a
policy política ⨍ po·*lee*·tee·ka
policy (insurance) póliza ⨍ *po*·lee·tha
politician político ⓜ po·*lee*·tee·ko
politics política ⨍ po·*lee*·tee·ka
pollen polen ⓜ *po*·len
polls sondeos ⓜ pl son·*de*·os
pollution contaminación ⨍ kon·ta·mee·na·*thyon*
pool (swimming) piscina ⨍ pees·*thee*·na
poor pobre *po*·bre
popular popular po·poo·*lar*
pork cerdo ⓜ *ther*·do
pork sausage chorizo ⓜ cho·*ree*·tho
port puerto ⓜ *pwer*·to
port (wine) oporto ⓜ o·*por*·to
possible posible po·*see*·ble
post code código postal ⓜ *ko*·dee·go pos·*tal*
post office correos ⓜ ko·*re*·os
postage franqueo ⓜ fran·*ke*·o
postcard postal ⨍ pos·*tal*
poster póster ⓜ *pos*·ter
pot (kitchen) cazuela ⨍ ka·*thwe*·la
pot (plant) tiesto ⓜ *tyes*·to
potato patata ⨍ pa·*ta*·ta
pottery alfarería ⨍ al·fa·re·*ree*·a
pound (money) libra ⨍ *lee*·bra

poverty pobreza ⨍ po·*bre*·tha
power poder ⓜ po·*der*
prawns gambas ⨍ pl *gam*·bas
prayer oración ⨍ o·ra·*thyon*
prayer book devocionario ⓜ de·vo·thyo·na·*ryo*
prefer preferir pre·fe·*reer*
pregnancy test prueba ⨍ del embarazo *prwe*·ba del em·ba·*ra*·tho
pregnant embarazada ⨍ em·ba·ra·*tha*·da
premenstrual tension tensión ⨍ premenstrual ten·*syon* pre·mens·*trw...*
prepare preparar pre·pa·*rar*
president presidente/a ⓜ/⨍ pre·see·*den*·te/a
pressure presión ⨍ pre·*syon*
pretty bonito/a ⓜ/⨍ bo·*nee*·to/a
prevent prevenir pre·ve·*neer*
price precio ⓜ *pre*·thyo
priest sacerdote ⓜ sa·ther·*do*·te
prime minister primer ministro/ primera ministra ⓜ/⨍ pree·*mer* mee·*nees*·tro/pree·*me*·ra mee·*nees*·tra
prison cárcel ⨍ *kar*·thel
prisoner prisionero/a ⓜ/⨍ pree·syon·*ne*·ro/a
private privado/a ⓜ/⨍ pree·va·do/*...*
private hospital clínica ⨍ *klee*·nee
produce producir pro·doo·*theer*
profit beneficio ⓜ be·ne·*fee*·thyo
programme programa ⓜ pro·*gra*·m
projector proyector ⓜ pro·yek·*tor*
promise promesa ⨍ pro·*me*·sa
protect proteger pro·te·*kher*
protected (species) protegido/a ⓜ/⨍ pro·te·*khee*·do/a
protest protesta ⨍ pro·*tes*·ta
protest protestar pro·tes·*tar*
provisions provisiones ⨍ pl pro·vee·*syo*·nes
prune ciruela ⨍ pasa thee·*rwe*·la pa
pub pub ⓜ poob
public telephone teléfono ⓜ públic te·*le*·fo·no poo·*blee*·ko

public toilet servicios ⓜ pl
ser·*vee*·thyos
pull tirar tee·*rar*
pump bomba ⓕ *bom*·ba
pumpkin calabaza ⓕ ka·la·*ba*·tha
puncture pinchar peen·*char*
punish castigar kas·tee·*gar*
puppy cachorro ⓜ ka·*cho*·ro
pure puro/a ⓜ/ⓕ *poo*·ro/a
purple lila *lee*·la
push empujar em·poo·*khar*
put poner po·*ner*

Q

qualifications cualificaciones ⓕ pl
kwa·lee·fee·ka·*thyo*·nes
quality calidad ⓕ ka·lee·*da*
quarantine cuarentena ⓕ
kwa·ren·*te*·na
quarrel pelea ⓕ pe·*le*·a
quarter cuarto ⓜ *kwar*·to
queen reina ⓕ *rey*·na
question pregunta ⓕ pre·*goon*·ta
question cuestionar kwes·tyo·*nar*
queue cola ⓕ *ko*·la
quick rápido/a ⓜ/ⓕ *ra*·pee·do/a
quiet tranquilo/a ⓜ/ⓕ tran·*kee*·lo/a
quiet tranquilidad ⓕ tran·kee·*lee*·da
quit dejar de·*khar*

R

rabbit conejo ⓜ ko·*ne*·kho
race (people) raza ⓕ *ra*·tha
race (sport) carrera ⓕ ka·*re*·ra
racetrack (bicycles) velódromo ⓜ
e·*lo*·dro·mo
racetrack (cars) circuito ⓜ de
arreras theer·*kwee*·to de ka·*re*·ras
racetrack (horses) hipódromo ⓜ
e·*po*·dro·mo
racetrack (runners) pista ⓕ *pees*·ta
racing bike bicicleta ⓕ de carreras
ee·thee·*kle*·ta de ka·*re*·ras
racquet raqueta ⓕ ra·*ke*·ta
radiator radiador ⓜ ra·dya·*dor*
radish rábano ⓜ *ra*·ba·no

railway station estación ⓕ de tren
es·ta·*thyon* de tren
rain lluvia ⓕ *lyoo*·vya
raincoat impermeable ⓜ
eem·per·me·*a*·ble
raisin uva ⓕ pasa *oo*·va *pa*·sa
rally concentración ⓕ
kon·then·tra·*thyon*
rape violar vyo·*lar*
rare raro/a ⓜ/ⓕ *ra*·ro/a
rash irritación ⓕ ee·ree·ta·*thyon*
raspberry frambuesa ⓕ fram·*bwe*·sa
rat rata ⓕ *ra*·ta
rate of pay salario ⓜ sa·*la*·ryo
raw crudo/a ⓜ/ⓕ *kroo*·do/a
razor afeitadora ⓕ a·*fey*·ta·do·ra
razor blades cuchillas ⓕ pl de afeitar
koo·*chee*·lyas de a·fey·*tar*
read leer le·*er*
ready listo/a ⓜ/ⓕ *lees*·to/a
real estate agent agente inmobiliario
ⓜ a·*khen*·te een·mo·bee·*lya*·ryo
realise darse cuenta de *dar*·se
kwen·ta de
realistic realista re·a·*lees*·ta
reason razón ⓕ ra·*thon*
receipt recibo ⓜ re·*thee*·bo
receive recibir re·thee·*beer*
recently recientemente
re·thyen·te·*men*·te
recognise reconocer re·ko·no·*ther*
recommend recomendar
re·ko·men·*dar*
recording grabación ⓕ gra·ba·*thyon*
recyclable reciclable re·thee·*kla*·ble
recycle reciclar re·thee·*klar*
red rojo/a ⓜ/ⓕ *ro*·kho/a
referee árbitro ⓜ *ar*·bee·tro
reference referencias ⓕ pl
re·fe·*ren*·thyas
refrigerator nevera ⓕ ne·*ve*·ra •
frigerífico ⓕ free·ge·*ree*·fee·ko
refugee refugiado/a ⓜ/ⓕ
re·foo·*khya*·do/a
refund reembolso ⓜ re·em·*bol*·so
refund reembolsar re·em·bol·*sar*
refuse negar ne·*gar*

registered mail correo ⓜ certificado ko·re·o ther·tee·fee·ka·do

regret lamentar la·men·tar

relationship relación ⓕ re·la·thyon

relax relajarse re·la·khar·se

relic reliquia ⓕ re·lee·kya

religion religión ⓕ re·lee·khyon

religious religioso/a ⓜ/ⓕ re·lee·khyo·so/a

remember recordar re·kor·dar

remote remoto/a ⓜ/ⓕ re·mo·to/a

remote control mando ⓜ a distancia man·do a dees·tan·thya

rent alquiler ⓜ al·kee·ler

rent alquilar al·kee·lar

repair reparar re·pa·rar

repeat repetir re·pe·teer

republic república ⓕ re·poo·blee·ka

reservation reserva ⓕ re·ser·va

reserve reservar re·ser·var

rest descansar des·kan·sar

restaurant restaurante ⓜ res·tow·ran·te

retired jubilado/a ⓜ/ⓕ khoo·bee·la·do/a

return volver vol·ver

return ticket billete ⓜ de ida y vuelta bee·lye·te de ee·da ee vwel·ta

review crítica ⓕ kree·tee·ka

rhythm ritmo ⓜ reet·mo

rice arroz ⓜ a·roth

rich rico/a ⓜ/ⓕ ree·ko/a

ride paseo ⓜ pa·se·o

ride montar mon·tar

right (correct) correcto/a ⓜ/ⓕ ko·rek·to/a

right (not left) derecha de·re·cha

right-wing derechista de·re·chees·ta

ring (phone) llamada ⓕ lya·ma·da

ring llamar por teléfono lya·mar por te·le·fo·no

rip-off estafa ⓕ es·ta·fa

risk riesgo ⓜ ryes·go

river río ⓜ ree·o

road carretera ⓕ ka·re·te·ra

rob robar ro·bar

rock (stone) roca ⓕ ro·ka

rock (music) rock ⓜ rok

rock climbing escalada ⓕ es·ka·la·da

rock group grupo ⓜ de rock groo·po de rok

rollerblading patinar pa·tee·nar

romantic romántico/a ⓜ/ⓕ ro·man·tee·ko/a

room habitación ⓕ a·bee·ta·thyon

room number número ⓜ de la habitación noo·me·ro de la a·bee·ta·thyon

rope cuerda ⓕ kwer·da

round redondo/a ⓜ/ⓕ re·don·do/a

roundabout glorieta ⓕ glo·rye·ta

route ruta ⓕ roo·ta

rowing remo ⓜ re·mo

rubbish basura ⓕ ba·soo·ra

rug alfombra ⓕ al·fom·bra

rugby rugby ⓜ roog·bee

ruins ruinas ⓕ pl rwee·nas

rules reglas ⓕ pl re·glas

rum ron ron

run correr ko·rer

run out of quedarse sin ke·dar·se seen

S

sad triste trees·te

saddle sillín ⓜ see·lyeen

safe seguro/a ⓜ/ⓕ se·goo·ro/a

safe caja ⓕ fuerte ka·kha fwer·te

safe sex sexo ⓜ seguro sek·so se·goo·ro

saint santo/a ⓜ/ⓕ san·to/a

salad ensalada ⓕ en·sa·la·da

salami (Spanish sausage) chorizo cho·ree·tho

salary salario ⓜ sa·la·ryo

sales tax IVA ⓜ ee·va

salmon salmón ⓜ sal·mon

salt sal ⓕ sal

same igual ee·gwal

sand arena ⓕ a·re·na

sandals sandalias ⓕ pl san·da·lyas

sanitary napkins compresas ⓕ pl kom·pre·sas

auna sauna ① *sow*·na
ausage salchicha ① sal·*chee*·cha
ave salvar sal·*var*
ave (money) ahorrar a·o·*rar*
ay decir de·*theer*
cale/climb trepar tre·*par*
carf bufanda ① boo·*fan*·da
chool escuela ① es·*kwe*·la
cience ciencias ① pl *thyen*·thyas
cientist científico/a ⓜ/①
nyen·*tee*·fee·ko/a
cissors tijeras ① pl tee·*khe*·ras
core marcar mar·*kar*
coreboard marcador ⓜ mar·ka·*dor*
cotland Escocia ① es·*ko*·thya
creen pantalla ① pan·*ta*·lya
cript guión ⓜ gee·*on*
culpture escultura ① es·kool·*too*·ra
ea mar ⓜ mar
easick mareado/a ⓜ/①
na·re·a·do/a
easide costa ① *kos*·ta
eason estación ① es·ta·*thyon*
eason (in sport) temporada ①
em·po·*ra*·da
eat asiento ⓜ a·*syen*·to
eatbelt cinturón ⓜ de seguridad
heen·too·*ron* de se·goo·ree·*da*
econd (place) segundo/a ⓜ/①
se·*goon*·do/a
econd (time) segundo ⓜ se·*goon*·do
econdhand de segunda mano de
se·*goon*·da *ma*·no
ecretary secretario/a ⓜ/①
se·kre·*ta*·ryo/a
ee ver ver
elfish egoista e·go·*ees*·ta
elf-service autoservicio ⓜ
ow·to·ser·*vee*·thyo
ell vender ven·*der*
end enviar en·vee·*ar*
ensible prudente proo·*den*·te
ensual sensual sen·*swal*
eparate separado/a ⓜ/①
se·pa·*ra*·do/a
eparate separar se·pa·*rar*
eries serie ① *se*·rye

serious serio/a ⓜ/① *se*·ryo/a
service station gasolinera ①
ga·so·lee·*ne*·ra
service charge carga ① *kar*·ga
several varias/os ⓜ/① *va*·ryas/os
sew coser ko·*ser*
sex sexo ⓜ *sek*·so
sexism machismo ⓜ ma·*chees*·mo
sexy sexy *sek*·see
shadow sombra ① *som*·bra
shampoo champú ⓜ cham·*poo*
shape forma ① *for*·ma
share (a dorm) compartir (un
dormitorio) kom·par·*teer* (oon
dor·mee·*to*·ryo)
share (with) compartir kom·par·*teer*
shave afeitarse a·fey·*tar*·se
shaving cream espuma ① de afeitar
es·*poo*·ma de a·fey·*tar*
she ella ① *e*·lya
sheep oveja ① o·*ve*·kha
sheet (bed) sábana ① *sa*·ba·na
sheet (of paper) hoja ① o·kha
shelf estante ⓜ es·*tan*·te
ship barco ⓜ *bar*·ko
ship enviar en·vee·*ar*
shirt camisa ① ka·*mee*·sa
shoe shop zapatería ①
tha·pa·te·*ree*·a
shoes zapatos ⓜ pl tha·*pa*·tos
shoot disparar dees·pa·*rar*
shop tienda ① *tyen*·da
shoplifting ratería ① ra·te·*ree*·a
shopping centre centro ⓜ comercial
then·tro ko·mer·*thyal*
short (height) bajo/a ⓜ/① *ba*·kho/a
short (length) corto/a ⓜ/① *kor*·to/a
shortage escasez ① es·ka·*seth*
shorts pantalones ⓜ pl cortos
kor·tos pan·ta·*lo*·nes
shoulders hombros ⓜ pl *om*·bros
shout gritar gree·*tar*
show espectáculo ⓜ es·pek·*ta*·koo·lo
show mostrar mos·*trar*
show enseñar en·se·*nyar*
shower ducha ① *doo*·cha

S

shrine capilla ① ka·pee·lya

shut cerrado/a ⓜ/① the·ra·do/a

shut cerrar the·rar

shy tímido/a ⓜ/① tee·mee·do/a

sick enfermo/a ⓜ/① en·fer·mo/a

side lado ⓜ la·do

sign señal ① se·nyal

sign firmar feer·mar

signature firma ① feer·ma

silk seda ① se·da

silver plateado/a ⓜ/① pla·te·a·do/a

silver plata ① pla·ta

similar similar see·mee·lar

simple sencillo/a ⓜ/① sen·thee·lyo/a

since desde (mayo) des·de (ma·yo)

sing cantar kan·tar

Singapore Singapur ⓜ seen·ga·poor

singer cantante ⓜ&① kan·tan·te

single soltero/a ⓜ/① sol·te·ro/a

single room habitación ① individual a·bee·ta·thyon een·dee·vee·dwal

singlet camiseta ① ka·mee·se·ta

sister hermana ① er·ma·na

sit sentarse sen·tar·se

size (clothes) talla ① ta·lya

skateboarding monopatinaje ⓜ mo·no·pa·tee·na·khe

ski esquiar es·kee·ar

skiing esquí ⓜ es·kee

skimmed milk leche ① desnatada le·che des·na·ta·da

skin piel ① pyel

skirt falda ① fal·da

sky cielo ⓜ thye·lo

skydiving paracaidismo ⓜ pa·ra·kai·dees·mo

sleep dormir dor·meer

sleeping bag saco ⓜ de dormir sa·ko de dor·meer

sleeping car coche cama ⓜ ko·che ka·ma

sleeping pills pastillas ① pl para dormir pas·tee·lyas pa·ra dor·meer

(to be) sleepy tener sueño te·ner swe·nyo

slide diapositiva ① dya·po·see·tee·va

slow lento/a ⓜ/① len·to/a

slowly despacio des·pa·thyo

small pequeño/a ⓜ/① pe·ke·nyo/a

smell olor ⓜ o·lor

smell oler o·ler

smile sonreír son·re·eer

smoke fumar foo·mar

snack tentempié ⓜ ten·tem·pye

snail caracol ⓜ ka·ra·kol

snake serpiente ① ser·pyen·te

snorkel tubos ⓜ pl respiratorios too·bos res·pee·to·ryos

snorkel buceo ⓜ boo·the·o

snow nieve ① nye·ve

snowboarding surf ⓜ sobre la nieve soorf so·bre la nye·ve

soap jabón ⓜ kha·bon

soap opera telenovela ① te·le·no·ve·la

soccer fútbol ⓜ foot·bol

social welfare estado ⓜ del bienestar es·ta·do del byen·es·tar

socialist socialista ⓜ&① so·thya·lees·ta

socks calcetines ⓜ pl kal·the·tee·nes

soft drink refresco ⓜ re·fres·ko

soldier soldado ⓜ sol·da·do

some alguno/a ⓜ/① al·goon/al·goo·r

someone alguien al·gyen

something algo al·go

sometimes de vez en cuando de veth en kwan·do

son hijo ⓜ ee·kho

song canción ① kan·thyon

soon pronto pron·to

sore dolorido/a ⓜ/① do·lo·ree·do/a

soup sopa ① so·pa

sour cream nata ① agria na·ta a·grya

south sur ⓜ soor

souvenir recuerdo ⓜ re·kwer·do

souvenir shop tienda ① de recuerdos tyen·da de re·kwer·dos

soy milk leche ① de soja le·che de so·kha

soy sauce salsa ① de soja sal·sa de so·kha

	S
	ENGLISH *to* SPANISH

ace espacio ⓜ es·pa·thyo
ain España ⓕ es·pa·nya
arkling espumoso/a ⓜ/ⓕ poo·mo·so
eak hablar a·blar
ecial especial es·pe·thyal
ecialist especialista ⓜ&ⓕ pe·thya·lees·ta
eed velocidad ⓕ ve·lo·thee·da
eeding exceso ⓜ de velocidad s·the·so de ve·lo·thee·da
eedometer velocímetro ⓜ ·lo·thee·me·tro
ider araña ⓕ a·ra·nya
inach espinacas ⓕ pl ·pee·na·kas
oon cuchara ⓕ koo·cha·ra
ort deportes ⓜ pl de·por·tes
orts store tienda ⓕ deportiva en·da de·por·tee·va
ortsperson deportista ⓜ&ⓕ ·por·tees·ta
rain torcedura ⓕ tor·the·doo·ra
ring (wire) muelle ⓜ mwe·lye
ring (season) primavera ⓕ ee·ma·ve·ra
uare (shape) cuadrado ⓜ va·dra·do
nain) square plaza ⓕ (mayor) a·tha (ma·yor)
adium estadio ⓜ es·ta·dyo
age escenario ⓜ es·the·na·ryo
atue airway escalera ⓕ es·ka·le·ra
amp sello ⓜ se·lyo
andby ticket billete ⓜ de lista de pera bee·lye·te de lees·ta de es·pe·ra
ars estrellas ⓕ pl es·tre·lyas
art comenzar ko·men·thar
ation estación ⓕ es·ta·thyon
atue estatua ⓕ es·ta·twa
ay (remain) quedarse ke·dar·se lo·khar·se
ay (somewhere) alojarse
eak (beef) bistec ⓜ bees·tek
eal robar ro·bar
eep escarpado/a ⓜ/ⓕ s·kar·pa·do/a

step paso ⓜ pa·so
stereo equipo ⓜ de música e·kee·po de moo·see·ka
stingy tacaño/a ⓜ/ⓕ ta·ka·nyo/a
stock caldo ⓜ kal·do
stockings medias ⓕ pl me·dyas
stomach estómago ⓜ es·to·ma·go
stomachache dolor ⓜ de estómago do·lor de es·to·ma·go
stone piedra ⓕ pye·dra
stoned colocado/a ⓜ/ⓕ ko·lo·ka·do/a
stop parada ⓕ pa·ra·da
stop parar pa·rar
storm tormenta ⓕ tor·men·ta
story cuento ⓜ kwen·to
stove cocina ⓕ ko·thee·na
straight recto/a ⓜ/ⓕ rek·to/a
strange extraño/a ⓜ/ⓕ ek·stra·nyo/a
stranger desconocido/a ⓜ/ⓕ des·ko·no·thee·do/a
strawberry fresa ⓕ fre·sa
stream arroyo ⓜ a·ro·yo
street calle ⓕ ka·lye
string cuerda ⓕ kwer·da
strong fuerte fwer·te
stubborn testarudo/a ⓜ/ⓕ tes·ta·roo·do/a
student estudiante ⓜ&ⓕ es·too·dyan·te
studio estudio ⓜ es·too·dyo
stupid estúpido/a ⓜ/ⓕ es·too·pee·do/a
style estilo ⓜ es·tee·lo
subtitles subtítulos ⓜ pl soob·tee·too·los
suburb barrio ⓜ ba·ryo
subway parada ⓕ de metro pa·ra·da de me·tro
suffer sufrir soo·freer
sugar azúcar ⓜ a·thoo·kar
suitcase maleta ⓕ ma·le·ta
summer verano ⓜ ve·ra·no
sun sol ⓜ sol
sunblock crema ⓕ solar kre·ma so·lar
sunburn quemadura ⓕ de sol ke·ma·doo·ra de sol

T

sun-dried tomato tomate ⓜ secado al sol to·*ma*·te se·*ka*·do al sol
sunflower oil aceite ⓜ de girasol a·*they*·te de khee·ra·*sol*
sunglasses gafas ⓕ pl de sol ga·fas de sol
(to be) sunny hace sol a·the sol
sunrise amanecer ⓜ a·ma·ne·*ther*
sunset puesta ⓕ del sol *pwes*·ta del sol
supermarket supermercado ⓜ soo·per·mer·*ka*·do
superstition superstición ⓕ soo·pers·tee·*thyon*
supporters hinchas ⓜ&ⓕ pl *een*·chas
surf hacer surf a·*ther* soorf
surface mail por vía terrestre por *vee*·a te·*res*·tre
surfboard tabla de surf ⓕ *ta*·bla de soorf
surname apellido ⓜ a·pe·*lyee*·do
surprise sorpresa ⓕ sor·*pre*·sa
survive sobrevivir so·bre·vee·*veer*
sweater jersey ⓜ kher·*sey*
Sweden Suecia ⓕ *swe*·thya
sweet dulce *dool*·the
sweets (candy) dulces ⓜ pl *dool*·thes
swim nadar na·*dar*
swimming pool piscina ⓕ pees·*thee*·na
swimsuit bañador ⓜ ba·nya·*dor*
Switzerland Suiza ⓕ *swee*·tha
synagogue sinagoga ⓕ see·na·go·ga
synthetic sintético/a ⓜ/ⓕ seen·*te*·tee·ko/a
syringe jeringa ⓕ khe·*reen*·ga

T

table mesa ⓕ *me*·sa
table tennis ping pong ⓜ peeng pong
tablecloth mantel ⓜ man·*tel*
tail rabo ⓜ *ra*·bo
tailor sastre ⓜ *sas*·tre
take (away) llevar lye·*var*

take (the train) tomar to·*mar*
take (photo) sacar sa·*kar*
take photographs sacar fotos sa·*ka* *fo*·tos
talk hablar a·*blar*
tall alto/a ⓜ/ⓕ *al*·to/a
tampons tampones ⓜ pl tam·*po*·ne
tanning lotion bronceador ⓜ bron·the·a·*dor*
tap grifo ⓜ *gree*·fo
tasty sabroso/a ⓜ/ⓕ sa·*bro*·so/a
taxes impuestos ⓜ pl eem·*pwes*·to
taxi taxi ⓜ *tak*·see
taxi stand parada ⓕ de taxis pa·*ra*· de *tak*·sees
tea té ⓜ te
teacher profesor/profesora ⓜ/ⓕ pro·fe·*sor*/pro·fe·*so*·ra
team equipo ⓜ e·*kee*·po
teaspoon cucharita ⓕ koo·cha·ree·
technique técnica ⓕ *tek*·nee·ka
teeth dientes ⓜ pl *dyen*·tes
telegram telegrama ⓜ te·le·*gra*·ma
telephone teléfono ⓜ te·*le*·fo·no
telephone llamar (por teléfono) lya·*mar* (por te·*le*·fo·no)
telephone centre central ⓕ telefónica then·*tral* te·le·fo·nee·ka
telescope telescopio ⓜ te·les·*ko*·py
television televisión ⓕ te·le·vee·*syo*
tell decir de·*theer*
temperature (fever) fiebre ⓕ *fye*·b
temperature (weather) temperatur ⓕ tem·pe·ra·*too*·ra
temple templo ⓜ *tem*·plo
tennis tenis ⓜ *te*·nees
tennis court pista ⓕ de tenis *pees*·t
de *te*·nees
tent tienda ⓕ (de campaña) *tyen*·da
(de kam·*pa*·nya)
tent pegs piquetas ⓕ pl pee·*ke*·tas
terrible terrible te·*ree*·ble
test prueba ⓕ *prwe*·ba
thank dar gracias dar *gra*·thyas
theatre teatro ⓜ te·a·tro
their su soo

they ellos/ellas ⓜ/ⓕ e·lyos/e·lyas
thief ladrón/ladrona ⓜ/ⓕ la·dron/la·dro·na
thin delgado/a ⓜ/ⓕ del·ga·do/a
think pensar pen·sar
third tercio ⓜ ter·thyo
thirst sed ⓕ se
this éste/a ⓜ/ⓕ es·te/a
this month este mes es·te mes
thread hilo ⓜ ee·lo
throat garganta ⓕ gar·gan·ta
ticket billete ⓜ bee·lye·te
ticket collector revisor/revisora ⓜ/ⓕ re·vee·sor/re·vee·so·ra
ticket machine máquina ⓕ de billetes ma·kee·na de bee·lye·tes
ticket office taquilla ⓕ ta·kee·lya
tide marea ⓕ ma·re·a
tight apretado/a ⓜ/ⓕ a·pre·ta·do/a
time (watch) hora ⓕ o·ra
time (passing) tiempo ⓜ tyem·po
time difference diferencia ⓕ de horas dee·fe·ren·thya de o·ras
timetable horario ⓜ o·ra·ryo
tin hojalata ⓕ o·kha·la·ta
tin opener abrelatas ⓜ a·bre·la·tas
tiny pequeñito/a ⓜ/ⓕ pe·ke·nyee·to/a
tip propina ⓕ pro·pee·na
tired cansado/a ⓜ/ⓕ kan·sa·do/a
tissues pañuelos ⓜ pl de papel pa·nywe·los de pa·pel
toast tostada ⓕ tos·ta·da
toaster tostadora ⓕ tos·ta·do·ra
tobacco tabaco ⓜ ta·ba·ko
tobacconist estanquero ⓜ s·tan·ke·ro
tobogganing ir en tobogán eer en to·bo·gan
today hoy oy
toe dedo ⓜ del pie de·do del pye
tofu tofú ⓜ to·foo
together juntos/as ⓜ/ⓕ khoon·tos/as
toilet servicio ⓜ ser·vee·thyo
toilet paper papel ⓜ higiénico pa·pel e·khye·nee·ko

tomato tomate ⓜ to·ma·te
tomato sauce salsa ⓕ de tomate sal·sa de to·ma·te
tomorrow mañana ma·nya·na
tomorrow afternoon mañana por la tarde ma·nya·na por la tar·de
tomorrow evening mañana por la noche ma·nya·na por la no·che
tomorrow morning mañana por la mañana ma·nya·na por la ma·nya·na
tone tono ⓜ to·no
tonight esta noche es·ta no·che
too (expensive) demasiado (caro/a) ⓜ/ⓕ de·ma·sya·do (ka·ro/a)
tooth diente ⓜ dyen·te
tooth (back) muela ⓕ mwe·la
toothache dolor ⓜ de muelas do·lor de mwe·las
toothbrush cepillo ⓜ de dientes the·pee·lyo de dyen·tes
toothpaste pasta ⓕ dentífrica pas·ta den·tee·free·ka
toothpick palillo ⓜ pa·lee·lyo
torch linterna ⓕ leen·ter·na
touch tocar to·kar
tour excursión ⓕ eks·koor·syon
tourist turista ⓜ&ⓕ too·rees·ta
tourist (slang) guiri ⓜ gee·ree
tourist office oficina ⓕ de turismo o·fee·thee·na de too·rees·mo
towards hacia a·thya
towel toalla ⓕ to·a·lya
tower torre ⓕ to·re
toxic waste residuos ⓜ pl tóxicos re·see·dwos tok·see·kos
toyshop juguetería ⓕ khoo·ge·te·ree·a
track (car racing) autódromo ⓜ ow·to·dro·mo
track (footprints) rastro ⓜ ras·tro
trade comercio ⓜ ko·mer·thyo
traffic tráfico ⓜ tra·fee·ko
traffic lights semáforos ⓜ pl se·ma·fo·ros
trail camino ⓜ ka·mee·no
train tren ⓜ tren
train station estación ⓕ de tren es·ta·thyon de tren

U

tram tranvía ⓜ tran·vee·a
transit lounge sala ⓕ de tránsito sa·la de tran·see·to
translate traducir tra·doo·theer
transport medios ⓜ pl de transporte me·dyos de trans·por·te
travel viajar vya·khar
travel agency agencia ⓕ de viajes a·khen·thya de vya·khes
travel books libros ⓜ pl de viajes lee·bros de vya·khes
travel sickness mareo ⓜ ma·re·o
travellers cheque cheque ⓜ de viajero che·ke de vya·khe·ro
tree árbol ⓜ ar·bol
trip viaje ⓜ vya·khe
trousers pantalones ⓜ pl pan·ta·lo·nes
truck camión ⓜ ka·myon
trust confianza ⓕ kon·fee·an·tha
trust confiar kon·fee·ar
try probar pro·bar
try (to do something) intentar (hacer algo) een·ten·tar (a·ther al·go)
T-shirt camiseta ⓕ ka·mee·se·ta
tube (tyre) cámara ⓕ de aire ka·ma·ra de ai·re
tuna atún ⓜ a·toon
tune melodía ⓕ me·lo·dee·a
turkey pavo ⓜ pa·vo
turn doblar do·blar
TV tele ⓕ te·le
TV series serie ⓕ se·rye
tweezers pinzas ⓕ pl peen·thas
twice dos veces dos ve·thes
twin beds dos camas ⓕ pl dos ka·mas
twins gemelos ⓜ pl khe·me·los
type tipo ⓜ tee·po
type escribir a máquina es·kree·beer a ma·kee·na
typical típico/a ⓜ/ⓕ tee·pee·ko/a
tyre neumático ⓜ ne·oo·ma·tee·ko

U

ultrasound ecografía ⓕ e·ko·gra·fee·a
umbrella (rain) paraguas ⓜ pa·ra·gwas

umbrella (sun) parasol ⓜ pa·ra·sol
umpire árbitro ⓜ ar·bee·tro
uncomfortable incómodo/a ⓜ/ⓕ een·ko·mo·do/a
underpants (men) calzoncillos ⓜ pl kal·thon·thee·lyos
underpants (women) bragas ⓕ pl bra·gas
understand comprender kom·pren·der
underwear ropa interior ⓕ ro·pa een·te·ryor
unemployed en el paro en el pa·ro
unfair injusto een·khoos·to
uniform uniforme ⓜ oo·nee·for·me
universe universo ⓜ oo·nee·ver·so
university universidad ⓕ oo·nee·ver·see·da
unleaded sin plomo seen plo·mo
unsafe inseguro/a ⓜ/ⓕ een·se·goo·ro/a
until (June) hasta (junio) as·ta (khoo·nyo)
unusual extraño/a ⓜ/ⓕ eks·tra·nyo/a
up arriba a·ree·ba
uphill cuesta arriba kwes·ta a·ree·ba
urgent urgente oor·khen·te
USA Estados ⓜ pl Unidos es·ta·dos oo·nee·dos
useful útil oo·teel

V

vacant vacante va·kan·te
vacation vacaciones ⓕ pl va·ka·thyo·nes
vaccination vacuna ⓕ va·koo·na
vagina vagina ⓕ va·khee·na
validate validar va·lee·dar
valley valle ⓜ va·lye
valuable valioso/a ⓜ/ⓕ va·lyo·so/a
value valor ⓜ va·lor
van caravana ⓕ ka·ra·va·na
veal ternera ⓕ ter·ne·ra
vegetable verdura ⓕ ver·doo·ra
vegetables verduras ⓕ pl ver·doo·ra

vegetarian vegetariano/a ⓜ/ⓕ ve·khe·ta·*rya*·no/a
vein vena ⓕ *ve*·na
venereal disease enfermedad ⓕ venérea en·fer·me·*da* ve·ne·*re*·a
venue local ⓜ lo·*kal*
very muy mooy
video tape cinta ⓕ de vídeo *theen*·ta de *vee*·de·o
view vista ⓕ *vees*·ta
village pueblo ⓜ *pwe*·blo
vine vid ⓕ veed
vinegar vinagre ⓜ vee·*na*·gre
vineyard viñedo ⓜ vee·*nye*·do
virus virus ⓜ *vee*·roos
visa visado ⓜ vee·*sa*·do
visit visitar vee·see·*tar*
vitamins vitaminas ⓕ pl vee·ta·*mee*·nas
vodka vodka ⓕ *vod*·ka
voice voz ⓕ voth
volume volumen ⓜ vo·*loo*·men
vote votar vo·*tar*

W

wage sueldo ⓜ *swel*·do
wait esperar es·pe·*rar*
waiter camarero/a ⓜ/ⓕ ka·ma·*re*·ro/a
waiting room sala ⓕ de espera *sa*·la de es·*pe*·ra
walk caminar ka·mee·*nar*
wall (inside) pared ⓕ pa·*re*
wallet cartera ⓕ kar·*te*·ra
want querer ke·*rer*
war guerra ⓕ *ge*·ra
wardrobe vestuario ⓜ ves·*twa*·ryo
warm templado/a ⓜ/ⓕ tem·*pla*·do/a
warn advertir ad·ver·*teer*
wash (oneself) lavarse la·*var*·se
wash (something) lavar la·*var*
wash cloth toallita ⓕ to·a·*lyee*·ta
washing machine lavadora ⓕ la·va·*do*·ra
watch reloj ⓜ de pulsera re·*lokh* de pol·*se*·ra
watch mirar mee·*rar*

water agua ⓕ *a*·gwa
— tap del grifo del *gree*·fo
— bottle cantimplora ⓕ kan·teem·*plo*·ra
waterfall cascada ⓕ kas·*ka*·da
watermelon sandía san·*dee*·a
waterproof impermeable eem·per·me·*a*·ble
waterskiing esquí ⓜ acuático es·*kee* a·*kwa*·tee·ko
wave ola ⓕ *o*·la
way camino ⓜ ka·*mee*·no
we nosotros/nosotras ⓜ/ⓕ no·*so*·tros/no·*so*·tras
weak débil ⓜ&ⓕ *de*·beel
wealthy rico/a ⓜ/ⓕ *ree*·ko/a
wear llevar lye·*var*
weather tiempo ⓜ *tyem*·po
wedding boda ⓕ *bo*·da
wedding cake tarta ⓕ nupcial *tar*·ta noop·*thyal*
wedding present regalo ⓜ de bodas re·*ga*·lo de *bo*·das
weekend fin de semana ⓜ feen de se·*ma*·na
weigh pesar pe·*sar*
weight peso ⓜ *pe*·so
weights pesas ⓕ pl *pe*·sas
welcome bienvenida ⓕ byen·ve·*nee*·da
welcome dar la bienvenida dar la byen·ve·*nee*·da
welfare bienestar ⓜ byen·es·*tar*
well bien byen
well pozo ⓜ *po*·tho
west oeste ⓜ o·es·te
wet mojado/a ⓜ/ⓕ mo·*kha*·do/a
what lo que lo ke
wheel rueda ⓕ *rwe*·da
wheelchair silla ⓕ de ruedas *see*·lya de *rwe*·das
when cuando *kwan*·do
where donde *don*·de
whiskey güisqui ⓜ *gwees*·kee
white blanco/a ⓜ/ⓕ *blan*·ko/a
white-water rafting rafting ⓜ *rahf*·teen

Y

who quien kyen
why por qué por ke
wide ancho/a ⓜ/ⓕ an·cho/a
wife esposa ⓕ es·po·sa
win ganar ga·nar
wind viento ⓜ vyen·to
window ventana ⓕ ven·ta·na
window-shopping mirar los escaparates mee·rar los es·ka·pa·ra·tes
windscreen parabrisas ⓜ pa·ra·bree·sas
windsurfing hacer windsurf a·ther ween·soorf
wine vino ⓜ vee·no
wineglass copa ⓕ de vino ko·pa de vee·no
winery bodega ⓕ bo·de·ga
wings alas ⓕ pl a·las
winner ganador/ganadora ⓜ/ⓕ ga·na·dor/ga·na·do·ra
winter invierno ⓜ een·vyer·no
wire alambre ⓜ a·lam·bre
wish desear de·se·ar
with con kon
within (an hour) dentro de (una hora) den·tro de (oo·na o·ra)
without sin seen
woman mujer ⓕ moo·kher
wonderful maravilloso/a ⓜ/ⓕ ma·ra·vee·lyo·so/a
wood madera ⓕ ma·de·ra
wool lana ⓕ la·na
word palabra ⓕ pa·la·bra
work trabajo ⓜ tra·ba·kho
work trabajar tra·ba·khar
work experience experiencia ⓕ laboral eks·pe·ryen·thya la·bo·ral
work permit permiso ⓜ de trabajo

per·mee·so de tra·ba·kho
workout entreno ⓜ en·tre·no
workshop taller ⓜ ta·lyer
world mundo ⓜ moon·do
World Cup Copa ⓕ Mundial ko·pa moon·dyal
worms lombrices ⓕ pl lom·bree·thes
worried preocupado/a ⓜ/ⓕ pre·o·koo·pa·do/a
worship adoración ⓕ a·do·ra·thyon
wrist muñeca ⓕ moo·nye·ka
write escribir es·kree·beer
writer escritor/escritora ⓜ/ⓕ es·kree·tor/es·kree·to·ra
wrong equivocado/a ⓜ/ⓕ e·kee·vo·ka·do/a

Y

yellow amarillo/a ⓜ/ⓕ a·ma·ree·lyo/
yes sí see
(not) yet todavía (no) to·da·vee·a (no
yesterday ayer a·yer
yoga yoga ⓜ yo·ga
yogurt yogur ⓜ yo·goor
you inf sg tú too
you ⓜ/ⓕ inf pl vosotros/as vo·so·tros/as
you pol pl Ustedes oo·ste·des
you pol sg Usted oo·ste
young joven kho·ven
your pol sg su soo
your inf sg tu too
youth hostel albergue ⓜ juvenil al·ber·ge khoo·ve·neel

Z

zodiac zodíaco ⓜ tho·dee·a·ko
zoo zoológico ⓜ zo·o·lo·khee·ko

Dictionary
SPANISH *to* ENGLISH
español–inglés

A

Nouns in the dictionary have their gender indicated by ⓜ or ⓕ. If it's a plural noun, you'll also see pl. Where a word that could be either a noun or a verb has no gender indicated, it's a verb.

A

ⱥajo a·*ba*·kho below
ⱥanico ⓜ a·ba·*nee*·ko fan (hand held)
ⱥarrotado a·ba·ro·*ta*·do crowded
ⱥeja ⓕ a·*be*·kha bee
ⱥierto/a ⓜ/ⓕ a·*byer*·to/a open
ⱥogado/a ⓜ/ⓕ a·bo·*ga*·do/a lawyer
ⱥorto ⓜ a·*bor*·to abortion
ⱥrazo ⓜ a·*bra*·tho hug
ⱥrebotellas ⓜ a·bre·bo·*te*·lyas bottle opener
ⱥrelatas ⓜ a·bre·*la*·tas can opener • tin opener
ⱥrigo ⓜ a·*bree*·go overcoat
ⱥrir a·*breer* open
ⱥuela ⓕ a·*bwe*·la grandmother
ⱥuelo ⓜ a·*bwe*·lo grandfather
ⱥurrido/a ⓜ/ⓕ a·boo·*ree*·do/a bored • boring
ⱥabar a·ka·*bar* end
ⱥampar a·kam·*par* camp
ⱥantilado ⓜ a·kan·tee·*la*·do cliff
ⱥccidente ⓜ ak·thee·*den*·te accident
ⱥeite ⓜ a·*they*·te oil
ⱥeptar a·thep·*tar* accept
ⱥera ⓕ a·*the*·ra footpath

acondicionador ⓜ
a·kon·dee·thyo·na·*dor* conditioner
acoso ⓜ a·*ko*·so harassment
activista ⓜ&ⓕ ak·tee·*vees*·ta activist
actuación ⓕ ak·twa·*thyon*
performance
acupuntura ⓕ a·koo·poon·*too*·ra
acupuncture
adaptador ⓜ a·dap·ta·*dor* adaptor
adentro a·*den*·tro indoors
adivinar a·dee·vee·*nar* guess
administración ⓕ
ad·mee·nees·tra·*thyon* administration
admitir ad·mee·*teer* admit
adoración ⓕ a·do·ra·*thyon* worship
aduana ⓕ a·*dwa*·na customs
adulto/a ⓜ/ⓕ a·*dool*·to/a adult
aeróbic ⓜ ai·ro·*beek* aerobics
aerolínea ⓕ ai·ro·*lee*·nya airline
aeropuerto ⓜ ai·ro·*pwer*·to airport
afeitadora ⓕ a·fey·ta·*do*·ra razor
afeitarse a·fey·*tar*·se shave
afortunado/a ⓜ/ⓕ a·for·too·na·do/a
lucky
África ⓕ a·*free*·ka Africa
agencia ⓕ **de viajes** a·*khen*·thya de
vya·khes travel agency
agenda ⓕ a·*khen*·da diary

agente ⓜ inmobiliario a·*khen*·te een·mo·bee·*lya*·ryo real estate agent
agresivo/a ⓜ/ⓕ a·gre·*see*·vo/a aggressive
agricultor(a) ⓜ/ⓕ a·gree·kool·*tor*/ a·gree·kool·*to*·ra farmer
agricultura ⓕ a·gree·kool·*too*·ra agriculture
agua ⓕ *a*·gwa water
— caliente ka·*lyen*·te hot water
— mineral mee·ne·*ral* mineral water
aguacate ⓜ a·gwa·*ka*·te avocado
aguja ⓕ a·*goo*·kha needle (sewing)
ahora a·*o*·ra now
ahorrar a·o·*rar* save (money)
aire ⓜ *ai*·re air
— acondicionado
a·kon·dee·thyo·*na*·do air-conditioning
ajedrez ⓜ a·khe·*dreth* chess
al lado de al *la*·do de next to
alambre ⓜ a·*lam*·bre wire
alba ⓕ *al*·ba dawn
albaricoque ⓜ al·ba·ree·*ko*·ke apricot
albergue ⓜ juvenil al·*ber*·ge khoo·ve·*neel* youth hostel
alcachofa ⓕ al·ka·*cho*·fa artichoke
alcohol ⓜ al·*kol* alcohol
Alemania ⓕ a·le·*ma*·nya Germany
alérgia ⓕ a·*ler*·khya allergy
alérgia ⓕ al polen a·*ler*·khya al *po*·len hay fever
alfarería ⓕ al·fa·re·*ree*·a pottery
alfombra ⓕ al·*fom*·bra rug
algo *al*·go something
algodón ⓜ al·go·*don* cotton
alguien al·*gyen* someone
algún al·*goon* some
alguno/a ⓜ/ⓕ al·*goo*·no/a any
almendras ⓕ pl al·*men*·dras almonds
almohada ⓕ al·*mwa*·da pillow
almuerzo ⓜ al·*mwer*·tho lunch
alojamiento ⓜ a·lo·kha·*myen*·to accommodation
alojarse a·lo·*khar*·se stay (somewhere)

alpinismo ⓜ al·pee·*nees*·mo mountaineering
alquilar al·kee·*lar* hire • rent
alquiler ⓜ al·kee·*ler* rent
— de coche de *ko*·che car hire
altar ⓜ al·*tar* altar
alto/a ⓜ/ⓕ *al*·to/a high • tall
altura ⓕ al·*too*·ra altitude
ama ⓕ de casa a·ma de *ka*·sa homemaker
amable a·*ma*·ble kind
amanecer ⓜ a·ma·ne·*ther* sunrise
amante ⓜ&ⓕ a·*man*·te lover
amarillo/a ⓜ/ⓕ a·ma·ree·*lyo*/a yellow
amigo/a ⓜ/ⓕ a·*mee*·go/a friend
ampolla ⓕ am·*po*·lya blister
anacardo ⓜ a·na·*kar*·do cashew nut
analgésicos ⓜ pl a·nal·*khe*·see·kos painkillers
análisis de sangre ⓜ a·*na*·lee·sees de *san*·gre blood test
anarquista ⓜ/ⓕ a·nar·*kees*·ta anarchist
ancho/a ⓜ/ⓕ *an*·cho/a wide
andar an·*dar* walk
animal ⓜ a·nee·*mal* animal
Año ⓜ Nuevo a·nyo *nwe*·vo New Year
antes *an*·tes before
antibióticos ⓜ pl an·tee·*byo*·tee·kos antibiotics
anticonceptivos ⓜ pl an·tee·kon·thep·*tee*·vos contraceptives
antigüedad ⓕ an·tee·gwe·*da* antiqu
antiguo/a ⓜ/ⓕ an·*tee*·gwo/a ancie
antiséptico ⓜ an·tee·*sep*·tee·ko antiseptic
antología ⓕ an·to·lo·*khee*·a anthology
anuncio ⓜ a·*noon*·thyo advertisement
aparcamiento ⓜ a·par·ka·*myen*·to carpark
apellido ⓜ a·pe·*lyee*·do surname

apéndice ⓜ a·*pen*·dee·the the appendix
apodo ⓜ a·*po*·do nickname
aprender a·*pren*·der learn
apretado/a ⓜ/ⓕ a·pre·*ta*·do/a tight
apuesta ⓕ a·*pwes*·ta bet
apuntar a·poon·*tar* point
aquí a·*kee* here
araña ⓕ a·*ra*·nya spider
árbitro ⓜ *ar*·bee·tro referee
árbol ⓜ *ar*·bol tree
arena ⓕ a·*re*·na sand
armario ⓜ ar·*ma*·ryo cupboard
arqueológico/a ⓜ/ⓕ ·ar·ke·o·lo·*khee*·ko/a archaeological
arquitecto/a ⓜ/ⓕ ar·kee·*tek*·to/a architect
arquitectura ⓕ ar·kee·tek·*too*·ra architecture
arriba a·*ree*·ba above • up
arroyo ⓜ a·*ro*·yo stream
arroz ⓜ a·*roth* rice
arte ⓜ *ar*·te art
• **gráfico** *gra*·fee·ko graphic art
artes pl **marciales** *ar*·tes mar·*thya*·les martial arts
artesanía ⓕ ar·te·sa·*nee*·a crafts
artista ⓜ&ⓕ ar·*tees*·ta artist
ascensor ⓜ as·*then*·sor elevator
Asia ⓕ a·*sya* Asia
asiento ⓜ a·*syen*·to seat
• **de seguridad para bebés** de ·e·goo·ree·*da* pa·ra be·*bes* child seat
asma ⓜ *as*·ma asthma
aspirina ⓕ as·pee·*ree*·na aspirin
atascado/a ⓜ/ⓕ a·tas·*ka*·do/a locked
atletismo ⓜ at·le·*tees*·mo athletics
atmósfera ⓕ at·*mos*·fe·ra atmosphere
atún ⓜ a·*toon* tuna
audífono ⓜ ow·*dee*·fo·no hearing aid
Australia ⓕ ow·*stra*·lya Australia
autobús ⓜ ow·to·*boos* bus
autocar ⓜ ow·to·*kar* bus (intercity)
autódromo ⓜ ow·*to*·dro·mo track (car racing)

autoservicio ⓜ ow·to·ser·*vee*·thyo self-service
autovia ⓕ ow·to·*vee*·a motorway
avenida ⓕ a·ve·*nee*·da avenue
avergonzado/a ⓜ/ⓕ a·ver·gon·*tha*·do/a embarrassed
avión ⓜ a·*vyon* plane
ayer a·*yer* yesterday
ayudar a·yoo·*dar* help
azúcar ⓜ a·*thoo*·kar sugar
azul a·*thool* blue

B

bailar bai·*lar* dance
bajo/a ⓜ/ⓕ *ba*·kho/a low • short (height)
balcón ⓜ bal·*kon* balcony
ballet ⓜ ba·*le* ballet
baloncesto ⓜ ba·lon·*thes*·to basketball
bálsamo ⓜ **de aftershave** *bal*·sa·mo de af·ter·*sha*·eev aftershave
bálsamo ⓜ **de labios** *bal*·sa·mo de *la*·byos lip balm
bañador ⓜ ba·nya·*dor* bathing suit
banco ⓜ *ban*·ko bank
bandera ⓕ ban·*de*·ra flag
bañera ⓕ ba·*nye*·ra bath
baño ⓜ *ba*·nyo bathroom
bar ⓜ bar bar
barato/a ⓜ/ⓕ ba·*ra*·to/a cheap
barco ⓜ *bar*·ko boat
barrio ⓜ *ba*·ryo suburb
basura ⓕ ba·*soo*·ra rubbish
batería ⓕ ba·te·*ree*·a battery (car) • drums
bebé ⓜ be·*be* baby
béisbol ⓜ *beys*·bol baseball
beneficio ⓜ be·ne·*fee*·thyo profit
berenjenas ⓕ pl be·ren·*khe*·nas aubergine • eggplant
besar be·*sar* kiss
beso ⓜ *be*·so kiss
biblia ⓕ *bee*·blya bible
biblioteca ⓕ bee·blyo·*te*·ka library

C

bicho ⓜ *bee*·cho bug

bici ⓕ *bee*·thee bike

bicicleta ⓕ bee·thee·*kle*·ta bicycle

— de carreras de ka·*re*·ras racing bike

— de montaña de mon·*ta*·nya mountain bike

bien byen well

bienestar ⓜ byen·es·*tar* welfare

bienvenida ⓕ byen·ve·*nee*·da welcome

billete ⓜ bee·*lye*·te ticket

— de ida y vuelta de *ee*·da ee vwel·ta return ticket

— de lista de espera de *lees*·ta de es·*pe*·ra standby ticket

billetes ⓜ pl **de banco** bee·*lye*·tes de *ban*·ko banknotes

biografía ⓕ bee·o·gra·*fee*·a biography

bistec ⓜ bees·*tek* steak (beef)

blanco y negro *blan*·ko ee *ne*·gro B&W (film)

blanco/a ⓜ/ⓕ *blan*·ko/a white

boca ⓕ *bo*·ka mouth

bocado ⓜ bo·*ka*·do bite (food)

boda ⓕ *bo*·da wedding

bodega ⓕ bo·*de*·ga winery • liquor store

bol ⓜ bol bowl

bolas ⓕ pl **de algodón** *bo*·las de al·go·*don* cotton balls

bolígrafo ⓜ bo·*lee*·gra·fo pen

bollos ⓜ pl *bo*·lyos rolls (bread)

bolo ⓜ *bo*·lo gig

bolsillo ⓜ bol·*see*·lyo pocket

bolso ⓜ *bol*·so bag • handbag

bomba ⓕ *bom*·ba bomb • pump

bombilla ⓕ bom·*bee*·lya light bulb

bondadoso/a ⓜ/ⓕ bon·da·*do*·so/a caring

bonito/a ⓜ/ⓕ bo·*nee*·to/a pretty

bordo ⓜ *bor*·do edge

a bordo a *bor*·do aboard

borracho/a ⓜ/ⓕ bo·*ra*·cho/a drunk

bosque ⓜ *bos*·ke forest

botas ⓕ pl *bo*·tas boots

— de montaña de mon·*ta*·nya hiking boots

botella ⓕ bo·*te*·lya bottle

botones ⓜ pl bo·*to*·nes buttons

boxeo ⓜ bo·*kse*·o boxing

bragas ⓕ pl *bra*·gas underpants (women)

brazo ⓜ *bra*·tho arm

broma ⓕ *bro*·ma joke

bronceador ⓜ bron·the·a·*dor* tanning lotion

bronquitis ⓜ bron·*kee*·tees bronchitis

brotes ⓜ pl **de soja** *bro*·tes de so·*kh* bean sprouts

brújula ⓕ *broo*·khoo·la compass

brumoso broo·*mo*·so foggy

buceo ⓜ boo·*the*·o snorkelling

budista ⓜ&ⓕ boo·*dees*·ta Buddhist

bueno/a ⓜ/ⓕ *bwe*·no/a good

bufanda ⓕ boo·*fan*·da scarf

buffet ⓜ boo·*fe* buffet

bulto ⓜ *bool*·to lump

burlarse de boor·*lar*·se de make fun of

burro ⓜ *boo*·ro donkey

buscar boos·*kar* look for

buzón ⓜ boo·*thon* mailbox

C

caballo ⓜ ka·*ba*·lyo horse

cabeza ⓕ ka·*be*·tha head

cabina ⓕ **telefónica** ka·*bee*·na te·le·*fo*·nee·ka phone box

cable ⓜ *ka*·ble cable

cables ⓜ pl **de arranque** ka·bles de a·*ran*·ke jumper leads

cabra ⓕ *ka*·bra goat

cacahuetes ⓜ pl ka·ka·*we*·tes peanuts

cacao ⓜ ka·*kow* cocoa

cachorro ⓜ ka·*cho*·ro puppy

cada *ka*·da each

cadena ⓕ **de bici** ka·*de*·na de *bee*·thee bike chain

café ⓜ ka·*fe* coffee • cafe

caída ⓕ ka·*ee*·da fall

aja ① *ka*·kha box • cashier
· fuerte *fwer*·te safe
· registradora re·khees·tra·*do*·ra
ash register
ajero ⑩ **automático** ka·*khe*·ro
w·to·ma·tee·ko automatic teller
achine
alabacín ⑩ ka·la·ba·*theen* zucchini •
ourgette
alabaza ① ka·la·*ba*·tha pumpkin
alcetines ⑩ pl kal·the·*tee*·nes socks
alculadora ① kal·koo·la·*do*·ra
alculator
aldo ⑩ *kal*·do stock
alefacción ① **central** ka·le·fak·*thyon*
en·*tral* central heating
alendario ⑩ ka·len·*da*·ryo calendar
alidad ① ka·lee·*da* quality
aliente ka·*lyen*·te hot
alle ① *ka*·lye street
alor ⑩ ka·*lor* heat
alzoncillos ⑩ pl kal·thon·*thee*·lyos
nderpants (men)
alzones ⑩ pl kal·*tho*·nes boxer
horts
ama ① *ka*·ma bed
· de matrimonio de ma·tree·*mo*·nyo
ouble bed
ámara ① **(fotográfica)** *ka*·ma·ra
o·to·*gra*·fee·ka) camera
ámara ① **de aire** *ka*·ma·ra de *ai*·re
ube (tyre)
amarero/a ⑩/① ka·ma·*re*·ro/a
aiter
ambiar kam·*byar* change • exchange
money)
ambio *kam*·byo ⑩ loose change
· de dinero de dee·*ne*·ro currency
xchange
aminar ka·mee·*nar* walk
amino ⑩ ka·*mee*·no trail • way
aminos ⑩ pl **rurales** ka·*mee*·nos
oo·*ra*·les hiking routes
amión ⑩ ka·*myon* truck
amisa ① ka·*mee*·sa shirt

camiseta ① ka·mee·*se*·ta singlet •
T-shirt
cámping ⑩ *kam*·peen campsite
campo ⑩ *kam*·po countryside • field
Canadá ① ka·na·*da* Canada
canasta ① ka·*nas*·ta basket
cancelar kan·the·*lar* cancel
cáncer ⑩ *kan*·ther cancer
canción ① kan·*thyon* song
candado ⑩ kan·*da*·do padlock
cangrejo ⑩ kan·*gre*·kho crab
canguro ⑩ kan·*goo*·ro babysitter
cansado/a ⑩/① kan·*sa*·do/a tired
cantalupo ⑩ kan·ta·*loo*·po
cantaloupe
cantante ⑩&① kan·*tan*·te singer
cantar kan·*tar* sing
cantimplora ① kan·teem·*plo*·ra water
bottle
capa ① **de ozono** *ka*·pa de o·*tho*·no
ozone layer
capilla ① ka·*pee*·lya shrine
capote ⑩ ka·po·te cloak
cara ① *ka*·ra face
caracol ⑩ ka·ra·*kol* snail
caramelos ⑩ pl ka·ra·*me*·los lollies
caravana ① ka·ra·*va*·na caravan •
van • traffic jam
cárcel ① *kar*·thel prison
cardenal ⑩ kar·de·*nal* bruise
carne ① *kar*·ne meat
— de vaca de *va*·ka beef
— molida mo·*lee*·da mince meat
carnet ⑩ kar·*ne* licence
— de identidad de ee·den·tee·*da*
identification card
— de conducir de kon·doo·*theer*
drivers licence
carnicería ① kar·nee·the·*ree*·a
butcher's shop
caro/a ⑩/① *ka*·ro/a expensive
carpintero ⑩ kar·peen·*te*·ro
carpenter
carrera ① ka·*re*·ra race (sport)
carta ① *kar*·ta letter

C

cartas ① pl *kar*·tas cards
cartón ⓜ kar·*ton* carton • cardboard
casa ① *ka*·sa house
(en) casa (en) *ka*·sa (at) home
casarse ka·*sar*·se marry
cascada ① kas·*ka*·da waterfall
casco ⓜ *kas*·ko helmet
casete ⓜ ka·se·te cassette
casi *ka*·see almost
casino ⓜ ka·*see*·no casino
castigar kas·tee·*gar* punish
castillo ⓜ kas·*tee*·lyo castle
catedral ① ka·te·*dral* cathedral
católico/a ⓜ/① ka·to·lee·ko/a Catholic
caza ① *ka*·tha hunting
cazuela ① ka·*thwe*·la pot (kitchen)
cebolla ① the·*bo*·lya onion
celebración ① the·le·bra·*thyon* celebration
celebrar the·le·*brar* celebrate (an event)
celoso/a ⓜ/① the·*lo*·so/a jealous
cementerio ⓜ the·men·*te*·ryo cemetery
cena ① *the*·na dinner
cenicero ⓜ the·nee·*the*·ro ashtray
centavo ⓜ then·*ta*·vo cent
centímetro ⓜ then·*tee*·me·tro centimetre
central ① **telefónica** then·*tral* te·le·fo·nee·ka telephone centre
centro ⓜ *then*·tro centre
— comercial ko·mer·*thyal* shopping centre
— de la ciudad de la thyu·*da* city centre
cepillo ⓜ the·*pee*·lyo hairbrush
— de dientes de *dyen*·tes toothbrush
cerámica ① the·*ra*·mee·ka ceramic
cerca ① *ther*·ka fence
cerca *ther*·ka near • nearby
cerdo ⓜ *ther*·do pork • pig
cereales ⓜ pl the·re·*a*·les cereal
cerillas ① pl las the·*ree*·lyas matches
cerrado/a ⓜ/① the·*ra*·do/a closed
— con llave kon *lya*·ve locked

cerradura ① the·ra·*doo*·ra lock (padlock)
cerrar the·*rar* close • lock • shut
certificado ⓜ ther·tee·fee·*ka*·do certificate
cerveza ① ther·*ve*·tha beer
— rubia *roo*·bya lager
chaleco ⓜ **salvavidas** cha·*le*·ko sal·va·*vee*·das lifejacket
champán ⓜ cham·*pan* Champagne
champiñón ⓜ cham·pee·*nyon* mushrooms
champú ⓜ cham·*poo* shampoo
chaqueta ① cha·*ke*·ta jacket
cheque ⓜ *che*·ke check (bank)
cheques ⓜ pl **de viajero** *che*·kes de vya·*khe*·ro travellers cheque
chica ① *chee*·ka girl
chicle ⓜ *chee*·kle chewing gum
chico ⓜ *chee*·ko boy
chocolate ⓜ cho·ko·*la*·te chocolate
choque ⓜ *cho*·ke crash
chorizo ⓜ cho·*ree*·tho salami (Spanish sausage)
chupete ⓜ choo·*pe*·te dummy • pacifier
cibercafé ⓜ thee·ber·ka·*fe* internet cafe
ciclismo ⓜ thee·*klees*·mo cycling
ciclista ⓜ&① thee·*klees*·ta cyclist
ciego/a ⓜ/① *thye*·go/a blind
cielo ⓜ *thye*·lo heaven • sky
ciencias ① pl *thyen*·thyas science
científico/a ⓜ/① thyen·*tee*·fee·ko/a scientist
cigarrillo ⓜ thee·ga·*ree*·lyo cigarette
cigarro ⓜ thee·*ga*·ro cigarette
cine ⓜ *thee*·ne cinema
cinta ① **de vídeo** *theen*·ta de *vee*·de·o video tape
cinturón ⓜ **de seguridad** theen·too·*ron* de se·goo·ree·*da* seatbelt
circuito ⓜ **de carreras** theer·*kwee*·to de ka·*re*·ras racetrack (cars)
ciruela ① thee·*rwe*·la plum
— pasa *pa*·sa prune

…stitis ① thees·tee·tees cystitis

…ta ① *thee*·ta appointment

…tarse thee·*tar*·se date

…tología ① thee·to·lo·*khee*·a pap

…near

…udad ① thyu·*da* city

…udadanía ① thyu·da·da·*nee*·a

…tizenship

…ase ① preferente *kla*·se

…re·fe·*ren*·te business class

…ase ① turística *kla*·se

…o·*rees*·tee·ka economy class

…ásico/a ⓜ/① *kla*·see·ko/a classical

…ienta/e ⓜ/① klee·*en*·ta/e client

…ínica ① *klee*·nee·ka private hospital

…brar (un cheque) ko·*brar* (oon

…ne·ke) cash (a cheque)

…oca ① *ko*·ka cocaine

…ocaína ① ko·ka·ee·*na* cocaine

…oche ⓜ *ko*·che car

… cama *ka*·ma sleeping car

…ocina ① ko·*thee*·na kitchen • stove

…ocinar ko·thee·*nar* cook

…ocinero ⓜ ko·thee·*ne*·ro chef • cook

…oco ⓜ *ko*·ko coconut

…odeína ① ko·de·ee·*na* codeine

…ódigo ⓜ postal *ko*·dee·go pos·*tal*

…ost code

…ojonudo/a ⓜ/① ko·kho·*noo*·do/a

…ntastic

…ol ⓜ kol cabbage

…ola ① *ko*·la queue

…olchón ⓜ kol·*chon* mattress

…olega ⓜ&① ko·*le*·ga colleague • mate

…oles ⓜ pl **de Bruselas** *ko*·les de

…roo·se·las brussels sprouts

…oliflor ⓜ ko·lee·*flor* cauliflower

…olina ① ko·lee·*na* hill

…ollar ⓜ ko·*lyar* necklace

…olor ⓜ ko·*lor* colour

…omedia ① ko·*me*·dya comedy

…omenzar ko·men·*thar* begin • start

…omer ko·*mer* eat

…omerciante ⓜ&① ko·mer·*thyan*·te

…usiness person

comercio ⓜ ko·*mer*·thyo trade

comezón ① ko·me·*thon* itch

comida ① ko·*mee*·da food

— de bebé de be·*be* baby food

— en el campo en el *kam*·po picnic

comisaría ① ko·mee·sa·*ree*·a police

station

cómo *ko*·mo how

cómodo/a ⓜ/① ko·mo·do/a

comfortable

cómpact ⓜ *kom*·pak CD

compañero/a ⓜ/① kom·pa·*nye*·ro/a

companion

compañía ① kom·pa·*nyee*·a company

compartir kom·par·*teer* share (with)

comprar kom·*prar* buy

comprender kom·pren·*der*

understand

compresas ① pl kom·*pre*·sas

sanitary napkins

compromiso ⓜ kom·pro·*mee*·so

engagement

comunión ① ko·moo·*nyon*

communion

comunista ⓜ&① ko·moo·*nees*·ta

communist

con kon with

coñac ⓜ ko·*nyak* brandy

concentración ① kon·then·tra·*thyon*

rally

concierto ⓜ kon·*thyer*·to concert

condición ① cardíaca kon·dee·*thyon*

kar·*dee*·a·ka heart condition

condones ⓜ pl kon·do·nes condoms

conducir kon·doo·*theer* drive

conejo ⓜ ko·*ne*·kho rabbit

conexión ① ko·ne·*ksyon* connection

confesión ① kon·fe·*syon* confession

confianza ① kon·fee·*an*·tha trust

confiar kon·fee·*ar* trust

confirmar kon·feer·*mar* confirm

conocer ko·no·*ther* know (someone)

conocido/a ⓜ/① ko·no·*thee*·do/a

famous

consejo ⓜ kon·*se*·kho advice

conservador(a) ⓜ/ⓕ kon·ser·va·dor/ kon·ser·va·do·ra conservative

consigna ⓕ kon·seeg·na left luggage

— automática ow·to·ma·tee·ka luggage lockers

construir kons·troo·eer build

consulado ⓜ kon·soo·la·do consulate

contaminación ⓕ kon·ta·mee·na·thyon pollution

contar kon·tar count

contestador ⓜ **automático** kon·tes·ta·dor ow·to·ma·tee·ko answering machine

contrato ⓜ kon·tra·to contract

control ⓜ kon·trol checkpoint

convento ⓜ kon·ven·to convent

copa ⓕ ko·pa drink

— de vino de vee·no wineglass

Copa ⓕ **Mundial** ko·pa moon·dyal World Cup

copos de maíz ko·pos de ma·eeth corn flakes

corazón ⓜ ko·ra·thon heart

cordero ⓜ kor·de·ro lamb

cordillera ⓕ kor·dee·lye·ra mountain range

correcto/a ⓜ/ⓕ ko·rek·to/a right (correct)

correo ⓜ ko·re·o mail

— urgente oor·khen·te express mail

correos ko·re·os post office

correr ko·rer run

corrida ⓕ **de toros** ko·ree·da de to·ros bullfight

corriente ⓕ ko·ryen·te current (electricity)

corriente ko·ryen·te ordinary

corrupto/a ⓜ/ⓕ ko·roop·to/a corrupt

cortar kor·tar cut

cortauñas ⓜ pl kor·ta·oo·nyas nail clippers

corto/a ⓜ/ⓕ kor·to/a short (length)

cosecha ⓕ ko·se·cha crop

coser ko·ser sew

costa ⓕ kos·ta coast • seaside

costar kos·tar cost

crecer kre·ther grow

crema ⓕ kre·ma cream

— hidratante ee·dra·tan·te moisturising cream

— solar so·lar sunblock

críquet ⓜ kree·ket cricket

cristiano/a ⓜ/ⓕ krees·tya·no/a Christian

crítica ⓕ kree·tee·ka review

cruce ⓜ kroo·the intersection

crudo/a ⓜ/ⓕ kroo·do/a raw

cuaderno ⓜ kwa·der·no notebook • square

cualificaciones ⓕ pl kwa·lee·fee·ka·thyo·nes qualifications

cuando kwan·do when

cuánto kwan·to how much

cuarentena ⓕ kwa·ren·te·na quarantine

Cuaresma ⓕ kwa·res·ma Lent

cuarto ⓜ kwar·to quarter

cubiertos ⓜ pl koo·byer·tos cutlery

cubo ⓜ koo·bo bucket

cucaracha ⓕ koo·ka·ra·cha cockroach

cuchara ⓕ koo·cha·ra spoon

cucharita ⓕ koo·cha·ree·ta teaspoon

cuchillas ⓕ pl **de afeitar** koo·chee·lyas de a·fey·tar razor blade

cuchillo ⓜ koo·chee·lyo knife

cuenta ⓕ kwen·ta bill

— bancaria ban·ka·rya bank account

cuento ⓜ kwen·to story

cuerda ⓕ kwer·da rope • string

— para tender la ropa pa·ra ten·der la ro·pa clothes line

cuero ⓜ kwe·ro leather

cuerpo ⓜ kwer·po body

cuesta abajo kwes·ta a·ba·kho downhill

cuesta arriba kwes·ta a·ree·ba uphill

cuestionar kwes·tyo·nar question

cuevas ⓕ pl kwe·vas caves

...idar kwee·*dar* care for • mind (an ...ject)
...idar de kwee·*dar* de care (for ...meone)
...lo ⓜ *koo*·lo bum (of body)
...lpable kool·*pa*·ble guilty
...mbre ⓕ *koom*·bre peak
...mpleaños ⓜ koom·ple·*a*·nyos ...rthday
...rrículum ⓜ koo·*ree*·koo·loom ...sumé
...rry ⓜ *koo*·ree curry
...s cus ⓜ koos koos cous cous

D

...ados ⓜ pl *da*·dos dice (die)
...añar da·*nyar* hurt
...ar dar give
...de comer de ko·*mer* feed
...gracias *gra*·thyas thank
...la bienvenida la byen·ve·*nee*·da ...elcome
...una patada *oo*·na pa·*ta*·da kick
...arse cuenta de dar·se *kwen*·ta de ...alise
...e de from
...(cuatro) estrellas de (*kwa*·tro) ...s·*tre*·lyas (four-)star
...izquierdas de eeth·*kyer*·das ...ft-wing
...pena de *pe*·na terrible
...primera clase de pree·*me*·ra *kla*·se ...rst-class
...segunda mano de se·*goon*·da ...a·no second-hand
...vez en cuando de veth en *kwan*·do ...ometimes
...eber de·*ver* owe
...ébil de·*beel* weak
...ecidir de·thee·*deer* decide
...ecir de·*theer* say • tell
...edo ⓜ *de*·do finger
...del pie del pye toe
...efectuoso/a ⓜ/ⓕ de·fek·*two*·so/a ...ulty

deforestación ⓕ de·fo·res·ta·*thyon* deforestation
dejar de·*khar* leave • quit
delgado/a ⓜ/ⓕ del·*ga*·do/a thin
delirante de·lee·*ran*·te delirious
demasiado caro/a ⓜ/ⓕ de·ma·*sya*·do *ka*·ro/a too (expensive)
democracia ⓕ de·mo·*kra*·thya democracy
demora ⓕ de·*mo*·ra delay
dentista ⓜ&ⓕ den·*tees*·ta dentist
dentro de (una hora) *den*·tro de (*oo*·na *o*·ra) within (an hour)
deportes ⓜ pl de·*por*·tes sport
deportista ⓜ&ⓕ de·por·*tees*·ta sportsperson
depósito ⓜ de·po·*see*·to deposit
derecha ⓕ de·*re*·cha right (not left)
derechista de·re·*chees*·ta right-wing
derechos ⓜ **civiles** de·*re*·chos thee·*vee*·les civil rights
derechos ⓜ pl **humanos** de·*re*·chos oo·*ma*·nos human rights
desayuno ⓜ des·a·*yoo*·no breakfast
descansar des·kan·*sar* rest
descanso ⓜ des·*kan*·so intermission
descendiente ⓜ des·then·*dyen*·te descendant
descomponerse des·kom·po·*ner*·se decompose
descubrir des·koo·*breer* discover
descuento ⓜ des·*kwen*·to discount
desde (mayo) *des*·de (*ma*·yo) since (may)
desear de·se·*ar* wish
desierto ⓜ de·*syer*·to desert
desodorante ⓜ de·so·do·*ran*·te deodorant
despacio des·*pa*·thyo slowly
desperdicios ⓜ pl **nucleares** des·per·*dee*·thyos noo·kle·*a*·res nuclear waste
despertador ⓜ des·per·ta·*dor* alarm clock
después de des·*pwes* de after

D

E

destino ⓜ des·*tee*·no destination
destruir des·troo·*eer* destroy
detallado/a ⓜ/ⓕ de·ta·*lya*·do/a itemised
detalle ⓜ de·*ta*·lye detail
detener de·te·*ner* arrest
detrás de de·*tras* de behind
devocionario ⓜ de·vo·thyo·*na*·ryo prayer book
día ⓜ *dee*·a day
— festivo fes·*tee*·vo holiday
diabetes ⓕ dee·a·*be*·tes diabetes
diafragma ⓜ dee·a·*frag*·ma diaphragm
diapositiva ⓕ dya·po·see·*tee*·va slide
diariamente dya·rya·*men*·te daily
diarrea ⓕ dee·a·*re*·a diarrhoea
dieta ⓕ dee·*e*·ta diet
dibujar dee·boo·*khar* draw
diccionario ⓜ deek·thyo·*na*·ryo dictionary
diente (de ajo) *dyen*·te (de a·kho) clove (garlic)
dientes ⓜ pl *dyen*·tes teeth
diferencia ⓕ **de horas** dee·fe·*ren*·thya de o·ras time difference
diferente dee·fe·*ren*·te different
difícil dee·*fee*·theel difficult
dinero ⓜ dee·*ne*·ro money
— en efectivo en e·fek·*tee*·vo cash
Dios dyos god
dirección ⓕ dee·rek·*thyon* address
directo/a ⓜ/ⓕ dee·*rek*·to/a direct
director(a) ⓜ/ⓕ dee·rek·*tor*/dee·rek·*to*·ra director
disco ⓜ *dees*·ko disk
discoteca ⓕ dees·ko·*te*·ka disco
discriminación ⓕ dees·kree·mee·na·*thyon* discrimination
discutir dees·koo·*teer* argue
diseño ⓜ dee·*se*·nyo design
disparar dees·pa·*rar* shoot
DIU ⓜ de·ee·oo IUD
diversión ⓕ dee·ver·*syon* fun
divertirse dee·ver·*teer*·se enjoy (oneself)

doblar do·*blar* turn • bend
doble do·ble double
docena ⓕ do·*the*·na dozen
doctor(a) ⓜ/ⓕ dok·*tor*/dok·*to*·ra doctor
dólar ⓜ do·lar dollar
dolor ⓜ do·*lor* pain
— de cabeza de ka·*be*·tha headache
— de estómago de es·*to*·ma·go stomachache
— de muelas de *mwe*·las toothache
— menstrual mens·*trwal* period pai
dolorido/a ⓜ/ⓕ do·lo·*ree*·do/a sor
doloroso/a ⓜ/ⓕ do·lo·ro·so/a pain'
donde *don*·de where
dormir dor·*meer* sleep
dos ⓜ/ⓕ pl dos two
— camas *ka*·mas twin beds
— veces *ve*·thes twice
drama ⓜ *dra*·ma drama
droga ⓕ *dro*·ga drug • dope
drogadicción ⓕ dro·ga·deek·*thyon* drug addiction
drogas ⓕ pl *dro*·gas drugs
ducha ⓕ *doo*·cha shower
dueño/a ⓜ/ⓕ *dwe*·nyo/a owner
dulce *dool*·the sweet
dulces ⓜ pl *dool*·thes sweets
duro/a ⓜ/ⓕ *doo*·ro/a hard

E

eczema ⓕ ek·*the*·ma eczema
edad ⓕ e·*da* age
edificio ⓜ e·dee·*fee*·thyo building
editor(a) ⓜ/ⓕ e·dee·*tor*/e·dee·*to*·ra editor
educación ⓕ e·doo·ka·*thyon* educatio
egoísta e·go·*ees*·ta selfish
ejemplo ⓜ e·*khem*·plo example
ejército ⓜ e·*kher*·thee·to military
el ⓜ el the
él ⓜ el he
elecciones ⓕ pl e·lek·*thyo*·nes elections
electricidad ⓕ e·lek·tree·thee·*da* electricity

elegir e·le·*kheer* pick • choose

ella ① e·lya she

ellos/ellas ⓜ/① e·lyos/e·lyas they

embajada ① em·ba·*kha*·da embassy

embajador(a) ⓜ/① em·ba·kha·*dor*/ m·ba·kha·do·ra ambassador

embarazada em·ba·ra·*tha*·da regnant

embarcarse em·bar·*kar*·se board ship etc)

embrague ⓜ em·*bra*·ge clutch

emergencia ① e·mer·*khen*·thya mergency

emocional e·mo·thyo·*nal* emotional

empleado/a ⓜ/① em·ple·*a*·do/a mployee

empujar em·poo·*khar* push

en en on

– el extranjero el eks·tran·*khe*·ro broad

– el paro el *pa*·ro unemployed

encaje ⓜ en·*ka*·khe lace

encantador(a) ⓜ/① en·kan·ta·*dor*/ n·kan·ta·do·ra charming

encendedor ⓜ en·then·de·*dor* lighter

encontrar en·kon·*trar* find • meet

encurtidos ⓜ pl en·koor·*tee*·dos ickles

energía ① **nuclear** e·ner·*khee*·a oo·*kle*·ar nuclear energy

enfadado/a ⓜ/① en·fa·*da*·do/a ngry

enfermedad ① en·fer·me·*da* disease

– venérea ve·ne·*re*·a venereal disease

enfermero/a ⓜ/① en·fer·*me*·ro/a urse

enfermo/a ⓜ/① en·*fer*·mo/a sick

enfrente de en·*fren*·te de in front of

enorme e·*nor*·me huge

ensalada en·sa·*la*·da salad

enseñar en·se·*nyar* show • teach

entrar en·*trar* enter

entre *en*·tre among • between

entregar en·tre·*gar* deliver

entrenador(a) ⓜ/① en·tre·na·*dor*/ n·tre·na·do·ra coach

entreno ⓜ en·*tre*·no workout

entrevista ① en·tre·*vees*·ta interview

enviar en·vee·*ar* send • ship off

epilepsia ① e·pee·*lep*·sya epilepsy

equipaje ⓜ e·kee·*pa*·khe luggage

equipo ⓜ e·*kee*·po equipment • team

– de inmersión de een·mer·*syon* diving equipment

– de música ⓜ de moo·see·ka stereo

equitación ① e·kee·ta·*thyon* horse riding

equivocado/a ⓜ/① e·kee·vo·*ka*·do/a wrong

error ⓜ e·*ror* mistake

escalada ① es·ka·*la*·da rock climbing

escalera ① es·ka·*le*·ra stairway

escaleras ① pl **mecánicas** es·ka·*le*·ras me·*kan*·icas escalator

escarcha ① es·*kar*·cha frost

escarpado/a ⓜ/① es·kar·*pa*·do/a steep

escasez ① es·ka·*seth* shortage

escenario ⓜ es·the·*na*·ryo stage

Escocia ① e·*sko*·thya Scotland

escoger es·ko·*kher* choose

escribir es·kree·*beer* write

– a máquina a *ma*·kee·na type

escritor(a) ⓜ/① es·kree·*tor*/ es·kree·to·ra writer

escuchar es·koo·*char* listen

escuela ① es·*kwe*·la school

– de párvulos de *par*·voo·los kindergarten

escultura ① es·kool·*too*·ra sculpture

espacio ⓜ es·*pa*·thyo space

espalda ① es·*pal*·da back (body)

España ① es·*pa*·nya Spain

especial es·pe·*thyal* special

especialista ⓜ&① es·pe·thya·*lees*·ta specialist

especies ① pl **en peligro de extinción** es·pe·thyes en pe·*lee*·gro de eks·teen·*thyon* endangered species

espectáculo ⓜ es·pek·ta·koo·lo show

espejo ⓜ es·*pe*·kho mirror

esperar es·pe·*rar* wait

F

espinaca ⓕ es·pee·*na*·ka spinach
esposa ⓕ es·*po*·sa wife
espuma ⓕ **de afeitar** es·*poo*·ma de a·*fey*·tar shaving cream
espumoso/a ⓜ/ⓕ es·poo·*mo*·so/a sparkling • foamy
esquí ⓜ es·*kee* skiing
— acuático a·*kwa*·tee·ko waterskiing
esquiar es·kee·*ar* ski
esquina ⓕ es·*kee*·na corner
esta noche es·ta *no*·che tonight
éste/a ⓜ/ⓕ es·te/a this
estación ⓕ es·ta·*thyon* season • station
— de autobuses de ow·to·*boo*·ses bus station
— de metro de *me*·tro metro station
— de tren de tren railway station
estacionar es·ta·thyo·*nar* park (car)
estadio ⓜ es·*ta*·dyo stadium
estado ⓜ **civil** es·*ta*·do thee·*veel* marital status
estado ⓜ **del bienestar** es·*ta*·do del byen·es·*tar* social welfare • wellbeing
Estados ⓜ pl **Unidos** es·*ta*·dos oo·*nee*·dos USA
estafa ⓕ es·*ta*·fa rip-off
estanquero ⓜ es·tan·*ke*·ro tobacconist
estante ⓜ es·*tan*·te shelf
estar es·*tar* to be
— constipado/a ⓜ/ⓕ kons·tee·pa·do/a have a cold
— de acuerdo de a·*kwer*·do agree
estatua ⓕ es·*ta*·twa statue
este *es*·te east
esterilla ⓕ es·te·*ree*·lya mat
estilo ⓜ es·*tee*·lo style
estómago ⓜ es·*to*·ma·go stomach
estrellas ⓕ pl es·*tre*·lyas stars
estreñimiento ⓜ es·tre·nyee·*myen*·to constipation
estudiante ⓜ&ⓕ es·too·*dyan*·te student
estudio ⓜ es·*too*·dyo studio
estufa ⓕ es·*too*·fa heater

estúpido/a ⓜ/ⓕ es·*too*·pee·do/a stupid
etiqueta ⓕ **de equipaje** e·tee·*ke*·ta de e·kee·*pa*·khe luggage tag
euro ⓜ e·*oo*·ro euro
Europa ⓕ e·oo·*ro*·pa Europe
eutanasia ⓕ e·oo·ta·*na*·sya euthanasia
excelente eks·the·*len*·te excellent
excursión ⓕ eks·koor·*syon* tour
excursionismo ⓜ eks·koor·syo·*nees*·mo hiking
experiencia ⓕ eks·pe·*ryen*·thya experience
— laboral ⓕ la·bo·*ral* work experience
exponer eks·po·*ner* exhibit
exposición ⓕ eks·po·see·*thyon* exhibition
expreso eks·*pre*·so express
exterior ⓜ eks·te·*ryor* outside
extrañar eks·tra·*nyar* miss (feel sad)
extranjero/a ⓜ/ⓕ eks·tran·*khe*·ro/a foreign

F

fábrica ⓕ *fa*·bree·ka factory
fácil *fa*·theel easy
facturación ⓕ **de equipajes** fak·too·ra·*thyon* de e·kee·*pa*·khes check-in
falda ⓕ *fal*·da skirt
falta ⓕ *fal*·ta fault
familia ⓕ fa·*mee*·lya family
fantástico/a ⓜ/ⓕ fan·*tas*·tee·ko/a great
farmacia ⓕ far·*ma*·thya chemist (shop) • pharmacy
farmacéutico/a far·ma·thee·*oo*·tee·ko chemist (person)
faros ⓜ pl *fa*·ros headlights
fecha ⓕ *fe*·cha date (time)
— de nacimiento de na·thee·*myen*·to date of birth
feliz fe·*leeth* happy

G

erretería ⓕ fe·re·te·*ree*·a hardware store

estival ⓜ fes·tee·*val* festival

icción ⓕ feek·*thyon* fiction

ideos ⓜ pl fee·*de*·os noodles

iebre ⓕ *fye*·bre fever

- glandular glan·doo·*lar* glandular ever

esta ⓕ *fyes*·ta party

ilete ⓜ fee·*le*·te fillet

ilm ⓜ feelm film

in ⓜ feen end

- de semana de se·*ma*·na weekend

inal ⓜ fee·*nal* end

irma ⓕ *feer*·ma signature

irmar feer·*mar* sign

lor ⓕ flor flower

lorista ⓜ&ⓕ flo·*rees*·ta florist

olleto ⓜ fo·*lye*·to brochure

ooting ⓜ *foo*·teen jogging

orma ⓕ *for*·ma shape

otografía ⓕ fo·to·gra·*fee*·a photograph

otógrafo/a ⓜ/ⓕ fo·to·gra·fo/a photographer

otómetro ⓜ fo·to·me·tro light meter

rágil *fra*·kheel fragile

rambuesa ⓕ fram·*bwe*·sa raspberry

ranela ⓕ fra·*ne*·la flannel

ranqueo ⓜ fran·*ke*·o postage

reír fre·*eer* fry

renos ⓜ pl *fre*·nos brakes

rente a *fren*·te a opposite

resa ⓕ *fre*·sa strawberry

río/a ⓜ/ⓕ *free*·o/a cold

rontera ⓕ fron·*te*·ra border

ruta ⓕ *froo*·ta fruit

ruto ⓜ **seco** froo·to se·*ko* dried fruit

uego ⓜ *fwe*·go fire

uera de juego *fwe*·ra de *khwe*·go offside

uerte *fwer*·te strong

umar foo·*mar* smoke

unda ⓕ **de almohada** *foon*·da de al·*mwa*·da pillowcase

uneral ⓜ foo·ne·*ral* funeral

fútbol ⓜ *foot*·bol football • soccer

— australiano ow·stra·*lya*·no Australian Rules football

futuro ⓜ foo·*too*·ro future

G

gafas ⓕ pl ga·fas glasses

— de sol de sol sunglasses

— de submarinismo de soob·ma·ree·*nees*·mo goggles

galleta ⓕ ga·*lye*·ta biscuit • cookie

galletas ⓕ pl **saladas** ga·*lye*·tas sa·*la*·das biscuits • crackers

gambas ⓕ pl *gam*·bas prawns

ganador(a) ⓜ/ⓕ ga·na·*dor*/ga·na·*do*·ra winner

ganar ga·*nar* earn • win

garbanzos ⓜ pl gar·*ban*·thos chickpeas

garganta ⓕ gar·*gan*·ta throat

gasolina ⓕ ga·so·*lee*·na petrol

gasolinera ⓕ ga·so·lee·*ne*·ra service station

gatito/a ⓜ/ⓕ ga·*tee*·to/a kitten

gato/a ⓜ/ⓕ *ga*·to/a cat

gay gai gay

gemelos ⓜ pl khe·*me*·los twins

general khe·ne·*ral* general

gente ⓕ *khen*·te people

gimnasia ⓕ **rítmica** kheem·*na*·sya *reet*·mee·ka gymnastics

ginebra ⓕ khee·*ne*·bra gin

ginecólogo ⓜ khee·ne·*ko*·lo·go gynaecologist

gobierno ⓜ go·*byer*·no government

gol ⓜ gol goal

goma ⓕ *go*·ma condom • rubber

gordo/a ⓜ/ⓕ *gor*·do/a fat

grabación ⓕ gra·ba·*thyon* recording

gracioso/a ⓜ/ⓕ gra·*thyo*·so/a funny

gramo ⓜ *gra*·mo gram

grande *gran*·de big • large

grande almacene ⓜ *gran*·de al·ma·*the*·ne department store

granja ⓕ *gran*·kha farm

gratis *gra*·tees free (of charge)

grifo ⓜ *gree*·fo tap

gripe ⓕ *gree*·pe influenza

gris grees grey

gritar gree·*tar* shout

grupo ⓜ *groo*·po group

— de rock de rok rock band

— sanguíneo san·*gee*·ne·o blood group

guantes ⓜ pl *gwan*·tes gloves

guardarropa ⓜ gwar·da·*ro*·pa cloakroom

guardería ⓕ gwar·de·*ree*·a childminding service • creche

guerra ⓕ *ge*·ra war

guía ⓜ&ⓕ *gee*·a guide (person)

guía ⓕ *gee*·a guidebook

— audio *ow*·dyo audioguide

— del ocio del o·thyo entertainment guide

— telefónica te·le·fo·*nee*·ka phone book

guindilla ⓕ geen·*dee*·lya chilli

guión ⓜ gee·*on* script

guiri ⓜ *gee*·ree tourist (slang)

guisantes gee·*san*·tes peas

güisqui *gwees*·kee whiskey

guitarra ⓕ gee·*ta*·ra guitar

gustar(le) goos·*tar*(·le) like

H

habitación ⓕ a·bee·ta·*thyon* bedroom • room

— doble *do*·ble double room

— individual een·dee·vee·*dwal* single room

hablar a·*blar* speak • talk

hace sol a·the sol sunny

hacer a·*ther* do • make

— dedo *de*·do hitchhike

— surf soorf surf

— windsurf *ween*·soorf windsurfing

hachís ⓜ a·*chees* hash

hacia a·thya towards

— abajo a·*ba*·kho down

halal a·*lal* halal

hamaca ⓕ a·*ma*·ka hammock

hambriento/a ⓜ/ⓕ am·*bryen*·to/a hungry

harina ⓕ a·*ree*·na flour

hasta (junio) *as*·ta (*khoo*·nyo) until (June)

hecho/a ⓜ/ⓕ e·cho/a made

— a mano a *ma*·no handmade

— de (algodón) de (al·go·*don*) made of (cotton)

heladería ⓕ e·la·de·*ree*·a ice cream parlour

helado ⓜ e·*la*·do ice cream

helar e·*lar* freeze

hepatitis ⓕ e·pa·*tee*·tees hepatitis

herbolario ⓜ er·bo·*la*·ryo herbalist (shop)

herida ⓕ e·*ree*·da injury

hermana ⓕ er·*ma*·na sister

hermano ⓜ er·*ma*·no brother

hermoso/a ⓜ/ⓕ er·*mo*·so/a beautiful

heroína ⓕ e·ro·*ee*·na heroin

hielo ⓜ *ye*·lo ice

hierba ⓕ *yer*·ba grass

hierbas ⓕ pl *yer*·bas herbs

hígado ⓜ *ee*·ga·do liver

higos ⓜ pl *ee*·gos figs

hija ⓕ *ee*·kha daughter

hijo ⓜ *ee*·kho son

hijos ⓜ pl *ee*·khos children

hilo ⓜ thread *ee*·lo

— dental den·*tal* dental floss

hinchas ⓜ&ⓕ pl *een*·chas supporters

hindú een·*doo* Hindu

hipódromo ⓜ ee·*po*·dro·mo racetrack (horses)

historial ⓜ **profesional** ees·to·*ryal* pro·fe·syo·*nal* CV

histórico/a ⓜ/ⓕ ees·to·*ree*·ko/a historical

hockey ⓜ *kho*·kee hockey

— sobre hielo so·bre *ye*·lo ice hockey

hoja ⓕ o·kha leaf • sheet (of paper)

ojalata ① o·kha·*la*·ta tin
olanda ① o·*lan*·da Netherlands
ombre ⓜ *om*·bre man
ombros ⓜ pl *om*·bros shoulders
omosexual ⓜ&① o·mo·se·*kswal* omosexual
ora ① o·ra time
orario ⓜ o·*ra*·ryo timetable
oras ① pl **de abrir** o·ras de a·*breer* pening hours
ormiga ① or·*mee*·ga ant
orno ⓜ or·no oven
oróscopo ⓜ o·ros·ko·po horoscope
ospital ⓜ os·pee·*tal* hospital
osteleria ① os·te·le·*ree*·a hospitality
otel ⓜ o·*tel* hotel
oy oy today
ueso ⓜ we·so bone
uevo ⓜ we·vo egg
umanidades ① pl oo·ma·nee·*da*·des umanities

I

dentificación ①
e·den·tee·fee·ka·*thyon* identification
diomas ⓜ pl ee·*dyo*·mas languages
diota ⓜ/① ee·*dyo*·ta idiot
glesia ① ee·*gle*·sya church
gual ee·*gwal* same
gualdad ① ee·gwal·*da* equality
mpermeable ⓜ eem·per·me·*a*·ble aincoat
mpermeable eem·per·me·*a*·ble vaterproof
mportante eem·por·*tan*·te important
mpuesto ⓜ eem·*pwes*·to tax
— sobre la renta so·bre la *ren*·ta ncome tax
ncluido een·kloo·ee·do included
ncómodo/a ⓜ/① een·*ko*·mo·do/a uncomfortable
ndia ① *een*·dya India
ndicador ⓜ een·dee·ka·*dor* indicator
ndigestión ① een·dee·khes·*tyon* ndigestion

industria ① een·*doos*·trya industry
infección ① een·fek·*thyon* infection
inflamación ① een·fla·ma·*thyon* inflammation
informática ① een·for·*ma*·tee·ka IT
ingeniería ① een·khe·nye·*ree*·a engineering
ingeniero/a ⓜ/① een·khe·*nye*·ro/a engineer
Inglaterra ① een·gla·*te*·ra England
inglés ⓜ een·*gles* English • English language
ingrediente ⓜ een·gre·*dyen*·te ingredient
injusto/a ⓜ/① een·*khoos*·to/a unfair
inmigración ① een·mee·gra·*thyon* immigration
inocente ee·no·*then*·te innocent
inseguro/a ⓜ/① een·se·*goo*·ro/a unsafe
instituto ⓜ eens·tee·*too*·to high school
intentar (hacer algo) een·ten·*tar* (a·*ther al*·go) try (to do something)
interesante een·te·re·*san*·te interesting
internacional een·ter·na·thyo·*nal* international
Internet ⓜ *een*·ter·net Internet
intérprete ⓜ&① een·*ter*·pre·te interpreter
inundación ① ee·noon·da·*thyon* flooding
invierno ⓜ een·*vyer*·no winter
invitar een·vee·*tar* invite
inyección ① een·yek·*thyon* injection
inyectar(se) een·yek·*tar*(·se) inject (oneself)
ir eer go
— de compras de *kom*·pras go shopping
— de excursión de eks·koor·*syon* hike
— en tobogán en to·bo·*gan* tobogganing
Irlanda ① eer·*lan*·da Ireland

irritación ⓕ ee·ree·ta·*thyon* rash
— de pañal de pa·*nyal* nappy rash
isla ⓕ *ees*·la island
itinerario ⓜ ee·tee·ne·*ra*·ryo
itinerary
IVA ⓜ *ee*·va sales tax
izquierda ⓕ eeth·*kyer*·da left

J

jabón ⓜ kha·*bon* soap
jamón ⓜ kha·*mon* ham
Japón ⓜ kha·*pon* Japan
jarabe ⓜ kha·*ra*·be cough medicine
jardín ⓜ **botánico** khar·*deen*
bo·*ta*·nee·ko botanic garden
jarra ⓕ *kha*·ra jar
jefe/a ⓜ/ⓕ *khe*·fe/a boss • leader
— de sección de sek·*thyon*
manager
jengibre ⓜ khen·*khee*·bre ginger
jeringa ⓕ khe·*reen*·ga syringe
jersey ⓜ kher·*sey* jumper • sweater
jet lag ⓜ dyet lag jet lag
jockey ⓜ *dyo*·kee jockey
joven *kho*·ven young
joyería ⓕ kho·ye·*ree*·a jeweller
(shop)
jubilado/a ⓜ/ⓕ khoo·bee·*la*·do/a
retired
judías ⓕ pl khoo·*dee*·as beans
judío/a ⓜ/ⓕ khoo·*dee*·o/a Jewish
juegos ⓜ pl **de ordenador** *khwe*·gos
de or·de·na·*dor* computer games
juegos ⓜ pl **olímpicos** *khwe*·gos
o·*leem*·pee·kos Olympic Games
juez ⓜ&ⓕ khweth judge
jugar khoo·*gar* play (sport/games)
jugo ⓜ *khoo*·go juice
juguetería ⓕ khoo·ge·te·*ree*·a
toyshop
juntos/as ⓜ/ⓕ pl *khoon*·tos/as
together

K

kilogramo ⓜ kee·lo·*gra*·mo kilogram
kilómetro ⓜ kee·*lo*·me·tro kilometre

kiwi ⓜ *kee*·wee kiwifruit
kosher *ko*·sher Kosher

L

labios ⓜ pl *la*·byos lips
lado ⓜ *la*·do side
ladrón ⓜ la·*dron* thief
lagartija ⓕ la·gar·*tee*·kha lizard
lago ⓜ *la*·go lake
lamentar la·men·*tar* regret
lana ⓕ *la*·na wool
lápiz ⓜ *la*·peeth pencil
— de labios de *la*·byos lipstick
largo/a ⓜ/ⓕ *lar*·go/a long
lata ⓕ *la*·ta can
lavadero ⓜ la·va·*de*·ro laundry
lavadora ⓕ la·va·*do*·ra washing
machine
lavandería ⓕ la·van·de·*ree*·a
laundrette
lavar la·*var* wash (something)
lavarse la·*var*·se wash (oneself)
leche ⓕ *le*·che milk
— de soja de so·kha soy milk
— desnatada des·na·*ta*·da skimmed
milk
lechuga ⓕ le·*choo*·ga lettuce
leer le·*er* read
legal le·*gal* legal
legislación ⓕ le·khees·la·*thyon*
legislation
legumbre ⓕ le·*goom*·bre legume
lejos *le*·khos far
leña ⓕ *le*·nya firewood
lentejas ⓕ pl len·*te*·khas lentils
lentes ⓜ pl **de contacto** *len*·tes de
kon·*tak*·to contact lenses
lento/a ⓜ/ⓕ *len*·to/a slow
lesbiana ⓕ les·bee·*a*·na lesbian
leve *le*·ve light
ley ⓕ ley law
libra ⓕ *lee*·bra pound (money)
libre *lee*·bre free (not bound)
librería ⓕ lee·bre·*ree*·a bookshop
libro ⓜ *lee*·bro book
— de frases de *fra*·ses phrasebook

M

…**ibros** ⑩ pl **de viajes** *lee*·bros de *ya*·khes travel books
…**der** ⑩ *lee*·der leader
…**igar** lee·*gar* pick up
…**ila** *lee*·la purple
…**ima** *lee*·ma lime
…**imite** ⑩ **de equipaje** *lee*·mee·te de *-kee·pa*·khe baggage allowance
…**món** ⑩ lee·*mon* lemon
…**imonada** ① lee·mo·*na*·da lemonade
…**mpio/a** ⑩/① *leem*·pyo/a clean
…**nea** ① *lee*·ne·a line
…**nterna** ① leen·*ter*·na flashlight • orch
…**sto/a** ⑩/① *lees*·to/a ready
…**amada** ① *lya*·ma·da phone call
— a cobro revertido a ko·bro ·e·ver·*tee*·do collect call
…**amar por telefono** lya·*mar* por ·e·*le*·fo·no to make a phone call
…**ano/a** ⑩/① *lya*·no/a flat
…**ave** ① *lya*·ve key
…**egadas** ① pl lye·*ga*·das arrivals
…**egar** lye·*gar* arrive
…**enar** lye·*nar* fill
…**eno/a** ⑩/① *lye*·no/a full
…**evar** lye·*var* carry • wear
…**luvia** ① *lyoo*·vya rain
…**o que** lo ke what
…**ocal** ⑩ lo·*kal* venue
…**ocal** lo·*kal* local
…**oco/a** ⑩/① *lo*·ko/a crazy
…**odo** ⑩ *lo*·do mud
…**ombrices** ① pl lom·*bree*·thes worms
…**os dos** los dos both
…**ubricante** ⑩ loo·bree·*kan*·te ·ubricant
…**uces** ① pl *loo*·thes lights
…**uchar contra** loo·*char* kon·tra fight ·against
…**ugar** ⑩ loo·*gar* place
— de nacimiento de na·thee·*myen*·to ·place of birth
…**ujo** ⑩ *loo*·kho luxury

luna ① *loo*·na moon
— llena *lye*·na full moon
— de miel de myel honeymoon
luz ① looth light

M

machismo ⑩ ma·*chees*·mo sexism
madera ① ma·*de*·ra wood
madre ① *ma*·dre mother
madrugada ① ma·droo·*ga*·da early morning
mago/a ⑩/① *ma*·go/a magician
maíz ⑩ ma·*eeth* corn
maleta ① ma·*le*·ta suitcase
maletín ⑩ ma·*le*·teen briefcase
— de primeros auxilios ⑩ de pree·*me*·ros ow·*ksee*·lyos first-aid kit
malo/a ⑩/① *ma*·lo/a bad
mamá ① ma·*ma* mum
mamograma ⑩ ma·mo·*gra*·ma mammogram
mañana ① ma·*nya*·na tomorrow • morning (6am–1pm)
— por la mañana por la ma·*nya*·na tomorrow morning
— por la noche por la *no*·che tomorrow evening
— por la tarde por la *tar*·de tomorrow afternoon
mandarina ① man·da·*ree*·na mandarin
mandíbula ① man·*dee*·boo·la jaw
mando a distancia *man*·do a dees·*tan*·thya remote control
mango ⑩ *man*·go mango
manifestación ① ma·nee·fes·ta·*thyon* demonstration
manillar ⑩ ma·nee·*lyar* handlebar
mano ① *ma*·no hand
manta ① *man*·ta blanket
manteca ① man·*te*·ka lard
mantel ⑩ man·*tel* tablecloth
mantequilla ① man·te·*kee*·lya butter
manzana ① man·*tha*·na apple
mapa ⑩ *ma*·pa map

M

maquillaje ⓜ ma·kee·*lya*·khe make-up

máquina ⓕ *ma*·kee·na machine

— de billetes de bee·*lye*·tes ticket machine

— de tabaco de ta·*ba*·ko cigarette machine

mar ⓜ mar sea

marido ⓜ ma·*ree*·do husband

maravilloso/a ⓜ/ⓕ ma·ra·vee·*lyo*·so/a wonderful

marcador ⓜ mar·ka·*dor* scoreboard

marcapasos ⓜ mar·ka·*pa*·sos pacemaker

marcar mar·*kar* score

marea ⓕ ma·*re*·a tide

mareado/a ⓜ/ⓕ ma·re·*a*·do/a dizzy • seasick

mareo ⓜ ma·*re*·o travel sickness

margarina ⓕ mar·ga·*ree*·na margarine

marihuana ⓕ ma·ree·*wa*·na marijuana

mariposa ⓕ ma·ree·*po*·sa butterfly

marrón ma·*ron* brown

martillo ⓜ mar·*tee*·lyo hammer

más cercano/a ⓜ/ⓕ mas ther·*ka*·no/a nearest

masaje ⓜ ma·*sa*·khe massage

masajista ⓜ&ⓕ ma·sa·*khees*·ta masseur

matar ma·*tar* kill

matrícula ⓕ ma·*tree*·koo·la license plate number

matrimonio ⓜ ma·tree·mo·*nyo* marriage

mayonesa ⓕ ma·yo·*ne*·sa mayonnaise

mecánico ⓜ me·*ka*·nee·ko mechanic

mechero ⓜ me·*che*·ro lighter

medianoche ⓕ me·dya·*no*·che midnight

medias ⓕ pl *me*·dyas stockings • pantyhose

medicina ⓕ me·dee·*thee*·na medicine

medico/a ⓜ/ⓕ *me*·dee·co/a doctor

medio ⓜ **ambiente** *me*·dyo am·*byen*·te environment

medio/a ⓜ/ⓕ *me*·dyo/a half

mediodía ⓜ me·dyo·*dee*·a noon

medios ⓜ pl **de comunicación** *me*·dyos de ko·moo·nee·ka·*thyon* media

medios ⓜ pl **de transporte** *me*·dyo de trans·*por*·te means of transport

meditación ⓕ meditation me·dee·ta·*thyon*

mejillones ⓜ pl me·khee·*lyo*·nes mussels

mejor me·*khor* better • best

melocotón ⓜ me·lo·ko·*ton* peach

melodía ⓕ me·lo·*dee*·a tune

melón ⓜ me·*lon* melon

mendigo/a ⓜ/ⓕ men·*dee*·go/a beggar

menos *me*·nos less

mensaje ⓜ men·*sa*·khe message

menstruación ⓕ mens·trwa·*thyon* menstruation

mentiroso/a ⓜ/ⓕ men·tee·ro·so/a liar

menú ⓜ me·*noo* menu

menudo/a ⓜ/ⓕ me·*noo*·do/a little

a menudo a me·*noo*·do often

mercado ⓜ mer·*ka*·do market

mermelada ⓕ mer·me·*la*·da jam • marmalade

mes ⓜ mes month

mesa ⓕ *me*·sa table

meseta ⓕ me·se·ta plateau

metal ⓜ me·*tal* metal

meter (un gol) me·*ter* (oon gol) kick (a goal)

metro ⓜ *me*·tro metre

mezclar meth·*klar* mix

mezquita ⓕ meth·*kee*·ta mosque

mi mee my

microondas ⓜ mee·kro·*on*·das microwave

miel ⓕ myel honey

miembro ⓜ *myem*·bro member
migraña ⓕ mee·*gra*·nya migraine
milímetro ⓜ mee·*lee*·me·tro millimetre
millón ⓜ mee·*lyon* million
minusválido/a ⓜ/ⓕ nee·noos·*va*·lee·do/a disabled
minuto ⓜ mee·*noo*·to minute
mirador ⓜ mee·ra·*dor* lookout
mirar mee·*rar* look • watch
– los escaparates los es·ka·pa·*ra*·tes window-shopping
misa ⓕ *mee*·sa mass
mochila ⓕ mo·*chee*·la backpack
módem ⓜ *mo*·dem modem
(carne) molida (*kar*·ne) mo·*lee*·da mince (meat)
mojado/a ⓜ/ⓕ mo·*kha*·do/a wet
monasterio ⓜ mo·nas·*te*·ryo monastery
monedas ⓕ pl mo·*ne*·das coins
monja ⓕ *mon*·kha nun
monopatinaje ⓜ no·no·pa·tee·*na*·khe skateboarding
montaña ⓕ mon·*ta*·nya mountain
montar mon·*tar* ride
– en bicicleta en bee·thee·*kle*·ta cycle
monumento ⓜ mo·noo·*men*·to monument
mordedura ⓕ mor·de·*doo*·ra bite (dog)
morir mo·*reer* die
mosquitera ⓕ mos·kee·*te*·ra mosquito net
mosquito ⓜ mos·*kee*·to mosquito
mostaza ⓕ mos·*ta*·tha mustard
mostrador ⓜ mos·tra·*dor* counter
mostrar mos·*trar* show
motocicleta ⓕ mo·to·thee·*kle*·ta motorcycle
motor ⓜ mo·*tor* engine
motora ⓕ mo·*to*·ra motorboat
muchas/os ⓜ/ⓕ pl *moo*·chas/os many

N

mudo/a ⓜ/ⓕ *moo*·do/a mute
muebles ⓜ pl *mwe*·bles furniture
muela ⓕ *mwe*·la tooth (back)
muelle ⓜ *mwe*·lye spring
muerto/a ⓜ/ⓕ *mwer*·to/a dead
muesli ⓜ *mwes*·lee muesli
mujer ⓕ moo·*kher* woman
multa ⓕ *mool*·ta fine
mundo ⓜ *moon*·do world
muñeca ⓕ moo·*nye*·ka doll • wrist
murallas ⓕ pl moo·*ra*·lyas city walls
músculo ⓜ *moos*·koo·lo muscle
museo ⓜ moo·*se*·o museum
— de arte de *ar*·te art gallery
música ⓕ *moo*·see·ka music
músico/a ⓜ/ⓕ *moo*·see·ko/a musician
— ambulante am·boo·*lan*·te busker
muslo ⓜ *moos*·lo drumstick (chicken)
musulmán(a) ⓜ/ⓕ moo·sool·*man*/moo·sool·*ma*·na Muslim
muy mooy very

N

nacionalidad ⓕ na·thyo·na·lee·*da* nationality
nada *na*·da none • nothing
nadar na·*dar* swim
naranja ⓕ na·*ran*·kha orange
nariz ⓕ na·*reeth* nose
nata ⓕ agria *na*·ta *a*·grya sour cream
naturaleza ⓕ na·too·ra·*le*·tha nature
naturopatía ⓕ na·too·ro·pa·*tee*·a naturopathy
náusea ⓕ *now*·se·a nausea
náuseas ⓕ pl **del embarazo** *now*·se·as del em·ba·*ra*·tho morning sickness
navaja ⓕ na·*va*·kha penknife
Navidad ⓕ na·vee·*da* Christmas
necesario/a ⓜ/ⓕ ne·the·*sa*·ryo/a necessary
necesitar ne·the·see·*tar* need
negar ne·*gar* deny

O

negar ne·*gar* refuse

negocio Ⓜ ne·go·thyo business

— de artículos básicos de ar·*tee*·koo·los ba·*see*·kos convenience store

negro/a Ⓜ/Ⓕ ne·gro/a black

neumático Ⓜ ne·oo·*ma*·tee·ko tyre

nevera Ⓕ ne·*ve*·ra refrigerator

nieto/a Ⓜ/Ⓕ nye·to/a grandchild

nieve Ⓕ *nye*·ve snow

niño/a Ⓜ/Ⓕ *nee*·nyo/a child

no no no

— fumadores foo·ma·*do*·res non-smoking

— incluido een·kloo·ee·do excluded

noche Ⓕ no·che evening • night

Nochebuena Ⓕ no·che·*bwe*·na Christmas Eve

Nochevieja Ⓕ no·che·*vye*·kha New Year's Eve

nombre Ⓜ *nom*·bre name

— de pila de *pee*·la Christian name

norte Ⓜ *nor*·te north

nosotros/as Ⓜ/Ⓕ pl no·so·tros/ no·so·tras we

noticias Ⓕ pl no·*tee*·thyas news

— de actualidad de ak·twal·ee·*da* current affairs

novia Ⓕ *no*·vya girlfriend

novio Ⓜ *no*·vyo boyfriend

nube Ⓕ *noo*·be cloud

nublado noo·*bla*·do cloudy

nueces *nwe*·thes nuts

— crudas *kroo*·das raw nuts

— tostadas tos·*ta*·das roasted nuts

nuestro/a Ⓜ/Ⓕ *nwes*·tro/a our

Nueva Zelanda Ⓕ *nwe*·va the·*lan*·da New Zealand

nuevo/a Ⓜ/Ⓕ *nwe*·vo/a new

número Ⓜ *noo*·me·ro number

— de la habitación de la a·bee·ta·*thyon* room number

— de pasaporte de pa·sa·*por*·te passport number

nunca *noon*·ka never

O

o o or

obra Ⓕ *o*·bra play • building site

obrero/a Ⓜ/Ⓕ o·*bre*·ro/a factory worker • labourer

océano Ⓜ o·*the*·a·no ocean

ocupado/a Ⓜ/Ⓕ o·koo·*pa*·do/a busy

ocupar o·koo·*par* live (somewhere)

oeste Ⓜ o·es·te west

oficina Ⓕ o·fee·*thee*·na office

— de objetos perdidos de ob·*khe*·tos per·*dee*·dos lost property office

— de turismo de too·rees·mo tourist office

oír o·eer hear

ojo Ⓜ o·kho eye

ola Ⓕ o·la wave

olor Ⓜ o·lor smell

olvidar ol·vee·*dar* forget

ópera Ⓕ o·pe·ra opera

operación Ⓕ o·pe·ra·*thyon* operation

opinión Ⓕ o·pee·*nyon* opinion

oporto Ⓜ o·*por*·to port (wine)

oportunidad Ⓕ o·por·too·nee·*da* chance

oración Ⓕ o·ra·*thyon* prayer

orden Ⓜ *or*·den order (placement)

ordenador Ⓜ or·de·na·*dor* computer

— portátil por·ta·teel laptop

ordenar or·de·*nar* order

oreja Ⓕ o·*re*·kha ear

orgasmo Ⓜ or·*gas*·mo orgasm

original o·ree·khee·*nal* original

orquesta Ⓕ or·*kes*·ta orchestra

oscuro/a Ⓜ/Ⓕ os·koo·ro/a dark

ostra Ⓕ os·tra oyster

otoño Ⓜ o·*to*·nyo autumn

otra vez o·tra veth again

otro/a Ⓜ/Ⓕ o·tro/a other • another

oveja Ⓕ o·ve·kha sheep

oxígeno Ⓜ o·*ksee*·khe·no oxygen

P

padre Ⓜ pa·dre father

padres Ⓜ pl pa·dres parents

P

pagar pa·*gar* pay
página ① *pa*·khee·na page
pago ⓜ *pa*·go payment
país ⓜ pa·ees country
pájaro ⓜ *pa*·kha·ro bird
palabra ① pa·*la*·bra word
palacio ⓜ pa·*la*·thyo palace
palillo ⓜ pa·*lee*·lyo toothpick
pan ⓜ pan bread
— **integral** in·te·*gral* wholemeal bread
— **moreno** mo·*re*·no brown bread
panadería ① pa·na·de·*ree*·a bakery
pañal ⓜ pa·*nyal* diaper • nappy
pantalla ① pan·*ta*·lya screen
pantalones ⓜ pl pan·ta·*lo*·nes
pants • trousers
— **cortos** kor·tos shorts
pañuelos ⓜ pl **de papel** pa·*nywe*·los
de pa·*pel* tissues
papá ⓜ pa·*pa* dad
papel ⓜ pa·*pel* paper
— **de fumar** de foo·*mar* cigarette
papers
— **higiénico** ee·*khye*·nee·ko toilet
paper
paquete ⓜ pa·*ke*·te packet • package
para llevar pa·ra lye·*var* to take away
parabrisas ⓜ pa·ra·*bree*·sas
windscreen
paracaidismo ⓜ pa·ra·kai·dees·mo
skydiving
parada ① pa·*ra*·da stop
— **de autobús** de ow·to·*boos* bus stop
— **de taxis** de *ta*·ksees taxi stand
paraguas ⓜ pa·*ra*·gwas umbrella
parapléjico/a ⓜ/①
pa·ra·*ple*·khee·ko/a paraplegic
parar pa·*rar* stop
pared ① pa·*re* wall (inside)
pareja ① pa·*re*·kha pair (couple)
parlamento ⓜ par·la·*men*·to
parliament
paro ⓜ *pa*·ro dole
parque ⓜ *par*·ke park
— **nacional** na·thyo·*nal* national park

parte ① *par*·te part
partida ① **de nacimiento** par·*tee*·da
de na·thee·*myen*·to birth certificate
partido ⓜ par·*tee*·do match (sport) •
(political) party
pasado ⓜ pa·*sa*·do past
pasado mañana pa·sa·do ma·*nya*·na
day after tomorrow
pasado/a ⓜ/① pa·sa·do/a off (food)
pasajero ⓜ pa·sa·*khe*·ro passenger
pasaporte ⓜ pa·sa·*por*·te passport
Pascua ① *pas*·kwa Easter
pase ⓜ *pa*·se pass
paseo ⓜ pa·*se*·o street
paso ⓜ *pa*·so step
— **de cebra** de *the*·bra pedestrian
crossing
pasta ① *pas*·ta pasta
— **dentífrica** den·*tee*·free·ka
toothpaste
pastel ⓜ pas·*tel* cake • pie
— **de cumpleaños** de
koom·ple·a·nyos birthday cake
pastelería ① pas·te·le·*ree*·a cake
shop
pastilla ① pas·*tee*·lya pill
pastillas ① pl **de menta** pas·*tee*·lyas
de *men*·ta mints
pastillas ① pl **para dormir**
pas·*tee*·lyas pa·ra dor·*meer* sleeping
pills
patata ① pa·*ta*·ta potato
paté ⓜ pa·*te* pate (food)
patinar pa·tee·*nar* rollerblading • ice
skating
pato ⓜ *pa*·to duck
pavo ⓜ *pa*·vo turkey
paz ① path peace
peatón ⓜ&① pe·a·*ton* pedestrian
pecho ⓜ *pe*·cho chest
pechuga ① pe·*choo*·ga breast
(poultry)
pedal ⓜ pe·*dal* pedal
pedazo ⓜ pe·*da*·tho piece
pedir pe·*deer* ask (for something)

peine ⓜ *pey*·ne comb

pelea ⓕ pe·*le*·a a fight

película ⓕ pe·*lee*·koo·la movie • film (camera)

— en color en ko·*lor* colour film

peligroso/a ⓜ/ⓕ pe·lee·*gro*·so/a dangerous

pelo ⓜ *pe*·lo hair

pelota ⓕ pe·*lo*·ta ball

— de golf de golf golf ball

peluquero/a ⓜ/ⓕ pe·loo·*ke*·ro/a hairdresser

pendientes ⓜ pl pen·*dyen*·tes earrings

pene ⓜ *pe*·ne penis

pensar pen·*sar* think

pensión ⓕ pen·*syon* boarding house

pensionista ⓜ&ⓕ pen·syo·*nees*·ta pensioner

pepino ⓜ pe·*pee*·no cucumber

pequeñito/a ⓜ/ⓕ pe·ke·*nyee*·to/a tiny

pequeño/a ⓜ/ⓕ pe·*ke*·nyo/a small

pera ⓕ *pe*·ra pear

perder per·*der* lose

perdido/a ⓜ/ⓕ per·*dee*·do/a lost

perdonar per·do·*nar* forgive

perejil ⓜ pe·re·*kheel* parsley

perfume ⓜ per·*foo*·me perfume

periódico ⓜ pe·*ryo*·dee·ko newspaper

periodista ⓜ&ⓕ pe·ryo·*dees*·ta journalist

permiso ⓜ per·*mee*·so permission • permit

— de trabajo ⓜ de tra·*ba*·kho work permit

permitir per·mee·*teer* allow • permit

pero *pe*·ro but

perro/a ⓜ/ⓕ *pe*·ro/a dog

perro lazarillo *pe*·ro la·tha·*ree*·lyo guide dog

persona ⓕ per·*so*·na person

pesado/a ⓜ/ⓕ pe·*sa*·do/a heavy

pesar pe·*sar* weigh

pesas ⓕ pl *pe*·sas weights

pesca ⓕ *pes*·ka fishing

pescadería ⓕ pes·ka·de·*ree*·a fish shop

pescado ⓜ pes·*ka*·do fish (as food)

peso ⓜ *pe*·so weight

petición ⓕ pe·tee·*thyon* petition

pez ⓜ peth fish

picadura ⓕ pee·ka·*doo*·ra bite (insect)

picazón ⓕ pee·ka·*thon* itch

pie ⓜ pye foot

piedra ⓕ *pye*·dra stone

piel ⓕ pyel skin

pierna ⓕ *pyer*·na leg

pila ⓕ *pee*·la battery (small)

píldora ⓕ *peel*·do·ra the Pill

pimienta ⓕ pee·*myen*·ta pepper

pimiento ⓜ pee·*myen*·to capsicum • bell pepper

— rojo ro·kho red capsicum

— verde *ver*·de green capsicum

piña ⓕ *pee*·nya pineapple

pinchar peen·*char* puncture

ping pong ⓜ peeng pong table tennis

pintar peen·*tar* paint

pintor(a) ⓜ/ⓕ peen·*tor*/peen·*to*·ra painter

pintura ⓕ peen·*too*·ra painting

pinzas ⓕ pl *peen*·thas tweezers

piojos ⓜ pl *pyo*·khos lice

piqueta ⓕ pee·*ke*·ta pickaxe

piquetas ⓕ pl pee·*ke*·tas tent pegs

piscina ⓕ pees·*thee*·na swimming pool

pista ⓕ *pees*·ta court (tennis)

— de tenis de *te*·nees tennis court

pistacho ⓜ pees·*ta*·cho pistachio

plancha ⓕ *plan*·cha iron

planeta ⓜ pla·*ne*·ta planet

planta ⓕ *plan*·ta plant

plástico ⓜ *plas*·tee·ko plastic

plata ⓕ *pla*·ta silver

plataforma ⓕ pla·ta·*for*·ma platform

plátano ⓜ *pla*·ta·no banana

plateado/a ⓜ/ⓕ pla·te·a·do/a silver
plato ⓜ pla·to plate
playa ⓕ pla·ya beach
plaza ⓕ pla·tha square
— **de toros** de to·ros bullring
pobre po·bre poor
pobreza ⓕ po·bre·tha poverty
pocos po·kos few
poder po·der can (be able)
poder po·der power
poesía ⓕ po·e·see·a poetry
polen ⓜ po·len pollen
policía ⓕ po·lee·thee·a police
política ⓕ po·lee·tee·ka policy •
politics
político ⓜ po·lee·tee·ko politician
póliza ⓕ po·lee·tha policy (insurance)
pollo ⓜ po·lyo chicken
pomelo ⓜ po·me·lo grapefruit
poner po·ner put
popular po·poo·lar popular
póquer ⓜ po·ker poker
por (dia) por (dee·a) per (day)
por ciento por thyen·to percent
por qué por ke why
por vía aérea por vee·a a·e·re·a air
mail
por vía terrestre por vee·a te·res·tre
surface mail
porque por·ke because
portero/a ⓜ/ⓕ por·te·ro/a
goalkeeper
posible po·see·ble possible
postal ⓕ pos·tal postcard
póster ⓜ pos·ter poster
potro ⓜ po·tro foal
pozo ⓜ po·tho well
precio ⓜ pre·thyo price
— **de entrada** de en·tra·da admission
price
— **del cubierto** del koo·byer·to cover
charge
preferir pre·fe·reer prefer
pregunta ⓕ pre·goon·ta question
preguntar pre·goon·tar ask
(a question)

preocupado/a ⓜ/ⓕ
pre·o·koo·pa·do/a worried
preocuparse por pre·o·koo·par·se por
care (about something)
preparar pre·pa·rar prepare
presidente/a ⓜ/ⓕ pre·see·den·te/a
president
presión ⓕ pre·syon pressure
— **arterial** ar·te·ryal blood pressure
prevenir pre·ve·neer prevent
primavera ⓕ pree·ma·ve·ra spring
(season)
primer ministro ⓜ pree·mer
mee·nees·tro prime minister
primera ministra ⓕ pree·me·ra
mee·nees·tra prime minister
primero/a ⓜ/ⓕ pree·me·ro/a first
principal preen·thee·pal main
prisa ⓕ pree·sa hurry
prisionero/a ⓜ/ⓕ pree·syon·ne·ro/a
prisoner
privado/a ⓜ/ⓕ pree·va·do/a private
probar pro·bar try
producir pro·doo·theer produce
productos ⓜ pl **congelados**
pro·dook·tos kon·khe·la·dos frozen
foods
profesor(a) ⓜ/ⓕ pro·fe·sor/
pro·fe·so·ra lecturer • instructor •
teacher
profundo/a ⓜ/ⓕ pro·foon·do/a deep
programa ⓜ pro·gra·ma programme
prolongación ⓕ pro·lon·ga·thyon
extension (visa)
promesa ⓕ pro·me·sa promise
prometida ⓕ pro·me·tee·da fiancee
prometido ⓜ pro·me·tee·do fiance
pronto pron·to soon
propietaria ⓕ pro·pye·ta·rya landlady
propietario ⓜ pro·pye·ta·ryo landlord
propina ⓕ pro·pee·na tip
proteger pro·te·kher protect
protegido/a ⓜ/ⓕ pro·te·khee·do/a
protected
protesta ⓕ pro·tes·ta protest

P

Q

provisiones ⓕ pl pro·bee·syo·nes provisions
proyector ⓜ pro·yek·tor projector
prudente proo·den·te sensible
prueba ⓕ prwe·ba test
— del embarazo del em·ba·ra·tho pregnancy test kit
pruebas ⓕ pl **nucleares** prwe·bas noo·kle·a·res nuclear testing
pub ⓜ poob bar (with music) • pub
pueblo ⓜ pwe·blo village
puente ⓜ pwen·te bridge
puerro ⓜ pwe·ro leek
puerta ⓕ pwer·ta door
puerto ⓜ pwer·to port • harbour
puesta ⓕ **del sol** pwes·ta del sol sunset
pulga ⓕ pool·ga flea
pulmones ⓜ pl pool·mo·nes lungs
punto ⓜ poon·to point (tip/score)
puro ⓜ poo·ro cigar
puro/a ⓜ/ⓕ poo·ro/a pure

Q

(el mes) que viene (el mes) ke vye·ne next (month)
quedar ke·dar leave (behind)
quedarse ke·dar·se stay (remain)
quedarse sin ke·dar·se seen run out of
quejarse ke·khar·se complain
quemadura ⓕ ke·ma·doo·ra burn
— de sol de sol sunburn
querer ke·rer love • want
queso ⓜ ke·so cheese
— crema kre·ma cream cheese
— de cabra de ka·bra goat's cheese
quien kyen who
quincena ⓕ keen·the·na fortnight
quiosco ⓜ kyos·ko news stand • newsagency
quiste ⓜ **ovárico** kees·te o·va·ree·ko ovarian cyst
quizás kee·thas maybe

R

rábano ⓜ ra·ba·no radish
— picante pee·kan·te horseradish
rápido/a ⓜ/ⓕ ra·pee·do/a fast
raqueta ⓕ ra·ke·ta racquet
raro/a ⓜ/ⓕ ra·ro/a rare (item)
rastro ⓜ ras·tro track (footprints)
rata ⓕ ra·ta rat
ratón ⓜ ra·ton mouse
raza ⓕ ra·tha race (people)
razón ⓕ ra·thon reason
realista re·a·lees·ta realistic
recibir re·thee·beer receive
recibo ⓜ re·thee·bo receipt
reciclable re·thee·kla·ble recyclable
reciclar re·thee·klar recycle
recientemente re·thyen·te·men·te recently
recogida ⓕ **de equipajes** re·ko·khee·da de e·kee·pa·khes baggage claim
recolección ⓕ **de fruta** re·ko·lek·thyon de froo·ta fruit picking
recomendar re·ko·men·dar recommend
reconocer re·ko·no·ther recognise
recordar re·kor·dar remember
recorrido ⓜ **guiado** re·ko·ree·do gee·a·do guided tour
recto/a ⓜ/ⓕ rek·to/a straight
recuerdo ⓜ re·kwer·do souvenir
red ⓕ red net
redondo/a ⓜ/ⓕ re·don·do/a round
reembolsar re·em·bol·sar refund
reembolso ⓜ re·em·bol·so refund
referencias ⓕ pl re·fe·ren·thyas references
refresco ⓜ re·fres·ko soft drink
refugiado/a ⓜ/ⓕ re·foo·khya·do/a refugee
regalar re·ga·lar exchange (gifts)
regalo ⓜ re·ga·lo gift
— de bodas de bo·das wedding present
régimen ⓜ re·khee·men diet
reglas ⓕ pl re·glas rules
reina ⓕ rey·na queen
reírse re·eer·se laugh

relación ① re·la·*thyon* relationship

relajarse re·la·*khar*·se relax

religión ① re·lee·*khyon* religion

religioso/a ⑩/① re·lee·*khyo*·so·a religious

reliquia ① re·lee·kya relic

reloj ⑩ re·*lokh* clock

— de pulsera de pool·*se*·ra watch

remo ⑩ *re*·mo rowing

remolacha ① re·mo·*la*·cha beetroot

remoto/a ⑩/① re·mo·*to*·a remote

reparar re·pa·*rar* repair

repartir re·par·*teer* divide up (share)

repetir re·pe·*teer* repeat

república ① re·*poo*·blee·ka republic

requesón ⑩ re·ke·*son* cottage cheese

reserva ① re·*ser*·va reservation

reservar re·ser·*var* book (make a reservation)

resfriado ⑩ res·free·a·do cold

residencia ① **de estudiantes** e·see·*den*·thya de es·too·*dyan*·tes college

residuos ⑩ pl **tóxicos** re·*see*·dwos *to*·ksee·kos toxic waste

respirar res·pee·*rar* breathe

respuesta ① res·*pwes*·ta answer

restaurante ⑩ res·tow·*ran*·te restaurant

revisar re·vee·*sar* check

revisor(a) ⑩/① re·vee·*sor*/ re·vee·*so*·ra ticket collector

revista ① re·*vees*·ta magazine

rey ⑩ rey king

rico/a ⑩/① *ree*·ko·a rich

riesgo ⑩ *ryes*·go risk

río ⑩ *ree*·o river

ritmo ⑩ *reet*·mo rhythm

robar ro·*bar* rob • steal

roca ① *ro*·ka rock

rock ⑩ rok rock (music)

rodilla ① ro·*dee*·lya knee

rojo/a ⑩/① *ro*·kho·a red

rollo ⑩ **repelente contra mosquitos** *ro*·lyo re·pe·*len*·te *kon*·tra mos·*kee*·tos mosquito coil

romántico/a ⑩/① ro·*man*·tee·ko·a romantic

romper rom·*per* break

ron ⑩ ron rum

ropa ① *ro*·pa clothing

— de cama de *ka*·ma bedding

— interior een·te·*ryor* underwear

rosa *ro*·sa pink

roto/a ⑩/① *ro*·to·a broken

rueda ① *rwe*·da wheel

rugby ⑩ *roog*·bee rugby

ruidoso/a ⑩/① rwee·*do*·so·a loud

ruinas ① pl *rwee*·nas ruins

ruta ① *roo*·ta route

S

S

sábado ⑩ *sa*·ba·do Saturday

sábana ① *sa*·ba·na sheet (bed)

saber sa·*ber* know (something)

sabroso/a ⑩/① sa·*bro*·so·a tasty

sacar sa·*kar* take out • take (photo)

sacerdote ⑩ sa·ther·*do*·te priest

saco ⑩ **de dormir** *sa*·ko de dor·*meer* sleeping bag

sal ① sal salt

sala ① **de espera** *sa*·la de es·*pe*·ra waiting room

sala ① **de tránsito** *sa*·la de *tran*·see·to transit lounge

salario ⑩ sa·*la*·ryo rate of pay • salary

salchicha ① sal·*chee*·cha sausage

saldo ⑩ *sal*·do balance (account)

salida ① sa·*lee*·da departure • exit

saliente ⑩ sa·*lyen*·te ledge

salir con sa·*leer* kon go out with

salir de sa·*leer* de depart

salmón ⑩ sal·*mon* salmon

salón de belleza ⑩ sa·*lon* de be·*lye*·tha beauty salon

salsa ① *sal*·sa sauce

— de guindilla de geen·*dee*·lya chilli sauce

— de soja de *so*·kha soy sauce

— de tomate de to·*ma*·te tomato sauce • ketchup

saltar sal·*tar* jump

salud ⓕ sa·*loo* health

salvaeslips ⓜ pl sal·va·e·*sleeps* panty liners

salvar sal·*var* save

sandalias ⓕ pl san·*da*·lyas sandals

sandía ⓕ san·dee·a watermelon

sangrar san·*grar* bleed

sangre ⓕ *san*·gre blood

santo/a ⓜ/ⓕ *san*·to/a saint

sarampión ⓜ sa·ram·*pyon* measles

sartén ⓕ sar·*ten* frying pan

sastre ⓜ *sas*·tre tailor

sauna ⓕ *sow*·na sauna

secar se·*kar* dry

secretario/a ⓜ/ⓕ se·kre·*ta*·ryo/a secretary

sed ⓕ se thirst

seda ⓕ *se*·da silk

seguir se·*geer* follow

segundo/a ⓜ/ⓕ se·*goon*·do/a second

seguro ⓜ se·*goo*·ro insurance

seguro/a ⓜ/ⓕ se·*goo*·ro/a safe

sello ⓜ *se*·lyo stamp

semáforos ⓜ pl se·*ma*·fo·ros traffic lights

Semana ⓕ **Santa** se·*ma*·na *san*·ta Easter Week

sembrar sem·*brar* plant

semidirecto/a ⓜ/ⓕ se·mee·dee·*rek*·to/a non-direct

señal ⓕ se·*nyal* sign

sencillo/a ⓜ/ⓕ sen·*thee*·lyo/a simple

(un billete) sencillo ⓜ (oon bee·*lye*·te) sen·*thee*·lyo one-way (ticket)

sendero ⓜ sen·*de*·ro mountain path · path

senos ⓜ pl *se*·nos breasts

sensibilidad ⓕ sen·see·bee·lee·*da* sensitivity · film speed

sensual sen·*swal* sensual

sentarse sen·*tar*·se sit

sentimientos ⓜ pl sen·tee·*myen*·tos feelings

sentir sen·*teer* feel

separado/a ⓜ/ⓕ se·pa·*ra*·do/a separate

separar se·pa·*rar* separate

ser ser be

serie ⓕ *se*·rye series

serio/a ⓜ/ⓕ se·ryo/a serious

seropositivo/a ⓜ/ⓕ se·ro·po·see·*tee*·vo/a HIV positive

serpiente ⓕ ser·*pyen*·te snake

servicio ⓜ ser·*vee*·thyo service charge

— militar mee·lee·*tar* military service

— telefónico automático te·le·fo·*nee*·ko ow·to·*ma*·tee·ko direct-dial

servicios ⓜ pl ser·*vee*·thyos toilets

servilleta ⓕ ser·vee·*lye*·ta napkin

sexo ⓜ *sek*·so sex

— seguro se·*goo*·ro safe sex

sexy *sek*·see sexy

si see if

sí see yes

SIDA ⓜ *see*·da AIDS

sidra ⓕ *see*·dra cider

siempre *syem*·pre always

silla ⓕ *see*·lya chair

— de ruedas de *rwe*·das wheelchair

sillín ⓜ see·*lyeen* saddle

similar see·mee·*lar* similar

simpático/a ⓜ/ⓕ seem·*pa*·tee·ko/a nice

sin seen without

— hogar o·*gar* homeless

— plomo *plo*·mo unleaded

sinagoga ⓕ see·na·go·ga synagogue

Singapur ⓜ seen·ga·*poor* Singapore

sintético/a ⓜ/ⓕ seen·*te*·tee·ko/a synthetic

soborno ⓜ so·*bor*·no bribe

sobre *so*·bre about · on top of

sobre ⓜ *so*·bre envelope

sobredosis ⓕ so·bre·*do*·sees overdos

T

sobrevivir so·bre·vee·*veer* survive

socialista ⓜ&ⓕ so·thya·*lees*·ta socialist

sol ⓜ sol sun

soldado ⓜ sol·*da*·do soldier

sólo *so*·lo only

solo/a ⓜ/ⓕ *so*·lo/a alone

soltero/a ⓜ/ⓕ sol·*te*·ro/a single

sombra ⓕ *som*·bra shadow

sombrero ⓜ som·*bre*·ro hat

soñar so·*nyar* dream

sondeos ⓜ pl son·*de*·os polls

sonreír son·re·*eer* smile

sopa ⓕ *so*·pa soup

sordo/a ⓜ/ⓕ *sor*·do/a deaf

sorpresa ⓕ sor·*pre*·sa surprise

su soo her • his • their

subir soo·*beer* climb

submarinismo ⓜ soob·ma·ree·*nees*·mo diving

subtítulos ⓜ pl soob·*tee*·too·los subtitles

sucio/a ⓜ/ⓕ *soo*·thyo/a dirty

sucursal ⓕ soo·koor·*sal* branch office

sudar soo·*dar* perspire

suegra ⓕ *swe*·gra mother-in-law

suegro ⓜ *swe*·gro father-in-law

sueldo ⓜ *swel*·do wage

suelo ⓜ *swe*·lo floor

suerte ⓕ *swer*·te luck

suficiente soo·fee·*thyen*·te enough

sufrir soo·*freer* suffer

sujetador ⓜ soo·khe·ta·*dor* bra

supermercado ⓜ soo·per·mer·*ka*·do supermarket

superstición ⓕ soo·pers·tee·*thyon* superstition

sur ⓜ soor south

surf ⓜ **sobre la nieve** soorf *so*·bre la *nye*·ve snowboarding

T

tabaco ⓜ ta·*ba*·ko tobacco

tabla ⓕ **de surf** *ta*·bla de soorf surfboard

tablero ⓜ **de ajedrez** ta·*ble*·ro de a·khe·*dreth* chess board

tacaño/a ⓜ/ⓕ ta·*ka*·nyo/a stingy

talco ⓜ *tal*·ko baby powder

talla ⓕ *ta*·lya size (clothes)

taller ⓜ ta·*lyer* workshop

también tam·*byen* also

tampoco tam·po·ko neither

tampones ⓜ pl tam·po·nes tampons

tanga ⓕ *tan*·ga g-string

tapones ⓜ pl **para los oídos** ta·po·nes pa·ra los o·ee·dos earplugs

taquilla ⓕ ta·*kee*·lya ticket office

tarde *tar*·de late

tarjeta tar·*khe*·ta card

— de crédito de *kre*·dee·to credit card

— de embarque de em·*bar*·ke boarding pass

— de teléfono de te·*le*·fo·no phone card

tarta ⓕ **nupcial** *tar*·ta noop·*thyal* wedding cake

tasa ⓕ **del aeropuerto** *ta*·sa del ay·ro·*pwer*·to airport tax

taxi ⓜ *ta*·ksee taxi

taza ⓕ *ta*·tha cup

té ⓜ te tea

teatro ⓜ te·*a*·tro theatre

teclado ⓜ te·*kla*·do keyboard

técnica ⓕ *tek*·nee·ka technique

tela ⓕ *te*·la fabric

tele ⓕ *te*·le TV

teleférico ⓜ te·le·*fe*·ree·ko cable car

teléfono ⓜ te·*le*·fo·no telephone

— móvil mo·*veel* mobile phone

— público poo·blee·ko public telephone

telegrama ⓜ te·le·*gra*·ma telegram

telenovela ⓕ te·le·no·*ve*·la soap opera

telescopio ⓜ te·les·*ko*·pyo telescope

televisión ⓕ te·le·vee·*syon* television

temperatura ⓕ tem·pe·ra·*too*·ra temperature (weather)

templado/a ⓜ/ⓕ tem·*pla*·do/a warm

T

templo ⓜ *tem*·plo temple
temporada ⓕ tem·po·*ra*·da season (in sport)
temprano tem·*pra*·no early
tenedor ⓜ te·ne·*dor* fork
tener te·*ner* have
— **hambre** *am*·bre to be hungry
— **prisa** *pree*·sa to be in a hurry
— **sed** seth to be thirsty
— **sueño** *swe*·nyo to be sleepy
tenis ⓜ *te*·nees tennis
tensión ⓕ **premenstrual** ten·*syon* pre·mens·*trwal* premenstrual tension
tentempié ⓜ ten·tem·*pye* snack
tercio ⓜ *ter*·thyo third
terminar ter·mee·*nar* finish
ternera ⓕ ter·*ne*·ra veal
ternero ⓜ ter·*ne*·ro calf
terremoto ⓜ te·re·*mo*·to earthquake
testarudo/a ⓜ/ⓕ tes·ta·*roo*·do/a stubborn
tía ⓕ *tee*·a aunt
tiempo ⓜ *tyem*·po time • weather
a— a *tyem*·po on time
a— completo/parcial a *tyem*·po kom·*ple*·to/par·*thyal* full-time/part-time
tienda ⓕ **(de campaña)** *tyen*·da (de kam·*pa*·nya) tent
tienda ⓕ *tyen*·da shop
— **de comestibles** de ko·mes·*tee*·bles grocery
— **de fotografía** de fo·to·gra·*fee*·a camera shop
— **de eléctrodomésticos** de e·*lek*·tro·do·mes·*tee*·kos electrical store
— **de cámping** de *kam*·peen camping store
— **de recuerdos** de re·*kwer*·dos souvenir shop
— **de ropa** de *ro*·pa clothing store
— **deportiva** de·por·*tee*·va sports store
Tierra ⓕ *tye*·ra Earth

tierra ⓕ *tye*·ra land
tiesto ⓜ *tyes*·to pot (plant)
tijeras ⓕ pl tee·*khe*·ras scissors
tímido/a ⓜ/ⓕ *tee*·mee·do/a shy
típico/a ⓜ/ⓕ *tee*·pee·ko/a typical
tipo ⓜ *tee*·po type
— **de cambio** de *kam*·byo exchange rate
tirar tee·*rar* pull
tiritas ⓕ pl tee·*ree*·tas band-aids
título ⓜ *tee*·too·lo degree
toalla ⓕ to·*a*·lya towel
toallita ⓕ to·a·*lyee*·ta face cloth
tobillo ⓜ to·*bee*·lyo ankle
tocar to·*kar* touch
— **la guitarra** la gee·*ta*·ra play guitar
tocino ⓜ to·*thee*·no bacon
todavía (no) to·da·*vee*·a (no) (not) yet
todo *to*·do all • everything
tofú ⓜ to·*foo* tofu
tomar to·*mar* take • drink
tomate ⓜ to·*ma*·te tomato
— **secado al sol** se·*ka*·do al sol sun-dried tomato
tono ⓜ *to*·no tone
torcedura ⓕ tor·the·*doo*·ra sprain
tormenta ⓕ tor·*men*·ta storm
toro ⓜ *to*·ro bull
torre ⓕ *to*·re tower
tos ⓕ tos cough
tostada ⓕ tos·*ta*·da toast
tostadora ⓕ tos·ta·*do*·ra toaster
trabajar tra·ba·*khar* work
trabajo ⓜ tra·*ba*·kho job • work
— **administrativo** ad·mee·nees·tra·*tee*·vo paperwork
— **de camarero/a** ⓜ/ⓕ de ka·ma·*re*·ro/a bar work
— **de casa** de *ka*·sa housework
— **de limpieza** de leem·*pye*·tha cleaning
— **eventual** e·ven·*twal* casual work
traducir tra·doo·*theer* translate
traer tra·*er* bring
traficante ⓜ&ⓕ **de drogas** tra·fee·*kan*·te de *dro*·gas drug dealer

ráfico ⓜ *tra*·fee·ko traffic

ramposo/a ⓜ/ⓕ tram·po·so/a
heat

ranquilo/a ⓜ/ⓕ tran·*kee*·lo/a quiet

ranvía ⓜ tran·*vee*·a tram

través a tra·ves across

ren ⓜ tren train

– de cercanías de ther·ka·*nee*·as
ocal train

repar tre·*par* climb • scale

res en raya tres en *ra*·ya noughts &
rosses

riste *trees*·te sad

ú inf too you

u too your

ubo ⓜ **de escape** *too*·bo de es·*ka*·pe
xhaust

umba ⓕ *toom*·ba grave

umbarse toom·*bar*·se lie (not stand)

urista ⓜ&ⓕ too·*rees*·ta tourist

– operador(a) ⓜ/ⓕ o·pe·ra·*dor*/
·pe·ra·*do*·ra tourist operator

U

niforme ⓜ oo·nee·*for*·me uniform

niversidad ⓕ oo·nee·ver·*see*·da
niversity

niverso ⓜ oo·nee·*ver*·so universe

rgente oor·*khen*·te urgent

ǁtil *oo*·teel useful

sted pol oos·*te* you

stedes pol pl oos·*te*·des you

vas ⓕ pl *oo*·vas grapes

– pasas *pa*·sas raisins

V

aca ⓕ *va*·ka cow

acaciones ⓕ pl va·ka·*thyo*·nes
olidays • vacation

acante va·*kan*·te vacant

acío/a ⓜ/ⓕ va·*thee*·o/a empty

acuna ⓕ va·*koo*·na vaccination

agina ⓕ va·*khee*·na vagina

agón ⓜ **restaurante** va·*gon*
es·tow·*ran*·te dining car

---

validar va·lee·*dar* validate

valiente va·*lyen*·te brave

valioso/a ⓜ/ⓕ va·*lyo*·so/a valuable

valle ⓜ *va*·lye valley

valor ⓜ va·*lor* value

vaqueros ⓜ pl va·*ke*·ros jeans

varios/as ⓜ/ⓕ pl *va*·ryos/as several

vaso ⓜ *va*·so (drinking) glass

vegetariano/a ⓜ/ⓕ
ve·khe·ta·*rya*·no/a vegetarian

vela ⓕ *ve*·la candle

velocidad ⓕ ve·lo·thee·*da* speed

velocímetro ⓜ ve·lo·*thee*·me·tro
speedometer

velódromo ⓜ ve·*lo*·dro·mo racetrack
(bicycles)

vena ⓕ *ve*·na vein

vendaje ⓜ ven·*da*·khe bandage

vendedor(a) ⓜ/ⓕ **de flores**
ven·de·*dor*/ven·de·*do*·ra de *flo*·res
florist

vender ven·*der* sell

venenoso/a ⓜ/ⓕ ve·ne·*no*·so/a
poisonous

venir ve·*neer* come

ventana ⓕ ven·*ta*·na window

ventilador ⓜ ven·tee·la·*dor* fan
(machine)

ver ver see

verano ⓜ ve·*ra*·no summer

verde *ver*·de green

verdulería ⓕ ver·doo·le·*ree*·a
greengrocery (shop)

verdulero/a ⓜ/ⓕ ver·doo·le·ro/a
grocer (shopkeeper)

verduras ⓕ pl ver·*doo*·ras vegetables

vestíbulo ⓜ ves·*tee*·boo·lo foyer

vestido ⓜ ves·*tee*·do dress

vestuario ⓜ ves·*twa*·ryo wardrobe

vestuarios ⓜ pl ves·*twa*·ryos
changing room

vez ⓕ veth once

viajar vya·*khar* travel

viaje ⓜ *vya*·khe trip

vid ⓕ veed vine

Y

vida ① *vee*·da life
vidrio ⓜ *vee*·dryo glass
viejo/a ⓜ/① *vye*·kho/a old
viento ⓜ *vyen*·to wind
vinagre ⓜ vee·*na*·gre vinegar
viñedo ⓜ vee·*nye*·do vineyard
vino ⓜ *vee*·no wine
violar vyo·*lar* rape
virus ⓜ *vee*·roos virus
visado ⓜ vee·*sa*·do visa
visitar vee·see·*tar* visit
vista ① *vees*·ta view
vitaminas ① pl vee·ta·*mee*·nas
vitamins
víveres ⓜ pl *vee*·ve·res food supplies
vivir vee·*veer* live (life)
vodka ① *vod*·ka vodka
volar vo·*lar* fly
volumen ⓜ vo·*loo*·men volume
volver vol·*ver* return
vosotros/as ⓜ/① pl inf
vo·*so*·tros/as you
votar vo·*tar* vote

voz ① voth voice
vuelo ⓜ **doméstico** *vwe*·lo
do·*mes*·tee·ko domestic flight

Y

y ee and
ya ya already
yip ⓜ yeep jeep
yo yo I
yoga ⓜ *yo*·ga yoga
yogur ⓜ yo·*goor* yogurt

Z

zanahoria ① tha·na·o·rya carrot
zapatería ① tha·pa·te·*ree*·a shoe
shop
zapatos ⓜ pl tha·*pa*·tos shoes
zodíaco ⓜ tho·*dee*·a·ko zodiac
zoológico ⓜ zo·o·*lo*·khee·ko zoo
zumo ⓜ *thoo*·mo juice
— de naranja de na·*ran*·kha orange
juice

Index

índice

For topics that are covered in several sections of this book, we've
indicated the most relevant page number in bold.

10 Ways to Start a Sentence

When's (the next flight)?	¿Cuándo sale (el próximo vuelo)?	*kwan*·do *sa*·le (el *prok*·see·mo *vwe*·lo)
Where's (the station)?	¿Dónde está (la estación)?	*don*·de es·*ta* (la es·ta·*thyon*)
Where can I (buy a ticket)?	¿Dónde puedo (comprar un billete)?	*don*·de *pwe*·do (kom·*prar* oon bee·*lye*·te)
How much is (a room)?	¿Cuánto cuesta (una habitación)?	*kwan*·to *kwes*·ta (*oo*·na a·bee·ta·*thyon*)
Do you have (a map)?	¿Tiene (un mapa)?	*tye*·ne (oon *ma*·pa)
Is there (a toilet)?	¿Hay (servicios)?	ai (ser·*vee*·thyos)
I'd like (a coffee).	Quisiera (un café).	kee·*sye*·ra (oon ka·*fe*)
Can I (enter)?	¿Se puede (entrar)?	se *pwe*·de (en·*trar*)
Could you please (help me)?	¿Puede (ayudarme), por favor?	*pwe*·de (a·*yoo*·dar·me) por fa·*vor*
Do I have to (get a visa)?	¿Necesito (obtener un visado)?	ne·the·*see*·to (ob·te·*ner* oon vee·*sa*·do)

SOCIAL

My name is ...	Me llamo ...	me *lya*·mo ...
I'm from ...	Soy de ...	soy de ...
I work in (education).	Trabajo en (enseñanza).	tra·*ba*·kho en (en·se·*nyan*·tha)
I'm ... years old.	Tengo ... años.	*ten*·go ... a·nyos
And you?	¿Y Usted/tú? **pol/inf**	ee oos·*te*/too

SAFE TRAVEL

Help!	¡Socorro!	so·*ko*·ro
There's been an accident.	Ha habido un accidente.	a a·*bee*·do oon ak·thee·*den*·te
It's an emergency!	¡Es una emergencia!	es *oo*·na e·mer·*khen*·thee·ya

FOOD

Can you recommend a restaurant?	¿Puede recomendar un restaurante?	*pwe*·de re·ko·men·*dar* oon res·tow·*ran*·te
I'd like a table for two, please.	Quisiera una mesa para dos, por favor.	kee·*sye*·ra oo·na *me*·sa *pa*·ra dos por fa·*vor*
I'd like the menu, please.	Quisiera el menu, por favor.	kee·*sye*·ra el me·*noo* por fa·*vor*
I'd like ...	Quisiera ...	kee·*sye*·ra ...
Please bring the bill.	Por favor nos trae la cuenta.	por fa·*vor* nos *tra*·e la *kwen*·ta

SURVIVAL PHRASES

Hello.	¡Hola!	o·la
Goodbye.	¡Adiós!	a·dyos
Please.	Por favor.	por fa·vor
Thank you.	(Muchas) Gracias.	(moo·chas) gra·thyas
You're welcome.	De nada.	de na·da
Yes./No.	Sí./No.	see/no
Excuse me.	Perdón.	per·don
Sorry!	¡Perdón!	per·don
I understand.	Entiendo.	en·tyen·do
I don't understand.	No entiendo.	no en·tyen·do
One moment.	Un momento.	oon mo·men·to
Help!	¡Socorro!	so·ko·ro
How much is this?	¿Cuánto cuesta esto?	kwan·to kwes·ta es·to
Where are the toilets?	¿Dónde están los servicios?	don·de es·tan los ser·vee·thyos
Cheers!	¡Salud!	sa·loo

NUMBERS

1	uno	oo·no	**6**	seis	seys
2	dos	dos	**7**	siete	sye·te
3	tres	tres	**8**	ocho	o·cho
4	cuatro	kwa·tro	**9**	nueve	nwe·ve
5	cinco	theen·ko	**10**	diez	dyeth

10 WAYS TO START A SENTENCE

When's (the next flight)?	¿Cuándo sale (el próximo vuelo)?	*kwan·do sa·le (el prok·see·mo vwe·lo)*
Where's (the station)?	¿Dónde está (la estación)?	*don·de es·ta (la es·ta·thyon)*
Where can I (buy a ticket)?	¿Dónde puedo (comprar un billete)?	*don·de pwe·do (kom·prar oon bee·lye·te)*
Do you have (a map)?	¿Tiene (un mapa)?	*tye·ne (oon ma·pa)*
Is there (a toilet)?	¿Hay (servicios)?	*ai (ser·vee·thyos)*
I'd like (a coffee).	Quisiera (un café).	*kee·sye·ra (oon ka·fe)*
How much is (a room)?	¿Cuánto cuesta (una habitación)?	*kwan·to kwes·ta (oo·na a·bee·ta·thyon)*
Can I (enter)?	¿Se puede (entrar)?	*se pwe·de (en·trar)*
Could you please (help me)?	¿Puede (ayudarme), por favor?	*pwe·de (a·yoo·dar·me) por fa·vor*
Do I have to (book a seat)?	¿Necesito (obtener un visado)?	*ne·the·see·to (ob·te·ner oon vee·sa·do)*

español es·pa·*nyol*

BASICS

Do you speak English?	¿Habla inglés?	*ab*·la een·*gles*
I (don't) understand.	(No) Entiendo.	(no) en·*tyen*·do
What does ... mean?	¿Qué significa ...?	ke seeg·nee·*fee*·ka ...

PRACTICAL

At what time's the next bus?	¿A qué hora es el próximo autobús?	a ke *o*·ra es el *prok*·see·mo ow·to·*boos*
One ... ticket, please.	Un ... billete, por favor.	oon ... bee·*lye*·te, por *fa*·vor
Can you tell me when we get to (Valladolid)?	¿Puede avisarme cuando lleguemos a (Valladolid)?	*pwe*·de a·vee·*sar*·me *kwan*·do lye·*ge*·mos a (va·lya·do·*leeth*)
Please take me to this address.	Por favor, lléveme a esta dirección.	por fa·*vor* *lye*·ve·me a *es*·ta dee·rek·*thyon*
I'd like to hire a car.	Quisiera alquilar un coche.	kee·*sye*·ra al·kee·*lar* oon *ko*·che